JEAN BÉLIVEAU

MY LIFE IN HOCKEY

JEAN BÉLIVEAU

with **CHRYS GOYENS & ALLAN TUROWETZ**

Jean Béliveau

MY LIFE IN HOCKEY

GREYSTONE BOOKS
Vancouver/Berkeley

First Greystone Books edition 2005
14 15 16 17 18 8 7 6 5 4

Greystone Books Ltd.
www.greystonebooks.com

Cataloguing data available from Library and Archives Canada
ISBN 978-1-55365-149-9 (pbk.)
ISBN 978-1-77164-183-8 (epub)

Editing by Jan Walter
Cover design by Jessica Sullivan
Text design by Lisa Hemingway
Cover photograph courtesy Hockey Online
Interior photographs courtesy the private collection of Jean Béliveau, unless otherwise credited. Copyright is retained by the original photographers.
Printed and bound in Canada by Houghton Boston
Distributed in the U.S. by Publishers Group West

We gratefully acknowledge the financial support of the Canada Council for the Arts, the British Columbia Arts Council, the Province of British Columbia through the Book Publishing Tax Credit, and the Government of Canada through the Canada Book Fund for our publishing activities.

Greystone Books is committed to reducing the consumption of old-growth forests in the books it publishes. This book is one step towards that goal.

This is a rare opportunity for one to reflect upon and rejoice in his family.

This book is dedicated to my wife Élise, my daughter Hélène, and granddaughters Mylène and Magalie, with all of my love.

As well, I dedicate this work to my father Arthur and my mother Laurette, who were inspirations and examples to me of the benefits of hard work, love, and faith, and to my stepmother Mida, who made my father so happy in his later years. Finally, to my brothers and sisters, living and passed away: Guy, Michel, Mimi, Madeleine, Hélène, Pierre, and André.

CONTENTS

Jean Béliveau

MY LIFE IN HOCKEY

FOREWORD

by

WAYNE GRETZKY

THE "C" THAT JEAN BÉLIVEAU wore so proudly on his Montreal Canadiens jersey could as well have stood for "class" as it did for "captain" of the perennial Stanley Cup champions.

I clearly remember watching *Hockey Night in Canada* on Saturday nights as a child, sitting with my dad at my grandma's farmhouse. We all marveled at the command displayed on the ice by big Jean Béliveau. It was obvious that he was the leader of those great teams. He carried himself like a leader, he competed like a leader, and he won with dignity like a leader. My father often remarked that whenever Jean Béliveau spoke, his comments were intelligent and humble. When Jean's team won, he was gracious in describing the Canadiens' opponents. Even at the age of six or seven, I could see there was something special about the Habs' big number 4—on and off the ice.

Many years later, I had lunch in Atlantic City with Jean and his beautiful wife, Élise. I had been playing in the National Hockey

League for only two years at the time, and Jean was firmly fixed in the executive offices of the Canadiens and Molson Companies Limited after eighteen glorious NHL seasons. Many legends of sport attended that event, and I watched as several of the biggest names in the history of the NFL, NBA, and professional baseball came to our table to greet the distinguished Jean Béliveau and his wife.

Having had the good fortune to win four Stanley Cups in my career and to experience the satisfaction and lifelong friendships that are generated by such a difficult and collective effort, it is mind-boggling to recall that Jean Béliveau accomplished the feat no fewer than ten times as a player and seven times more as a senior executive with the same organization. I don't think there can be any other figure in the history of professional team sports who better exemplifies the word "winner."

Jean's induction to the Hockey Hall of Fame was automatic. I'm sure the decision came as naturally to the selection committee as scoring the big goal, winning the big game, and conducting himself with grace and distinction did to Jean Béliveau.

INTRODUCTION

by
ALLAN TUROWETZ

IN THE SPRING OF 2004, I was the guest of Jean Béliveau at a Canadiens game at Montreal's dazzling Bell Centre. Inside the vast arena, the decibel level was so sharp and so annoying that I almost expected to see fans clutch their bleeding ears in agony.

A petite woman stood at the Canadiens' blue line, brandishing a microphone and exhorting the crowd in a high-pitched screech. It was yet another intermission promotion, to this fan nothing more than an irritating delay of the work of the ice-resurfacing crew after the previous period.

On the ice beside her teetered three giddy contest winners, all wearing Montreal Canadiens team jerseys and preparing to shoot pucks into an undersized opening in a net at one end of the rink. Big money was at stake, but it rarely left the building after these spectacles. If the Montreal Canadiens can miss their share of open nets, the average fan in street shoes is no match for the problematic logistics of composite stick, a vulcanized rubber disk, a significant distance over a tricky ice surface, and the vagaries of friction.

I silently bet on a shutout while voicing to my host my disapproval of this circus act. A second seatmate commented on the "marketing idiocy that masquerades as entertainment these days." While the goal-scoring competition went on, the Jumbotron sound system kicked in periodically with the earsplitting heavy-metal chords that some call music.

I felt suddenly guilty for my part in the original negotiations that brought that Jumbotron into this space. It seemed to pose a threat to the health of all who were its captives; perhaps I owed everyone in these seats an apology. And I knew this was only the beginning: when the game finally began, all senses would be assailed by a wall of sound so piercing that it would almost eviscerate us every time play was stopped. I wondered if today's sports entrepreneurs feared silence above all else.

"Who is this aimed at?" I whined, as the crowd cheered and groaned at misdirected pucks and the "color commentary" of the woman with the mike.

Jean Béliveau was as gracious and unperturbed as ever, an island of calm dignity in this raucous amphitheater. He is a man more accustomed to the ballads of Charles Trenet, to *chansonniers* like Brel, Montand, and Piaf, to music lovingly rendered in a *boîte à chansons* or piano bar, his wife at his side and a civilized drink on the table.

A faint smile on his face, he nodded to a spot three rows down. There, two preteeners bopped to the beat, so caught up in the energy of the place that they could hardly sit still. They were bedecked head-to-toe in Canadiens merchandise—jerseys, pants and caps—with one waving a Canadiens pennant and the other an outsize logo-bearing sponge-rubber index finger—number 1—that identifies the hard-core fan everywhere.

"It's aimed at them," he said matter-of-factly. These were the fans of the new millennium, high on the Hockey Show. When the game was over, they'd go home and relive it on their PlayStations or Xboxes. He directed my attention back to the Jumbotron. The house cameras panned over the crowd, and every time the house director spotted a young fan in Canadiens paraphernalia, the camera lingered just long enough for friends and seatmates to acknowledge the moment with friendly shoves and squeals of delight. Then the camera moved on to the next target in the roiling mass of this NHL-branded mosh pit.

The Hockey Show circa 2004 bore no resemblance to the game Jean Béliveau played at the venerable Montreal Forum fifty years ago. But, as he gently reminded me, "it is still the National Hockey League and we are still here to see hockey. Canadians define themselves by this sport, and although much has changed, that fact never has."

Jean Béliveau should know; he's been there for the entire journey, for half a century of hockey and all the changes those decades have seen.

And he understands it all.

PROLOGUE

IN THE ELEVEN YEARS since the publication of the first edition of this memoir of my life in and around hockey, nothing has changed more for the hockey fan than the game experience itself.

Indeed, if you had been stuck in a time warp for the past decade, you might have had a hard time even finding your old arena. Nearly every team in the National Hockey League has opened a new rink since the late 1990s; in Canada, new buildings were inaugurated in Vancouver, Montreal, Ottawa, and Toronto in the four-year period between 1995 and 1999 alone. South of the border, the NHL outfitted itself with no fewer than eighteen state-of-the-art venues, beginning with the Arrowhead Pond for the Anaheim Mighty Ducks in 1993 and ending with the Glendale Arena for the Phoenix Coyotes in 2003. All are beautifully designed, computerized facilities that can be adapted to many audiences and needs: small sites for a couple of hundred patrons in an intimate nightclub setting, medium bowls for solo performers or comedians, halved facilities for rock groups just breaking onto the scene, or full-size arenas for the headline acts.

I recall a similar buzz of "out with the old, in with the new" at the Montreal Forum in 1993 when I was preparing for official retirement from the Canadiens organization. In those days it seemed that team president Ronald Corey was constantly surrounded by scrums of gentlemen in tweed jackets, bulky blueprints under their arms and safety helmets on their heads. His pace quickened by the challenge, the Canadiens' president was overseeing the construction of what would become the Molson Centre (later the Bell Centre), and everyone in our front office was caught up in his enthusiasm. Parties of officials were forever returning from a trek to the construction site in the city center or heading there for a day of consultations and supervision. As they say, no boy of any age can pass a construction site without stopping and marveling at the trucks and cranes.

And when the architects and engineers were too busy to drop by, Ronald would invite his executives in to view the architectural models and artists' renditions of his fabulous arena. The last time I'd seen someone this excited was in 1968, when the Forum was rebuilt from floor to roof and Sam Pollock was readying his franchise for the miracle of color television.

Like Pollock before him, Ronald Corey was right on his game, in the vanguard of the new-look NHL in the mid-1990s. The league was hastily vacating the rinks of the game's Golden Age in favor of surroundings more in tune with the new century. Venues boasting between fifty and a hundred corporate boxes each were a large part of the picture.

The Molson Centre in downtown Montreal, the Palladium in Kanata, just outside Ottawa, and General Motors Place in Vancouver all opened in the 1995–96 season. The Winnipeg Arena and the Colisée in Quebec City were deemed "old league," and when it became evident that no new buildings would replace them, the teams in those cities headed south.

New-hockey hype was rampant, but there were dark clouds on the horizon. Team and league management and the players' association obviously held different visions of the future, and they were soon at an impasse in contract negotiations. In the fall of 1994, the hockey season came to a halt in a bitter labor dispute. Thankfully, play resumed in January 1995.

Montreal's baseball fans were not so lucky. The Expos were running away from the National League and were arguably the best team in baseball when that sport shut down on August 12, 1994. The players did not take to the field again that year and the 1994 World Series was canceled.

THAT WAS THEN, this is now. While I prepared this updated edition in the winter of 2005, another lockout paralyzed the league, and this time there was no January recovery. After a winter without professional hockey, both sides realized that they had gone to the edge of the precipice and taken a long look down.

That winter, too, as a direct result of the original 1994 baseball shutdown, the Expos left the city of their birth for Washington, D.C., after thirty-six seasons in Montreal. The city's sports fans put on a brave face, but they were hurting.

For the hockey fan, there can be nothing more alienating than endless wrangling over collective-bargaining agreements. Denying fans the game they love, and then replacing the on-ice action with the sight of lawyers, union representatives and league officials bickering over money in expensive hotel rooms, is a fatal combination. It's no surprise that the league and the game are in trouble as a result.

Closer to home, I cannot help but note that for the first time in my lifetime and my fifty years in and around the NHL, the Montreal

Canadiens have gone more than a decade without winning the Stanley Cup. That's the real bottom line in that city.

On the personal front, I have to acknowledge that old teammates are moving on and that when *les anciens* gather today it is most often for memorial services. Another novelty: I am a recovering cancer patient, with the emphasis on the word "recovering"—one of my favorites in the vocabulary of this disease, along with two others, "in remission."

It has been an eventful decade between editions, with experiences both life-altering and highly rewarding for me, my family, my fellow and former teammates, and for the game we love. I hope you will enjoy catching up.

1

THE BEST SEATS IN THE HOUSE

Adieu, Rocket.

ON THIS LAST DAY in May 2000, the hockey world has gathered to share in Maurice "Rocket" Richard's greatness for one last time. A collection of former teammates, six of them members of the Hockey Hall of Fame, as the Rocket was, occupy the best seats in the house—as usual.

We had enjoyed a privileged view from the team bench while the Rocket torched opposition netminders for 544 regular-season and eighty-two play-off goals during an eighteen-year career in the National Hockey League. We were young and proud then, draped in the *bleu-blanc-rouge* of the fabled Montreal Canadiens, hockey's winningest team. Every two minutes, over the boards we'd go to wage war against the rest of the NHL.

The Canadiens' team benches at the Montreal Forum were the only seats in the house that could not be bought. Howie Morenz and Aurel Joliat had sat there. Albert "Battleship" Leduc, Joe Malone, the brothers Mantha and Cleghorn, Johnny "Black Cat" Gagnon, Georges Vezina, George Hainsworth, and Edouard "Newsy" Lalonde had mounted their Stanley Cup campaigns from that very spot. And it was from there that my teammates and I watched *l'héros d'un peuple*—"the hero of a people"—elevate hockey to high drama.

Half a century later, Maurice Richard still commands center stage, but today we aren't hopping over the boards to spell him and his linemates. Forty years and a month after his last game for the *Sainte-Flanelle*—literally "the Holy Cloth," the beloved Habs—the Rocket still has the *feu sacré* to bring an entire province to its feet. We are in Notre-Dame Cathedral instead of the Forum, yet once again we're all present to honor him. Outside, a million Montrealers have lined the streets of his hometown for a final farewell.

Instead of the *tricolore* of the Montreal Canadiens, we wear black mourning suits, a sharp contrast to the white hair that identifies us as the older generation. The always combative and supremely talented Dickie Moore sits to my left; beside him, the veteran defensive pair of Ken Reardon and Émile "Butch" Bouchard. All-purpose winger Kenny Mosdell comes next, then goalie Gerry McNeil and Elmer Lach, the Rocket's first center and partner on the famed Punch Line, along with Hector "Toe" Blake.

The Rocket's younger brother, Henri, one of our delegation of pallbearers, sits across the aisle with the rest of the Richard family. Behind us in the pews sit "Mr. Hockey," Gordie Howe, and a contingent of hockey stars from six decades.

As a young player in the Canadiens' organization, I had studied the pictures on the Forum walls of the famous funeral for Howie Morenz in 1937. Like most players of my age, I had had trouble conceiving of such an outpouring of emotion by Montreal sports fans, especially during the Great Depression. How had they packed the Forum with fifteen thousand people when the seating capacity back then was barely nine thousand?

It took the Rocket to teach me what that emotional connection was all about, sixty-three years later. I saw a profound sense of loss in the faces of hundreds of thousands of people all along the processional route from the Molson Centre to Notre-Dame.

FUNERALS LEAD INEVITABLY to reflection and recollection, in my case to the so-called golden age of the National Hockey League in the 1950s and 1960s. As a player, that was my era and all of my memories of it are a young man's memories, of vibrant, brash hockey players and the fast game we played for a living.

Later, long after we'd left the locker room behind, they called us "the Lions in Winter," and by the time of the publication of the first edition of this book, in 1994, we had aged gracefully and still basked in the glow of the fans' appreciation. Our "team" remained intact, and we were feted at special ceremonies almost annually to keep our memories fresh and, occasionally, to distract Montreal fans from the weaknesses of the current squad.

Today, time has caught up with us in the corners, stopping us cold with a well-directed elbow and skating away up the ice with the future. In other words, we have been forced to confront our mortality with the passing of some of our own. Daily practices are a thing of the past; reading the obituaries is our ritual nowadays, as we rush headlong into our seventh and eighth decades.

Claude Provost, Doug Harvey, Jacques Plante, Jean-Claude Tremblay, Bob Turner, and Gerry McNeil also have left us in the past decade. The loss of Provost, Tremblay, Plante, and Rocket Richard in particular were very personal to me, each for quite different reasons.

October 28, 1994, turned out to be Jean-Claude Tremblay's last public outing. The occasion was the launch of the first edition of this work, and it was wall-to-wall people at the Forum's Mise Au Jeu lounge. Scores of family members, friends, media, players, and other colleagues were packed into that room, and everywhere there were faces I hadn't seen in years.

I had overlooked "J.-C." on my invitation list, believing he was in

Switzerland, where he served as the Canadiens' head scout in Europe. A few days before the party, I received a telephone call from his long-time companion.

"J.-C. would like to come to your launch," she said.

"*Mon Dieu,* I thought he was out of the country! Of course, he must come."

J.-C. was there, but few people in the room knew that he was in the last stages of a futile battle against pancreatic cancer. He moved from group to group, smiling, kibitzing with the likes of Marcel Bonin, Yvan Cournoyer, the Richards, Dickie Moore, Dollard St. Laurent, Réjean Houle, and Phil Goyette. He posed proudly with his former teammates for a picture of *les anciens.*

Five weeks later, I visited him at Montreal General Hospital. He lay quietly, his eyes closed, suddenly very frail. The Jean-Claude Tremblay I had known was a barrel-chested man who would have earned a living out of doors if it hadn't been for his extraordinary talents on the ice.

I gently shook his foot. "How are you, old friend?"

He opened his eyes, taking a long time to focus. I could detect the moment of recognition, but all he could say was, "Jean."

The next day, I was scheduled for a pair of book signings in the Ottawa-Hull area when CKAC radio host Pierre Trudel tracked me down in the early afternoon to ask for my comments on the passing of J.-C. Tremblay.

J.-C. was just six weeks short of his fifty-sixth birthday when he breathed his last. I was very glad that he had been able to make a final public appearance at the book launch. With the 1994 NHL lockout in effect and no games being played, there were no other opportunities to gather *les anciens* as a group. The book's send-off proved to be a last good-bye to J.-C. from many of his friends.

However cheery he may have seemed that day, the severity of his illness could not fool the neutral and all-seeing eye of the camera lens.

When the first pictures from the event came back, I was amazed to see how gray and aged J.-C. looked. And I could not help but wonder what kind of pain he had endured and how much strength it had taken for him to attend.

Jean-Claude was a good friend, a teammate for many years, and a very important cog in the Canadiens' machine. Although his style of play exemplified finesse and skill, J.-C. was a gruff person in crowds, and he never seemed to settle into the social side of hockey life. In fact, when he later went to the World Hockey Association and single-handedly rescued the Quebec Nordiques from premature extinction, he was known as *le vieux grogneux*—"the old growler" or grouser, a grinch even. While some might interpret that to mean J.-C. was always moaning and griping, those who knew him recognized an essentially shy man, a bit of a loner who, like a bear, might growl a little to maintain his distance. His courage, however, was never questioned.

The first death in our close group was that of Claude Provost, on a tennis court in Florida in 1984. Jos, as we called him, was barely fifty years of age. I went to the memorial service in Boucherville, where his urn remains at its columbarium. His son told me that Claude had probably suffered previous heart attacks; an autopsy revealed two telltale scars on his heart. Claude was tough, not an ounce of fat on him, and he might not have realized that any discomfort was a serious matter. He died as he had played: silently, uncomplaining, with no fuss at all.

Doug Harvey's death five years later also hit hard. Doug was perhaps the most accomplished athlete ever to play with the Canadiens. The best defenseman of his day, and to my mind the best in NHL history, Doug was an all-round athlete who played professional football with the Quebec Rifles of the Continental Football League, semipro baseball with a variety of teams in Quebec, and in every pickup basketball game at the YMCA when he had the free time.

He left us for the New York Rangers in 1962 and played for the Detroit Red Wings as well before moving into the minors with the Kansas City organization and the top farm team for the St. Louis Blues, as a player-coach. When injuries overtook the Blues in the 1967–68 play-offs, Doug was asked to send up reinforcements to help the parent club. He was one of the reinforcements, and he played magnificently against us in the Stanley Cup final. We swept St. Louis in four straight, but it wasn't easy; every game against the expansion team was a one-goal decision (3–2, 1–0, 4–3, 3–2), thanks in large part to Doug's presence on the ice.

Doug bounced around the hockey world and a half-dozen years later, when he was an executive with the Houston Aeros of the World Hockey Association, he played Gordie Howe together with his sons Mark and Marty, in one of the sport's most imaginative combinations. Shortly after, Doug was out of hockey and a problem with drink surfaced. Montrealers, remembering the triumphs of his youth, were gentle with the man who was still very much a local hockey hero. A *Globe and Mail* reporter from Toronto wasn't as charitable, publishing a profile that was long on accusation and innuendo and short on understanding. I remember that the entire Canadiens family felt violated.

When Doug was in his early sixties, Joe Gorman, son of Ottawa-born sports executive and icon Tommy Gorman, hired him as a handyman at his racetrack, just outside Ottawa. Doug stayed away from the bottle and was the picture of health for a few years. But too many more years of hard living finally caught up with him, and the damage done to his liver could not be repaired.

In December 1989, just before Christmas, he checked himself out of the Montreal General and came to a Canadiens practice with one of his grandsons. I was in my office on the second floor when a security official phoned.

"Jean, Doug is sitting behind the net and he doesn't look very good." I went down right away. It was a sign of the respect Doug commanded at the Forum that he had been welcomed into the building without question.

The Doug Harvey I encountered was shockingly emaciated, his facial features ravaged by time and disease, his clothes hanging limply. But he still had that impish smile, one we describe in French as *mesquin*, or "naughty," and his blue eyes were still lively when he greeted me. We sat watching the practice, talking very little while he pointed out the finer points to his grandson. Truth be told, I had always enjoyed Doug's company and I was happy to be there with him. My presence was also a deterrent; we didn't want passersby bothering him for autographs—was he still able to write in his condition?—and possibly ruining a precious family moment for him. He died just a few days later, on Boxing Day, at the age of sixty-five.

IN FEBRUARY 1986, I returned from a Chamber of Commerce luncheon in St. Jean on the South Shore to find a Longueuil police patrol car waiting in my driveway. My wife, Élise, was in Barbados, and there had been no one home all day.

"A break-in?" I asked the officer. Several years earlier, thieves had ransacked our house during a hockey game, assured of my absence because they were following my progress on television—my television, which they then carried away. Domestic security had been a concern ever since.

"No, no, Mr. Béliveau," he replied. "The Forum has been trying to get hold of you all afternoon. Please call your office."

It was François Seigneur, the Canadiens' vice-president of communications, who had an urgent request.

"Jean, we've just learned that Jacques Plante will be buried in Switzerland on Saturday," he told me. We had learned of Jacques' passing the previous day and had assumed that his remains would be returned to Canada for burial. It was 4 PM on a Thursday in Montreal, already 10 PM in Sierre, Switzerland, and Jacques would be laid to rest there in thirty-six hours.

"We've found a ticket on Air Canada to Zurich via Paris," François continued, "and the plane leaves at seven fifty tonight from Mirabel. You knew him best of anyone still with the team and the league needs representation too. Can you make it?"

Jacques was special to me, a colleague in hockey since my first year in junior, when my Victoriaville team faced off against his Quebec Citadels. I threw a few things into an overnight bag, then plunged into rush-hour traffic, heading for Mirabel International Airport, twenty-five miles on the other side of the city and almost forty miles from my house.

By 11 AM Friday local time, I was in Zurich. It took another three hours by car to reach Sierre, the small town where Jacques Lemaire had gone to coach after he retired from the Canadiens in 1979. The Valais region is very beautiful, and I was amazed to see that spring had already arrived in the valley, while up on the heights winter maintained its hold.

I arrived at my hotel at two o'clock in the afternoon and tried to nap for a bit; I'd only managed to doze lightly on the plane. When sleep wouldn't come, I went for a short walk in the fresh air, then returned to my hotel and telephoned Raymonde, Jacques' wife. She was pleased to hear my voice and thanked me for coming.

The visitation at the funeral home started at 6 PM. I stayed until nine o'clock and heard from Raymonde the story of Jacques' final year. I'd last seen him in January 1985, when the Canadiens celebrated a double anniversary: the team's seventy-fifth year and the Forum's sixtieth. As part of the festivities, the fans had been invited to vote for an all-time Canadiens dream team. Jacques was the people's choice for goalie, edging out Ken Dryden, with Doug Harvey and Larry Robinson on defense, Maurice Richard on right wing, Dickie Moore on left, and Béliveau at center. Aurel Joliat represented the players of the 1920s and 1930s.

Jacques' selection in 1985 and the special anniversary gala at the Queen Elizabeth Hotel brought him back to Canada. He spent several days in Montreal, and we had occasion to talk more than once. It was clear that he was supremely happy in Switzerland with Raymonde, his second wife, and that he had found the life he had always sought.

Later that fall, Jacques returned to North America to work with the goaltenders of the St. Louis Blues. On his way to St. Louis, he experienced stomach pains and could hardly eat. When he reached Missouri, he visited the team doctor, who in turn consulted a specialist. The diagnosis was stomach cancer. Jacques returned to Switzerland and was admitted to a hospital in Geneva, one of the world's foremost medical centers. Doctors operated immediately and he underwent therapy while still hospitalized.

On the night Jacques Plante would die, Raymonde stayed with her husband until ten o'clock. After they'd watched the late news in his hospital room, she returned home. A few hours later, Jacques' aorta burst and he died of the resulting hemorrhage.

His funeral took place in a small church that was packed to overflowing. Raymonde had told me that she and Jacques had many friends in the area; clearly, given the number of mourners, this was true. Raymonde led me to the first row of family mourners, and I sat beside her during the service.

Afterward, two teams of peewee hockey players, wearing their sweaters over shirts and ties, formed an honor guard at the door. One of their coaches seemed familiar to me; I was staggered to learn that the peewees came from Victoriaville. They were scheduled to play an exhibition game in Sierre later that day, having just crossed the Alps from Chamonix, France. When the coach heard of Jacques' death and learned that the funeral would take place on Saturday morning, he booked his teams on an earlier train to ensure they could pay their respects to a fellow Canadian and Quebecker. It was a gracious tribute appreciated by everyone.

Following the service, the funeral party moved in a procession to the cemetery gates where, according to Swiss custom, the priest said a few more words, then accompanied the casket to the gravesite for private burial. Later I returned to the graveside with Raymonde and her family, and a few more prayers were said. A huge bank of flowers identified the spot where Jacques lay. We stood quietly with our memories for several moments before leaving for a reception at his home.

Raymonde left me with two special mementos of her late husband. The first was her proposal that we go to a Swiss National League hockey game between Sierre and Kloten, a Zurich suburb, that very evening. Jacques often went to the Saturday afternoon games, so we followed his example by attending this one, which began with a moving moment of silence in his memory.

The next morning, Raymonde presented me with a bottle of wine from a nearby vineyard where Jacques had made his own wine, meticulously recording and numbering by hand all the bottles produced. Mine was bottle 187, a last personal gift from my friend.

Then it was back to Geneva for the flight home. Between the moment I'd first received news of the funeral on Thursday afternoon and the departure time of my plane at eleven on Sunday morning, I'd had less than ten hours of sleep. We landed at Mirabel at four in the afternoon, seventy-two hours after the original phone call and right in the middle of Sunday evening traffic, as thousands of skiers returned to the city from the Laurentians.

But my duties to the memory of Jacques Plante weren't finished quite yet. On Monday morning, I went in to see team president Ronald Corey first thing.

"There are other family members to be considered, people who have lost a husband and a father and a brother," I said. I was referring to Jacques' first wife, Jacqueline, to his son (another son had been killed in a motorcycle crash many years before), and to Jacques' surviving siblings. He had been the eldest of eleven children, and his brothers and sisters in his hometown of Shawinigan wanted a memorial of some kind.

"You're right," said Ronald. "See what you can do."

I called Marcel de la Sablonnière at Immaculate Conception Church. Père Sablon, as he was known to thousands, was Montreal's unofficial athletes' priest, and several times he had served as chaplain to Canadian Olympic teams. The following day, a second memorial was held for Jacques Plante. The extended Plante families were comforted to say good-bye to Jacques in this way, and they gathered around with me with questions about Sierre. In life, Jacques had been aloof. In death, he was surrounded by hundreds of friends.

CLAUDE PROVOST, Jacques Plante, Doug Harvey, Jean-Claude Tremblay, and, now, the Rocket. Maurice Richard's death was especially sobering for me since just a few days earlier I had been given some very unwelcome news.

I had detected a growth on the left side of my neck back in March, and when I returned from a boat cruise in late April, I went to see Dr. Doug Kinnear, the Canadiens' team doctor. He took one look and picked up the telephone. Moments later, I was in the office of Dr. Roger Tabah, an oncologist. It's a small world: I knew his father well; we lunched occasionally at The Texan restaurant across the street from the Forum. Dr. Tabah examined my neck, turning my head this way and that, and looked down my throat for long minutes while I inquired about his dad's health.

"We're not going to wait," he said at last, "we're taking a biopsy right away." Less than ten days before Maurice's funeral, I was given the results: "It's malignant, Jean."

In the 1950s and 1960s, cancer—the big C—was a death sentence. It felled even the famous; superstar actors like John Wayne and Steve

McQueen had succumbed to it. Those victims who could afford the expense chased hope to specialized clinics all over the world, institutions that promised relief like those in Mexico that offered a medicine derived from peach pits. Few such remedies proved effective.

Two decades later, research had developed many treatments for cancer and, happily, one's neighbors and coworkers were more often diagnosed, treated and returned to normal life. It wasn't as frightening as before, but it was cancer and scary enough. That small phrase—"It's malignant"—still had the power to knock someone to his or her knees.

Élise and I had spoken before my appointment with Dr. Tabah and we had reaffirmed our vows: we would be fully committed to fighting this disease together, and we would do everything that was expected of us. We had read that a positive mental outlook was crucial in the treatment of any life-threatening affliction, especially cancer. So positive we would be, embracing the team approach that had served me so well in my working life. My new linemates included Drs. Kinnear and Tabah, along with a radiation oncologist, Dr. Te Vuong. They and their colleagues at Montreal General, Dr. David Mulder and Dr. Rea Brown, were known as the all-stars of their field and were as famous among Montrealers as Guy Lafleur, Steve Shutt, and Bob Gainey.

Optimism and positive thoughts are helpful, but don't think for a minute that I was approaching this challenge naively. Over the next few months, there was enough pain to go around for both Élise and me.

On the Victoria Day weekend in May, we had visited Maurice at Hôtel-Dieu hospital. We found him restless, a little out of sorts, fidgety, and probably frustrated. He was unable to speak, so most of the conversation flowed between Élise and me on one side and his companion, Sonia, and one of his sons on the other. I remember his eyes still radiated that laser-beam intensity that could burn right through you.

The nursing staff had barely tucked the Rocket into his chair when one of them gave him a shot of what I guessed was morphine.

The fidgeting stopped and he became more peaceful. We sat with him and his family for about half an hour on that holiday Monday; he passed away on the following Saturday. In between, I had been given my own diagnosis.

On the day of his funeral, I was one of the team representatives who arrived at Notre-Dame well ahead of the rest. My position as an honorary pallbearer meant I would have to wait on the church steps for quite a while as the cortège wound its way through the streets of the city. The Canadiens front office had issued a press release about my condition several days before Maurice's funeral, and there was a tacit agreement with the media that I would be available for brief interviews in the interim. That chore was done with when the hearse pulled into the square in front of the church, and I was ready to assume my duties as pallbearer.

Twenty-four hours later, on June 1, I had my first radiation therapy. I'm a morning person, so I asked Dr. Vuong if I could be among the first patients of the day at eight o'clock. The plan was for thirty-six treatments, five a week, with weekends off. That first week Élise and I left home at six thirty in the morning to beat the traffic and find a place to park. We would stop in at the cafeteria on the sixth floor for a muffin and coffee before the treatments. But by week 2, solid food and drink were out of the question.

Each treatment lasted only fifteen or twenty seconds, but over time radiation therapy takes a toll. I lost twenty-eight pounds during the course of the thirty-six sessions, and it seemed that Élise had the blender going day and night. My last appointment was on July 26, 2000. By then the tumor in my neck was gone; as of this writing, it has not returned.

What bothered me the most then and does now is that I can no longer produce saliva. Those on various kinds of special medication for diseases such as diabetes will tell you stories about the discomfort of a dry mouth. The first year, my taste buds disappeared, too, and if you don't taste food, you don't eat as much, accelerating weight loss. The taste buds returned eventually, but my saliva production is still off more than five years later. And I take pills for my thyroid every day to combat one of the side effects of the radiation treatment.

One afternoon the medical team dispatched me to Sherbrooke because the university hospital there has a positron emission tomography (PET) scanner. There was only one such scanner in Montreal at the time, at the Montreal Neurological Institute, and it was calibrated for brain scans. During my first briefing with the doctors, they had warned me the cancer could be anywhere, even though it appeared to be confined to my neck. (Ironically, when the Canadiens' Saku Koivu contracted and defeated cancer a couple of years later, he established a charitable foundation that led to the purchase of a PET scanner for the Montreal General. He, too, had had to make the trip to Sherbrooke.)

After the first twenty-five treatments, which covered both sides of my neck, Dr. Vuong told me that all the scans showed that the tumor was localized on the left side of the neck. But, she said, "we're going for full prevention," so they scanned the throat, the top of the stomach and elsewhere. The last ten treatments focused on the tumor itself, and I developed a deep burn at the site on my neck. It took three weeks to clear it up with a special first-aid cream.

When you undergo facial radiation therapy, you must wear a form-fitting mask, not unlike a goalie mask, during treatment. At that point, about halfway through the schedule, I had lost some twenty pounds. They had to mold another mask because my face had become so thin in the process.

To prevent flinching or movement of my shoulders while undergoing radiation, my wrists were tied down and I was instructed to push my shoulders into the table in order to minimize any nervous twitches. The mask itself was attached to the table on which I lay and, once it was tied on, it was impossible to move my head or neck.

This would be agony for anyone suffering from claustrophobia. I once asked the technician, "What do you do when somebody can't keep that mask on?" The answer was a weak smile and a shrug.

What I found most difficult had nothing to do with personal physical discomfort. It was my family's distress that I felt most acutely. I watched my wife, my daughter, and my two granddaughters trying to be upbeat and positive, but they were suffering nonetheless. I'm not blind and I know them too well. Many times I reminded them that we had to hope for the best; I probably uttered variations of that homily countless times, attempting to raise their spirits and my own. As the doctors had predicted, there were a few dark days during those weeks of radiation treatment.

We were all comforted by the success stories of many young athletes who were similarly combating cancer and whose illnesses went into remission following treatment. Both Lance Armstrong, the top cyclist in the world, and Mario Lemieux, arguably the best hockey player in the world, vanquished cancers. Later on, Koivu and another athlete with Montreal connections, the Montreal Expos' Andres Galarraga, survived cancer as well.

When my illness became known, I received letters from people who had seriously ill spouses or other family members and who were reaching for a lifeline. Could I help with an encouraging telephone call, a word of advice? As it turned out, these calls were as therapeutic for my health and state of mind as they may have been helpful to those on the other end of the line. I heard from a few former teammates, too, but I derived the greatest benefits from total strangers.

When the wives called, their stories were almost identical: a husband sitting at home, too depressed to battle back. I'd chat with these men and we'd commiserate with each other, then we'd encourage each other. Finally, we'd pledge together to fight for our lives.

As I write, it's been fifty-five months since the end of my treatments and I'm officially in remission. My health is fairly good and today, when I have something to do, I do it. But I also experience days when simple tasks are a challenge. I tire more quickly and still take on more than a recovering cancer patient—or someone who is supposed to be retired—should. But that is my nature, and it is too late to change.

While working on this updated version of my memoirs, it occurred to me that "my life in hockey," as the subtitle reads, has come to embrace unexpected dimensions. In the last ten years, real life has parked itself in my driveway. Time has overtaken the Lions in Winter, and whatever the physical glories of our youth, inevitably we have aged along with the rest of the population. Indeed, that may be the greatest shock of them all. When you are at the top of the hill, in superb physical condition at a young age, the notion of deterioration and death seem very remote. But when the decline begins, as it must, you have that much farther to fall.

BACK AT NOTRE-DAME, the funeral Mass drawing to a close, we in the white hair and black suits take our positions as pallbearers. Entering the cathedral, I was in back and there was a reason for it; the center aisle slopes up several degrees, and my height helped to keep the casket level. Leaving the church, I move to the left side. The weight of our burden is lighter than I would have expected.

Maurice Richard finally leaves us when the casket is driven away to the cemetery. But the Rocket will never leave in our hearts. To most Quebeckers, he was a god; to us, he was something dearer still. He was our teammate.

2

THE TOWN

FROM THE SADNESS and heavy humidity of a funeral in the late spring of the new millennium, I want to take you back a season and about sixty years to a time long before Richard and Béliveau were household names, a time of freezing temperatures, pure light, and undying hope.

On the crisp winter day I am remembering, the snow was so brilliantly white it was blue, and so hard-packed that the crunch of heavy boots seemed to echo for miles. In 1943, there was no such thing as recognition of a wind-chill factor. Television and its temptations were still a generation away. With nothing to drive or lure us indoors on frigid Sunday afternoons, adults and children alike reveled in temperatures twenty-five degrees below zero Fahrenheit.

I was twelve years old and sat with Guy, my eight-year-old brother, at the kitchen table. Somehow, my mother had persuaded us to take off our toques and jackets, which now lay in a pile by the back door. Under the table, scarcely denting the kitchen's industrial-strength linoleum, were two pairs of skates, still on our feet. Guy and I had been skating on the rink that our father, Arthur Béliveau, built every winter in the family's backyard in Victoriaville. Melting ice chips dripped from the blades beneath our chairs.

Moments earlier, Laurette Dubé Béliveau had stood at the door and called out the magic words *vient manger,* "come and eat." The entire family gathered for a lunch of sandwiches and steaming bowls of soup. After several hours of nonstop shinny, the players were steaming as well, eager to rejoin the game. From time to time, Arthur Béliveau would have to reach across and gently swat one of his impatient sons, punishment for a breach of etiquette. Usually, however, all it took was a warning look from either parent, and order was restored.

The sounds of a puck booming on makeshift boards and the hiss of steel on ice had us leaning imperceptibly toward the door as we ate. Our friends and neighbors—Raymond, André, and Gilles Ducharme, Charles and Jean-Marie Dumas, Marcel Boutet, Joe Moore, and Léopold and Jean-Marc Côté—were continuing the play without us.

This was the beauty of marathon shinny. Whenever chores and staggered lunch hours called one or more of the regulars away, the teams reformed instantly and kept on skating. The only interruption of our weekend games occurred when altar-boy duty called us to the church of Les Saints-Martyrs Canadiens. On Saturday mornings, we older players would serve early Mass at seven or eight o'clock, before adjourning to the Béliveau kitchen for breakfast and the Béliveau rink for hockey. On Sundays, especially once we'd become senior altar boys, we would generally serve High Mass at ten o'clock, and then return home for a late lunch.

I took these church tasks very seriously. Both of my parents were religious and came from rural backgrounds. The Dubés were clustered in and around Charette, halfway between Shawinigan Falls and Trois-Rivières; the Béliveaus hailed from the Saint-Célestin area, near Nicolet.

My father's family traces its roots back to Antoine Béliveau, who settled in Port Royal, Nova Scotia, on the Bay of Fundy, in 1642. Port Royal, now Annapolis Royal, was once the most fought-over piece of real estate in Canada, the site of several eighteenth-century skirmishes between Britain and France that culminated in the great displacement of the Acadians in 1755. When some ten thousand of them refused to swear fealty to the British Crown, they were expelled, fanning out in many directions. Some went back to France, others journeyed to Louisiana, where they would become known as "Cajuns." Still others headed for the northeastern United States or toward Quebec. I've heard that some decided to travel as far away as possible and ended up in the Falkland Islands, off the coast of Argentina.

Our particular branch of the family lived in the Boston area before making its way back to Canada in the mid-1800s. Like many *Acadiens* who'd spent more than a generation south of the border, they may first have thought of settling in a French-speaking enclave in the Madawaska Valley of New Brunswick. But when they heard that the Quebec government was offering arable land in the Saint-Grégoire area, on the south shore of the St. Lawrence River near Trois-Rivières, they applied for and received a land grant there and stayed. At least, most of them stayed.

Around the time of the First World War, when my father was still a boy, four of his older brothers came to the same conclusion that had sent so many other young French-Canadian males to remote destinations across North America: Quebec's family farms simply could not provide a living for most of its grown sons. Large households were the norm then, and it was not uncommon for as many as ten children—including five or more boys—to reach maturity. A farm might be subdivided to accommodate the eldest two or three sons, but the rest would have to marry into families short of male offspring or move to the nearest city in search of work.

My father was barely in his teens when four of his brothers prepared to leave for western Canada and work in the fall harvest. He wanted to join them, but his mother objected and with good cause. After all, it was a rough trip to the wheat fields, sometimes clinging atop a railway car. Several young men from their region had lost their lives en route. Perhaps my grandmother sensed another danger in my uncles' trip that the rest of the family didn't, something that only time would prove right; the three months that her sons were supposed to be gone eventually stretched to many decades.

I finally met three of those uncles almost fifty years after they'd journeyed west. In 1959, Molson's Brewery, the firm that employed me, purchased a number of breweries in western Canada, and I was asked to tour them in the summer of 1960. Élise and I started out by car from Montreal and drove across Canada. In Wolseley, Saskatchewan, about seventy miles east of Regina, we met Antonio Béliveau. He was retired, and his children had taken over the family farm. His brothers Ernest and Armand were in Saskatchewan too, having settled and raised families to the west of Regina, in Moose Jaw and Ponteix. Sadly, none of them could tell me what had happened to the fourth brother, who had seemingly vanished many years before into the British Columbia interior. Perhaps a surprise yet awaits me in the form of long-lost relatives there.

The sixth and youngest Béliveau brother, Louis-Philippe, was not quite as adventurous as his siblings. In the 1930s, he moved to Montreal, where he was to work for Canadian National Railways for some forty years before retiring to a family farm in Saint-Célestin. I visited him there when he was well into his late eighties, and until he passed away a few years ago, he was a regular at our annual family reunions.

The Béliveaus who stayed in Quebec congregated near Saint-Célestin, then spread out toward Quebec City and Victoriaville. Like his brothers before him, my father eventually had to leave the family farm. During the Depression, he was hired by Shawinigan Water and Power Company, then one of the province's largest private utilities and later part of Hydro-Québec.

Arthur was stringing electrical line in Trois-Rivières when he met Laurette Dubé, the only daughter in an uncharacteristically small family of two children. Shortly thereafter a wedding took place, and on August 31, 1931, Arthur and Laurette's first child, christened Jean Arthur Béliveau, arrived just as the Depression reached its nadir. I was the first of eight in a family of five sons and three daughters. We lost my sister Hélène when she was only two, struck by a car in front of the house.

Because my father was wiring much of the Bois-Francs region, we followed the hydro poles a fair bit in my early years. When I was about three years old, the family moved to Plessisville, but resettled in Victoriaville shortly after my sixth birthday. There I attended elementary school at École Saint-David, was taught by the brothers of the Sacred Heart at L'Académie Saint-Louis de Gonzague in grades 5 through 9, and went to the Collège de Victoriaville for grade 10.

My childhood was in no way remarkable. It was a typical French-Canadian Catholic upbringing, one centered on family values, strict religious observance, hard work, conservatism, and self-discipline. We certainly weren't well-to-do in material terms, but in the 1940s you could raise a family on a working man's salary if you were careful, which of necessity we were. Our home was modest and very old. Shortly after my family moved to a new house across town in 1952, the old one was demolished to make a larger yard for the neighboring presbytery.

Despite reduced circumstances, we always had food on the table and clean clothes to wear. We had a backyard vegetable garden, raised rabbits in the summer, and heated the house on the "Shawinigan Water and Power Company Plan." Sometimes when those cedar hydro poles were blown down by windstorms or knocked over by reckless drivers, my father would "harvest" the casualties and bring them home. Then he and I would spend hours sawing and chopping them to size for burning in our furnace and kitchen stove. I'll always remember the aroma of cedar that permeated the house, and I believe that hewing those logs helped me develop a strong physique while still a teenager.

We all worked hard in those days, and after our chores were done at home and at Les Saints-Martyrs Canadiens, we got to play our favorite sports. Summertime meant baseball from dawn to dusk. In winter, the family rink was empty barely long enough for my father to flood it.

The wonders and distractions children experience today were, of course, unknown in the 1940s. Forget video games and iPods and rock concerts. At the same time, our entertainment wasn't over-organized by well-meaning adults. We were left to our own devices. As a result, shinny at the Béliveau Forum may have been technically primitive, devoid of positional play and five-on-five chalk-talk strategies, but we were allowed to concentrate on the basics, learning how to skate, stickhandle, and shoot.

Our rules were few, but then so were our disputes. Winning was secondary to enjoying ourselves. We kept score, of course, and often called our own play-by-play as we went along: "Richard goes around Schmidt, holds off Armstrong, leans low and sends a screaming backhand into the top corner! He shoots, he scores!" To keep things interesting, the teams' players would change every ten minutes or so. There were no losers and we were scrupulous in maintaining a well-matched equilibrium.

We learned by doing and by holding on to the puck. The bigger, older boys were obviously more adept and would control the play for long moments while their younger opponents attempted to check them. When the youngsters grew larger and more proficient, they in turn began to dominate the game, daring the newcomers to challenge them. Today's sports psychologists might call this Darwinian hockey, survival of the fittest. We called it fun.

I didn't play for a "real" team, with sweaters, coaches, and scheduled games, until I was twelve years old. The idea of sitting back and waiting for someone else to clear the rink was unheard of in my childhood crowd. Our version of power skating involved getting behind a scraper and plowing a path through foot-high snow until the ice below was cleared. And yet, without all the trappings that kids today have come to expect, I somehow learned to play the game, as did boys all over Quebec and the rest of Canada.

The next stage of my hockey development was fostered by the brothers of the Sacred Heart, at L'Académie. The first full-size rink I ever set skates on, one with a more or less regulation ice surface, proper lines, and boards and goals, was erected in the school yard every November and would be well used until the thaw of the following March.

At L'Académie, we played after school in a four-team house league. The brothers also formed the school's all-stars team that played on Saturday mornings at the Victoriaville Arena. In those days, Victoriaville was a relatively modest town of perhaps no more than ten thousand residents, and it was fortunate to have such a fine facility. The reason for the building's existence was simple: Victoriaville was the center of the Bois-Francs region, an important farming area, and the arena was home to the annual agricultural exhibition every summer.

Thanks to the Sacred Heart brothers and an accident of geography, I was able to play on weekends against a wide range of hockey talent. We didn't have organized divisions such as peewee or bantam; instead, our all-stars often faced off against teams composed of local factory workers that were sponsored by the town's businesses. Twenty-year-olds would sometimes be on the ice with kids of thirteen and fourteen. With the exception of myself and a boy named Cloutier, the academy all-stars were pretty small, and our lineup of Ducharme, Patry, Côté, Boutet, Houle, Métivier, and Filion intimidated no one. Still, we had our share of successes and learned a great deal in the process.

My hockey career took another step forward when, at fifteen, I went to the Collège de Victoriaville for grade 10. That year I played for both the college and the Victoriaville Panthers, a team in an Intermediate B league that included squads from Athabaska, Princeville, Plessisville, and Warwick. Now my winter weekends were consumed by travel as well as playing time.

Ironically, it was baseball, not hockey, that almost took me away from my home and family permanently. During the war years, an electrician named John Nault was known as "Mr. Baseball" in Victoriaville. He was what we call in French *mordu*—bitten by the game—and he couldn't do enough for any boy who showed an interest. He organized leagues and installed lighting at the park to allow night games. When I was fourteen, he packed four or five of us into his car for a Sunday excursion to Boston's Fenway Park. We couldn't understand a word of what was going on around us, but we needed no translation when Ted Williams hammered the ball more than four hundred feet, deep over the right centerfield fence.

It was a grueling twenty-hour round trip, but I've never forgotten it. All the way back to Victoriaville, through Massachusetts and Vermont, a carload of wide-eyed young French Canadians dreamed of playing for the Boston Red Sox, digging in against Allie Reynolds and other New York Yankee aces.

Another professional ballpark was even closer to hand, about a hundred miles away in Montreal. We sometimes went to Delormier Downs to watch the AAA Royals play, and I saw stars like pitchers Tommy Lasorda and Jean-Pierre Roy, as well as Chuck Connors, a towering first baseman who later starred on television in *The Rifleman* series. The only Royals player I don't remember seeing was perhaps the most famous of them all, the inimitable Jackie Robinson.

I loved watching the big hitters because I myself was a pitcher-infielder who knew the thrill of sending the ball out of sight. By the time I turned fifteen, my burgeoning growth had added several miles per hour to my fastball and thirty or forty feet to my occasional home runs.

That spring, after school let out at four o'clock, John Nault and I would sometimes drive to Trois-Rivières, where I would warm up with a senior team that played in the Canadian-American League. I didn't actually play in their games, but I had the opportunity to pitch to fellows who were twenty-five and older. The local baseball scouts began to take notice.

One scout was sufficiently impressed by my size, pitching arm, and hitting skills that he tried to sign me to a class C or D contract. Unfortunately, this meant that I'd be placed with a team somewhere in Alabama. The discussion didn't get far; needless to say, *maman* responded with an unequivocal *non*.

The following summer, however, I did leave home to play in a setting that was as foreign as Alabama to a sixteen-year-old from Victoriaville. In 1948, Val d'Or, Quebec, was still a rough, tough frontier town, the haunt of gold miners, prospectors, and lumberjacks. Long, hard winters meant that the townspeople cherished their summertime pursuits—hunting, fishing, and above all baseball. Val d'Or competed in the flourishing Abitibi Senior League, where teams were in the habit of importing players from elsewhere in Quebec and northern Ontario to bolster their fortunes. When the Val d'Or team lost a player through injury that summer, one of the players from Victoriaville said he knew of a young prospect back home who might be able to help them out.

"How young?" he was asked.

"I'm not sure, maybe sixteen. Plays with my kid brother."

"We can't hire him at the mine, then. He's too young. Can you think of someone else?"

"Nobody as good as him. He's a good relief pitcher, plays the corners and hits the ball for distance."

"In that case, maybe the city needs another kid to cut grass in the parks."

Which is how, a few days later, Jean Béliveau became a summer employee of the city of Val d'Or and a regular on the baseball team. I mowed by day and pitched in the evenings for seven weeks. What I remember most—not in this order—were the unpaved streets, the wooden sidewalks, and the tremendous kindness I was shown by everyone.

Later, of course, I would meet many great hockey players from the area. Dave Keon, Jacques Laperrière, and Réjean Houle were from Rouyn, Quebec, while Christian, Jean-Paul, and Paulin Bordeleau hailed from nearby Noranda. Ralph Backstrom, Dick Duff, Bob Murdoch, Larry and Wayne Hillman, and Mickey and Dick Redmond were just across the provincial border in Kirkland Lake, Ontario, and Timmins was home to Frank and Peter Mahovlich. After spending a summer in Val d'Or, I wondered what a winter in that wild country would be like. I know for a fact that the players who graduated from the northwestern junior leagues were well schooled and made rock-solid professionals. Toronto and Montreal competed fiercely to identify and sign them.

That Val d'Or summer was my first extended period away from home. All of my subsequent absences would be brought about by hockey. When I was thirteen or fourteen, I'd seen the Victoriaville Senior Tigers, an amateur team, play at the local arena. One player who quickly became a favorite of mine was a defenseman named Roland Hébert. Roland wasn't tall or particularly wide, but he had great hockey sense and a lot of heart, throwing himself in front of pucks at every opportunity. I revered him, as did many of my friends, but I had no idea that he would help send me farther down the road toward my destiny.

In 1946, Roland was invited to referee a game between our college all-stars and a team sponsored by Victoriaville Furniture. The brother who coached our team played me the entire sixty minutes on defense, and I managed to score three or four goals, many on rink-long rushes. Roland took note of my performance and my size, by this time six feet even and almost 180 pounds. After the game, he asked me how I felt about a career in hockey.

"The Montreal Junior Canadiens will be interested in hearing about you," he said, but I don't remember us pursuing the subject any further, perhaps because I couldn't believe he was serious.

Later that winter, however, one of the directors of the Senior Tigers, a man named Parenteau, invited me to practice with them. This proved to be enormously instructive, although the Seniors' culture came as quite a shock to a boy who had been playing académie hockey just a year before. On the ice with me were veterans such as Roland Hébert, Dick Wray, and Phil Vitali. Lucien Dechêne, a former player with New Westminster of the Western Hockey League, was in the net. In those days, team practices amounted to glorified scrimmages, and I found myself on the same ice as experienced former professionals and doing a lot better than I had realized I could, or so it seemed.

One day after practice, a man came by and introduced himself. His name was Jack Toupin, and he coached the Trois-Rivières Reds of the Quebec Junior A league. He was also a scout for the Toronto Maple Leafs.

"You're good enough to play with my team right now, Jean," he said. "All you have to do is give me the word, and I'll sign you. Besides, it would be exciting for you to play in your birthplace." I almost flew home that night. Junior A in Trois-Rivières, where I was born and my parents had been married! And close to the Béliveau and Dubé clans in Saint-Célestin and Charette! What could be better?

This time, it was my father who said no. "Not yet, Jean, you're still a bit too young, barely sixteen," he counseled. "I want you to continue your studies at the college. If you have the talent these people think you do, the hockey world won't forget you just because you choose to stay in Victoriaville another year or two." Case closed.

The following season, I rejoined the Victoriaville Panthers full-time as an intermediate. Unlike in today's strictly controlled and highly regimented hockey system, young men in the 1940s could play more or less wherever they were capable of playing. Talent, not age, was the determining factor. Intermediate hockey in particular was a place where players in their mid-twenties or even thirties who were a step too slow for the senior leagues could find a berth. But these guys knew what they were doing, and there was a whole lot more physical contact.

One of the attractions of intermediate hockey was that the whole community got behind the team. Among our most enthusiastic boosters was Adélard Morier, owner of a hardware and sporting goods store. Out of the blue one day, he gave me a pair of brand-new skates. Considering our family's finances, these were a luxury, and I never forgot his very generous gesture. But Mr. Morier was not alone. Several other local businessmen took it upon themselves to help out "their" Panthers.

That single season as an intermediate was an important springboard for my career. First and foremost, I became acquainted with new people in the community, including its leaders, whose support made life easier for the team. Second, I scored forty-seven goals and added twenty-one assists—the first yardstick of my progress in organized hockey. Third, I learned a very valuable lesson: to reach for the next rung on the ladder. When you're the best in your small corner, you can become too self-satisfied. You may achieve success, but you won't grow. Stand still, and you'll lose ground. Move on, and you'll continually test yourself, proving your worth anew.

While I was coming to this understanding, hockey's jungle drums were beating messages up and down the province of Quebec. Like their players, every coach and manager throughout the intermediate, junior, and senior leagues in the province aspired to move up in the hockey hierarchy, and the best way to do it was to ensure that the Montreal Canadiens knew what was happening in their backyard.

This sort of competition picked up steam in 1946 when Frank Selke joined the Canadiens as general manager. He immediately began to organize and encourage Quebec hockey (and hockey in other provinces, as well) at every level. Before Monsieur Selke arrived, the NHL's scouting system had been a hit-or-miss network of hot tips and tall tales. All that changed with his arrival, and Montreal's farm-club network became a production line, sending its output one-way to the Forum.

Time and money were no objects to Selke. He never hesitated to fund or create teams, sometimes intervening to enlarge the size of a particular league. He was patient, too, always working toward long-term results. He needed a constant flow of accurate information, and a coach's or manager's currency rose if he was the source of such intelligence.

My father was right, of course, to keep me back for a year, but when my season with the Panthers ended, Roland Hébert brought me to the attention of the Canadiens organization. A friend of his, a veteran goaltender named Paul Bibeault, happened to marry Frank Selke's daughter. At the wedding, Roland took Selke to one side. After recounting my scoring feats and describing how I'd fared in scrimmages with the senior players, Roland added the clincher: "And he's still growing."

And so the parade to Victoriaville began. One Sunday afternoon, after finishing a game of baseball, I was approached by two men while walking home. One spoke English only, the other acted as his interpreter. The man who appeared to be in charge introduced himself as Mickey Hennessey and said that he worked for Frank Selke and the Montreal Canadiens. He invited me into a snack bar "to talk a little business," and ordered a round of soft drinks. Once seated, he told me, "If you sign a C form with the Montreal Canadiens, I am authorized to give you a hundred dollars cash money, right here and now."

He extracted twenty $5 bills from his wallet and piled them before him on the table. This was serious money—more, I think, than I'd ever seen at one time. I used the interpreter to slow the bargaining process, asking him to clarify certain points and repeat others. It took me a while to grasp that the C form—a standard and legally binding document in those days—would link me directly to the Canadiens themselves, not to a junior team, although Montreal would have the right to assign me wherever they chose. I kept on asking questions, buying time, and trying desperately to think what to do next.

With each hesitation, a blue Canadian bank note was pushed across the tabletop, until $100 lay before me. Belong to the Montreal Canadiens? Play on the same team as Richard, Blake, and Lach? And get paid for it? At least I was smart enough not to tell these rather intimidating gentlemen that I would probably do it for free.

I was ready to go, lock, stock, and barrel—until, that is, I thought of the reception I'd get at home. Arthur Béliveau demanded respect and obedience from his children. If I was unwise enough to make such a commitment behind his back, I'd strike out on both counts. Summoning all my courage and pulling my eyes away from the money, I finished my drink and told Hennessey, "Please talk to my father. I can't sign any agreement without his approval."

Hennessey took me at my word and visited our home. Later, several other representatives of the Canadiens, including team captain Émile "Butch" Bouchard, paid calls. One after the other, my father turned them down. "My son will not sign something which gives someone else control over his life," said Arthur Béliveau, and he meant it.

Finally, however, an acceptable offer did arrive, albeit from another quarter. Sam Pollock's Junior Canadiens sent along a consent form—a totally different document that, if signed, meant only that I would report to their training camp for the following season and nothing more. I was free to go my own way afterward, whatever happened at the camp. My father and I signed this agreement on the recommendation of Roland Hébert and returned it to the team by mail.

That seemed to settle the matter. However, my father and I were unaware that Lucien Dechêne, the Senior Tigers' goaltender, had meanwhile contacted his friend Roland Mercier, the manager of the Quebec Citadels, a junior team owned by Frank Byrne. Mercier had been Lucien's coach in Junior B between 1941 and 1944. Dechêne had described me to Mercier, but Lucien wasn't sure of my first name. He knew me only as "the tall boy with the blue toque." As a result, Mercier had a hard time finding me, but he succeeded at last. Three weeks before my seventeenth birthday, I received a consent form similar to the one I'd already signed and returned to the Junior Canadiens, accompanied by a letter inviting me to the Quebec Citadels' training camp.

Had both invitations arrived simultaneously, there was a strong chance that I would have gone to Quebec City. The provincial capital was closer to Victoriaville and not quite the daunting metropolis that Montreal was. However, scant weeks before everyone's training camps began, Frank Selke changed the rules overnight by funding a drastic expansion of Quebec's junior league, almost tripling its size. One of the expansion centers that received a conditional franchise was Victoriaville, which suddenly found itself with both Senior and Junior Tigers, the latter being coached by none other than Roland Hébert.

Hébert immediately went to work on Selke: "Release Béliveau from the Junior Canadiens and let him play in his hometown. We're going to need all the help we can get to be competitive as an expansion team, and a local star will fill the rink. Besides, Sam Pollock has enough talent in Montreal already." Selke agreed, and Hébert came to me with the news that I could join the Tigers.

We didn't sign right away, though, figuring Roland Mercier's Citadels and Jack Toupin's Reds surely would submit counteroffers when they discovered that the Junior Canadiens had relinquished their claim. But when these were not forthcoming, I signed with Victoriaville three days before the season began. Only later did my father and I discover that Selke's release had been delivered to Hébert in secrecy; neither the Citadels nor the Reds knew anything about it. Frank Selke did not build a hockey dynasty by letting players get away.

Before I signed, my father had a long conversation with Roland Hébert. "Jean will play for you for one season only," he said. "After that, his rights revert to me."

"That's not how it works," Roland countered. "Players become the property of the team they sign with, unless they are traded or released."

"Not Jean Béliveau," my father replied, and we didn't sign the contract until that clause was added. Roland Hébert sensed my father's determination. Being from Victoriaville himself, he knew that while Arthur Béliveau would be scrupulously fair, he would stick to his guns when he felt he was right. After the season ended, I would be a free agent. End of discussion.

So it was that, when play in the Quebec Junior A Hockey League began in October 1948, I was wearing the gold-and-black of the Tigers. Like most of the other expansion teams, it was a diverse crew of castaways and newcomers. Still, we had some decent players, among them Denis Brodeur and André Belhumeur in nets, with Rémy Blais, Gordie Haworth, Roger Hayfield, and me up front, along with Gildor Lévesque and Marcel Chainey on defense.

The name "Brodeur" will be familiar. Denis went on to play goal for the Montreal Nationals at both junior and senior levels. He also represented Canada in Olympic hockey competition. He fathered Martin Brodeur, the superb young netminder of the New Jersey Devils, and he later became one of Montreal's foremost sports photographers. (The elder Brodeur's most difficult assignment came on Wednesday, December 8, 1993, when Martin, the same kid who used to tote Denis's equipment as a teenager, led his team against Montreal. There is nothing like a Forum homecoming for Canadiens' legends, and that night behind the Devils' bench were two well-known names, head coach Jacques Lemaire and defensive assistant Larry Robinson. Of course, Martin Brodeur earned the first star in a 4–2 win over the Canadiens, and Denis' lenses were fogged for all three periods.)

Besides myself and Paul Alain, very few local boys made the Tigers in 1948. The majority of players had come from far and wide. "Since you're living at home and you don't have to pay room and board, your salary will be $15 a week," said Hébert. I wasn't overwhelmed by his logic, figuring that on-ice performance, not my sleeping arrangements, should determine how much I was worth. Team management soon saw it my way: by Christmas I had as many goals as the rest of my teammates combined and a raise in pay to $35 a week. In those days, $35 a week could comfortably support a family of four.

Our season began promisingly with a 4–3 victory over the Verdun–LaSalle Cyclones. Roger Hayfield and I scored a pair of goals each against a fire-hydrant-shaped goalie named Lorne Worsley. At first, the Tigers did quite well for an expansion team, playing slightly less than .500 hockey through the fall as we approached a big game against the mighty Quebec Citadels on November 25. Going into that game, Quebec had fifteen wins and one tie for thirty-one points to lead the Southern Division, thirteen points more than the second-place Nationals and nineteen more than us, stuck in fourth place with six wins and nine losses.

That night proved auspicious for two reasons. It was my first appearance at Quebec City's Colisée and my introduction to a goaltender who would share a large part of my hockey career, Jacques Plante. We opened the scoring on a goal by Rémy Blais early in the second period, but the Citadels responded with a pair before the middle period was finished. My goal midway through the third sent the game into overtime.

Back then the rules called for a full, ten-minute overtime period, not a sudden-death finale. About three minutes in, I fed a pass to Gérard Théberge, who one-timed it into the Quebec goal. Several minutes later, the puck was cleared out of our zone and toward the Quebec goal. I took off after it, with no one in close pursuit. The Citadels' netminder, who I'd heard was infamous for his wandering ways, decided to come out after the puck. Just as he reached to poke it away, I managed to get my stick on it. The goalie sprawled at the Citadels' blue line while I swung around him and tucked the puck into the open net. We ended the extra-time period with a 4–2 win.

In later years I had many opportunities to kid Jacques about the night I deked him out of the rink and ruined his streak, but the true star that night was our goalie, Denis Brodeur, who stopped thirty-nine shots to keep the contest close.

My first experience with Junior A hockey was quite different from that of the majority of my teammates. I was living in my hometown and continuing my education, maintaining a hectic schedule even then. I was a regular eight-to-four daytime student at the college, which also required that we attend study hall between seven and nine o'clock in the evening, Monday through Thursday. However, the

Tigers held a practice at four o'clock and played their games at eight. On game nights, I'd make a token appearance in study hall, flash my special hockey player's pass, and receive permission to leave. Brother Fernand supervised the hall, and as I flew past him he'd often call after me, "Boy, you're in a hurry to avoid your studies." I never knew if he was upset because I had dispensation to play, or if he was only kidding.

Many years later, after I had joined the Canadiens, I was playing in Boston when I received a call from Brother Fernand, looking for a ticket. That night he sat right behind our bench and after the game we reminisced about the student hotfooting it by him at the study hall door. He had to admit that my alternative "studies" had gone fairly well.

The grade 10 students at Collège de Victoriaville were directed into one of three streams: business, technical, or science. I was enrolled in technical, in pre-electrical studies; I'd thought that perhaps I would follow my father into a job with the power company. But a year later, worn out by one too many five-in-the-morning returns from a road trip, I had to put an end to my formal schooling, and my father agreed.

The Tigers and I got off to a slow start that debut season in 1948–49. By early December, I was well back in the individual scoring statistics, with twenty-one points on thirteen goals and eight assists. Frankie Reid of Trois-Rivières was far in front with fifty-one points, three ahead of the Nationals' Bernard Geoffrion, with forty-eight. By season's end, Reid still led on points, but I had a league-leading forty-eight goals, which earned me dual honors as "rookie of the year" and "most promising professional prospect."

As the season progressed, it appeared that the Tigers would not make the play-offs, but we squeaked in when Roland Mercier reported that a Citadels player named Marius Groleau had been playing with false identification, namely his dead brother's birth certificate. Groleau was ruled ineligible and Quebec had to forfeit all the games in which he'd played. This moved us out of last place and into a best-of-five divisional semifinal. But our luck didn't hold. We were eliminated 3–1, and although I didn't yet know it, my hockey career in Victoriaville was over.

After the Tigers were bumped from play-off action, my father and I began to negotiate with the Quebec Citadels for the following season, 1949–50. Thanks to my father's insistence, I was a free agent, able to deal with anyone we chose. We met Roland Mercier, the Citadels' general manager, at a hotel in nearby Princeville and discussed contract terms. A few days later we reconvened and came to an agreement in principle. It appeared I would head for Quebec that autumn, barring unforeseen snags with the league or the Tigers.

In the meantime, however, Roland Hébert's excellent work in Victoriaville had not gone unnoticed. He accepted the post of head coach and general manager of the Chicoutimi Saguenéens of the Senior League, and he attempted to have the Junior Tigers declared an official Chicoutimi farm team. When this proved impossible under the league's bylaws, Roland rescinded Victoriaville's junior-league concession, and all of his players became free agents along with me.

Or at least that was the story as I understood it for more than forty years. While I was preparing the manuscript of this book, I had occasion to review those events with Roland Mercier, who revealed for the first time that other maneuvers were going on behind the scenes.

In fact, I was never a free agent and had belonged to the Citadels since November 1948. Without going into the fine print of league bylaws and hockey contracts, it seems any player who had signed with a given team—in my case, the 1948–49 Victoriaville Junior Tigers—could sign with another team—in my case, the Citadels—if one of three conditions applied: Either I would have had to obtain a release from the first team, which the Tigers wouldn't have granted; or I would have had to be an over-aged junior, which I wasn't. Or the first team would have had to cease operations, which in fact is what happened with the Tigers. But nobody knew they were going to disappear until they did, thanks to Roland Hébert's decision.

Despite my father's best intentions, the contract we signed with Hébert could have been contested by the league or by any other club. The clause that we added sounded fine, but it had no real validity.

In any event, Roland Mercier took his first step toward signing me with the Citadels in the fall of 1948, immediately after the game during which I scored on my future teammate, Jacques Plante. Roland came straight to the Tigers' dressing room and concluded a deal with the team that sent Leonard Shaw to Victoriaville for $100 and a player to be named later—"later" being the 1949–50 season. Roland felt no need to mention that the player he had in mind was me.

When the Tigers ran into financial difficulties a couple of months later, Roland returned their $100 cheque and informed them that he would waive the usual $100-per-game fee that the Citadels—a major draw—would receive for playing in the Victoriaville Arena. The Tigers were surprised by his generosity and asked him to name at last the player he wanted to complete their deal. When he uttered the name "Béliveau," the Tigers' directors were up in arms and threatened to renege. Roland calmly pointed out that the deal had been transacted in front of several witnesses and that he intended to hold them to it.

This also explains why, after the old Colisée in Quebec City burned down, the Citadels took up temporary residence in Victoriaville. In effect, I was already the Citadels' property, lent to the Tigers for the duration of the season, a fact that few people other than Roland Mercier have ever known.

None of which really matters, I suppose, because the rest of the story unfolded as described. I played the first two months of the 1949–50 season with the Citadels in Victoriaville, waiting for construction to be completed on the new, improved Colisée.

In all my conversations with Roland Mercier and owner Frank Byrne, they were very explicit as to why they wanted me on the team. The destroyed Colisée had been a glorified exhibition barn, but its replacement would be state of the hockey art.

"Our building opens in December," said Byrne, "and it is more than twice as big as the old Colisée. We need a star to fill those seats. We believe that star is you."

3

LA VIEILLE CAPITALE

MORE THAN FIFTY YEARS after my time as a young hockey player in Quebec City, I always find reasons to return. It was there that this small-town boy grew up, met and married his wife, forged hundreds of lifelong acquaintances and close friendships, and launched a career in the sport he loved. Through the decades, I've revisited the city for birthday celebrations, weddings, anniversaries, funerals, and for holidays, not to mention countless league and team functions. It still feels like home to Élise and me.

I could not have predicted the attachment I would develop for the city when, in late 1949, its opportunities beckoned me away from home and family. On December 13, the Citadels left Victoriaville to return to Quebec City and their new home rink, and I went with them. My mother served a hearty lunch to send me off and my father drove me to the arena where the team bus awaited its eager passengers.

It was a gray day and snowing heavily. My father and I spoke not a word during the five-minute ride, but he seemed composed and confident. He had met the Citadels management in his own backyard and he liked what he had seen. He knew I was in good hands. At the arena he reached into the back of his truck and swung out the suitcase. As he passed me the bag, he took my right hand in his and shook it once.

"Do your best, Jean. That will be enough."

He turned and climbed back into the cab, waved curtly, and drove away. The snow meant problems for the wires that sang overhead in Victoriaville, and Arthur Béliveau, crew foreman, was on the job.

The bus ride to Quebec City took a little more than three hours, twice as long as usual because of the weather. We went directly to the old Colisée and unloaded our equipment there. The previous spring's fire damage had not reached its dressing rooms, while the rooms at the new Colisée, about a hundred yards away across the parade grounds of the Exposition de Québec, were not yet completed. It had been decided that for the first month of the season we would dress, pick up our skates, and walk or take a shuttle bus from the old building to the new. Intermissions were spent in a freshly finished but very gloomy room redolent of fresh concrete and offering only a few bare planks on which to rest our weary behinds. When the game ended, we'd return to the old Colisée for a shower and a change into street clothes.

On our arrival that December afternoon, coach Pete Martin and Roland Mercier offered a few words of welcome, then sent us off in various directions to our billets. Milt Pridham, Dave O'Meara, and I had been assigned to the Paquette family's boardinghouse on St. Cyrille Boulevard, between Salaberry and Turnbull Streets in Upper Town, not far from the National Assembly. The rooms were tiny, but they were all we needed. Our lives would be taken up by hockey for the next five months.

I think the billeting arrangements were handled by Roland Mercier. Placing me with two English-speaking players was his way of accelerating my second-language proficiency. At that time, I could manage "yes" or "no," and several simple phrases, but that was it. All of my schooling and, of course, every conversation at home had been in French only. Milt and Dave were literally my first English teachers. The following year, I roomed with Gordie Haworth and Bruce Cline, who did their part to introduce me to unfamiliar nouns and verbs. English was the dominant language of the NHL, and Roland Mercier wanted to expose me to it early, another sign that those in my growing hockey family believed that I was going on beyond the junior ranks.

The Quebec Citadels of 1949–50 were a solid, tough team, led by Dave O'Meara and Marcel Paillé in goal. Spike Laliberté, Gordie Hudson, Bernard Lemonde, and Jean-Marie Plante were on defense. Up front with me were Roger Hayfield and Gordie Haworth, my former teammates from Victoriaville, plus Rainer Makila, Milt Pridham, Bruce Cline, Jean-Marc Pichette, Jules Tremblay, Roland Dubeau, Russell Tuer, Norman Diviney, and Gaston Gervais.

We had plenty of offensive power, but we played in a league of strong offensive teams. The Montreal Nationals counted Bernie Geoffrion and Fred "Skippy" Burchell among their ranks, and Sam Pollock's Junior Canadiens were spearheaded by Dickie Moore. In my first season with the Citadels I had fewer goals (thirty-five), but more assists (forty-five) than in previous years. Even so, my total of eighty points ranked second only to Geoffrion's, and I was glad to see the scoring responsibilities spread among my Citadels teammates.

As it turned out, we finished the regular season in second place and beat the third-place Nationals four straight in the semifinal, winning the last game 6–5 in overtime. It was an extremely close game, with both teams skating full tilt from the opening face-off. This spoke well for the Nationals, who trailed 3–0 in the series on our home ice but who refused to fold. We were down 5–4 when my second goal of the game at 19:06 of the third period sent the teams into overtime. I netted a hat trick with a breakaway goal at the forty-eight-second mark of extra time. The victim of all three goals was my former Tigers teammate Denis Brodeur.

Our semifinal victory was marred by an incident that rankled all of us for days afterward. With the completion of the new Colisée and the continued success of our team—remember, the Citadels had been a first-place club during my year in Victoriaville—the crowds began to swell. We played before more than ten thousand fans every night, a display of enthusiasm enjoyed by other teams in the league as well. Trois-Rivières, Verdun, and the three Montreal teams all drew capacity crowds. But with the increased attendance came increased rowdiness and occasional outright idiocy in the stands. When I scored that third-period goal against the Nationals in game 4, it prompted both a standing ovation and a shower of debris that littered the ice surface and delayed resumption of play for several minutes. Some fans threw rolls of toilet paper, streamers, or cardboard, but one individual thought it would be a good idea to toss a bottle from the upper seats. It struck a Nationals player on the head, and the Colisée fell silent as he was carried off on a stretcher. Fortunately, he was not seriously injured, but the episode was a disturbing one.

Still, the Nationals-Citadels series could be viewed as a fairly clean encounter compared with the league final against Sam Pollock's Junior Canadiens. That contest was all-out war. Sam's not-so-secret weapon was Dickie Moore, one of the fiercest competitors I've ever met. Dickie stood maybe five feet, ten inches tall, and weighed 170 pounds soaking wet. I was five inches taller and almost thirty pounds heavier, but every time we played the "Baby Habs" he was in my face. Our coach, Pete Martin, would put another man on against him, switch lines, double-shift me, or sit me out for a while, but Dickie was undeterred: whenever I came out, he'd be in front of me, always taking shots.

Bigger hockey players are often faulted for failing to take advantage of their size, for hesitating to use their bodies to lean on smaller but highly aggressive players. I heard that often enough during my junior career when I was repeatedly dubbed "the gentle giant," or "le Gros Bill." It didn't bother me, because I knew where my true strengths lay. Moreover, when we played the Junior Canadiens it wasn't true: Dickie and I were running at each other all the time. The high-sticking, cross-checking, elbowing, and roughing was relentless, and I'm not ashamed to admit that on certain occasions, Dickie wore me down. I wasn't a fighter, mostly by choice. I didn't like it, and I recognized my limitations in that area. But I tended to make an exception for Dickie, and he got as good as he gave. He was a wild man who on more than one occasion went up into the stands to confront his long-distance tormentors. You couldn't find a better teammate, though, as I would discover a few years later.

The Junior Habs of 1950–51 provided Moore with a formidable supporting cast: Bill Sinnett, Dave McCready, Donnie Marshall, Herb English, Ernie Roche, George McAvoy, Kenny Rocheford, Billy Rose, and Art Goold. These boys could skate like the wind, pass beautifully, and frustrate the opposition with their forechecking and control of the defensive zone. If you did manage to get past a defenseman like Kevin "Crusher" Conway, you would have to contend with either Charlie Hodge or Bill Harrington in nets.

Our best-of-seven series was deadlocked at two hard-fought wins apiece when Frank Selke decided to muddy the waters with a remark that anticipated Mario Puzo's *Godfather* by almost three decades. "When this season is over, I'm going to make Jean Béliveau an offer he can't refuse," he told the Montreal media. He went on to say that the Canadiens' weak spot that season was at center, where Elmer Lach, "the Old Reliable," wasn't getting any younger.

"I know that Jean Béliveau is only eighteen, but he is a big boy, and other boys of that age have broken into our league. I think he has demonstrated all the right qualities to be able to do this and to be a star in our league for a long, long time," said Selke.

Naturally, Frank Byrne and Pete Martin were incensed by this. It was galling enough that Papa Selke had told them in no uncertain terms that he intended to come and get me, a player with a year of junior eligibility still to go, which was akin to tampering. But Selke's announcement also had the effect of painting a bull's-eye on my back for any Junior Canadien who wished to make his mark.

Most observers felt that our series would not go the full seven games and that the Saturday-Sunday home-and-home series on March 25 and 26 would settle matters. They were right. The Canadiens came out with guns blazing on Saturday night. They followed Sam Pollock's script to perfection, and Rocheford scored on a goalmouth pass from Donnie Marshall at 5:20. Then Herbie English set up Ernie Roche a scant two minutes later.

We began to return, urged on by an impatient crowd, but lost momentum when the penalty box was filled after a scrap erupted between—no surprise—myself and Dickie Moore. Still, we managed to get one back before the period ended on a screen shot by Gordie Hudson, and we had the crowd back on our side midway through the second period when Gaston Gervais and Jean-Marc Pichette set me up for the equalizer. It wouldn't be enough. A knee injury to Bernard Lemonde hurt us on defense, and the Canadiens stepped up their relentless attack, with Herbie English putting them ahead to stay with less than two minutes remaining in the period.

We were hanging on by our fingertips when Dickie Moore decided to put us out of our misery, setting up Roche for his second goal at 12:17 of the third period. Milt Pridham brought us back to within one in the eighteenth minute, prompting Pete Martin to pull Marcel Paillé in favor of an extra attacker. Pridham took the face-off deep in the Montreal zone and I was at the point, ready to let go with my best shot. The puck went behind the net and up to Moore. He passed to Roche, who went one-on-one with me. I never was an NHL-caliber defenseman and even less an NHL-caliber goalie; Roche backed me into our net and easily put the puck behind me. The Junior Canadiens were one win away from the title.

The following night at the Forum, they were unstoppable, taking a 3–0 lead by the 13:10 mark on goals by Bill Sinnett, Art Goold, and Billy Rose. We replied with markers from Rainer Makila and Jules Tremblay, but Rose added two more in the middle period, to one of ours by Gervais, our best player in the final two games. Another two in the final period gave Sam Pollock a 7–3 win and his first-ever junior-league title. Later that spring, Dickie, Donnie, and company went on to defeat St. Mary's of Halifax, then the Guelph Biltmores, and finally the Regina Pats to win the 1950 Memorial Cup.

THE 1950–51 SEASON had been wonderful for me, even though the first few months in Quebec were tough for a newcomer. I was lonely, making a difficult adjustment to life away from home and family. I couldn't continue my high school studies in the technical course I'd begun in Victoriaville because the hockey schedule placed far too many demands on my time. I felt isolated, and my natural shyness inhibited me from meeting people my own age outside the rink. I was pretty much a loner that year, reluctant to initiate social contacts, and spent a lot of my newfound spare time reading or walking through Quebec City. If it wasn't too cold, I would stroll for miles along St. Jean Street and past Salaberry, Turnbull, Park, and Fraser, all around the Cartier Street neighborhood.

Rue Cartier in Upper Town is still a very popular street. In those days, there was a drugstore with a lunch counter and a soda fountain on the corner of St. Cyrille Boulevard, and another one farther up, where constables from the Royal Canadian Mounted Police (RCMP) office on Grande-Allée and Cartier would eat their lunch. I used to boast that I was the best-fed and best-protected hockey player in Quebec. My RCMP buddies would watch over me, and Mr. Laroche, the lunch counter's owner, would give me a free steak every time I scored three goals.

That summer I returned home to Victoriaville for the last time, living with my family and working days at the Fashion Craft apparel plant for $15 a week. Evenings were spent hitting home runs for the firm's team in a commercially sponsored softball league. It sounds like an ideal life, but there were one or two irritants. I worked in the shipping and receiving department in a warehouse without air conditioning. Since Fashion Craft's winter coats were manufactured in summer, we often had to wrestle with huge boxes and mountainous piles of thick, bulky material, in ninety- or hundred-degree-Fahrenheit temperatures. I put on weight that summer, all of it muscle in the back, shoulders, and upper arms. As fall approached, I was anxious to get back to Quebec City.

First, however, there was a stop in Montreal, where I'd been invited to attend the Canadiens' training camp. I enjoyed my three weeks there, but did not receive "an offer I couldn't refuse" from Frank Selke and returned to Quebec in late September. I felt reasonably comfortable playing with the Canadiens in intrasquad games and against senior-league opposition in exhibition contests, but I was determined to return to the Citadels for my final junior year. I had had several conversations with Roland Mercier and Frank Byrne in the off-season, and they'd assured me that the Citadels would be a serious challenger for the 1951 Memorial Cup.

Montreal hadn't given up hopes of luring me there. The prospect of Geoffrion, Moore, and Béliveau—three of Canada's most highly touted junior stars—in the same uniform had set Canadiens' fans and Montreal sportswriters to salivating. While I was skating with the big team, Frank Selke's emissaries had made forays to both Victoriaville and Quebec City but without success. The Canadiens offered the Citadels some of their top junior talent in exchange for me, but Arthur Béliveau and Frank Byrne stuck stubbornly to their agreement. Before I left to attend the Canadiens' camp, Frank had reiterated that money would not be an issue. "Whatever they offer you," he said, "we'll match or better. Just don't sign anything."

The Citadels had attracted record attendance the previous season. An overcapacity crowd of 13,714 paying customers had marched through the turnstiles for our fourth game against the Junior Canadiens in the league final. Quebec sportswriters such as Louis Fusk, Guy Lemieux, and Roland Sabourin regularly described the Colisée as "Château Béliveau," and the pressure was on for me to return to the provincial capital to help the Citadels' drive for the Canadian championship. Deep down, however, most Quebec fans and hockey pundits felt that I would yield to Frank Selke's overtures and that I had already played my final game for the Citadels.

What these people weren't considering were the lessons that Arthur and Laurette Béliveau had taught their children. Even Selke, a deeply religious and fair-minded man, no doubt respected our stand and secretly approved. "Loyalty is another form of responsibility," my father had often told me. "If you feel that you owe something to someone, no matter what the debt, it behooves you to pay it. Sometimes, those very people will indicate that they are discharging the debt, but only you will know what the best policy will be. Your good name is your greatest asset."

Call it loyalty or a debt of gratitude, I was determined to return to Quebec, and nothing Mr. Selke could say or do in the late summer of 1950 would alter my decision.

When I arrived in Quebec, I soon discovered that Frank Byrne had kept his end of the bargain. The Citadels had lost a number of valuable veterans, most notably Spike Laliberté, Milt Pridham, Jackie Leclair, Jean-Marc Pichette, and Jules Tremblay. But we had managed to retain a strong nucleus, including goalie Marcel Paillé, defensemen Gordie Hudson, Jean-Marie Plante, and Bernard

Lemonde, and forwards Rainer Makila, Gordie Haworth, Norm Diviney, Gaston Gervais, and Bernard Guay. Newcomers included left-winger Claude Larochelle, who would go on to become the dean of Quebec City sportswriters, Wilson "Copper" Leyte, Camille Henry, who would win the Calder Trophy as NHL rookie of the year in 1954, defensemen Neil Amodio and Jean-Paul Légault, and backup goalie Claude Senecal. Frank had promised performance, and this lineup delivered it.

A promise of off-ice employment turned out to be a public relations job with the Laval Dairy at $60 a week, a lot of money at that time. At age nineteen I was earning about $6,000 a year with the Citadels—a competitive NHL salary—and another $3,000 or so with Laval, where I began to pick up the off-ice skills that would help me later in life.

Part of my job was to cohost a Saturday morning children's program on radio station CHRC. We had all the ingredients for a successful format. After a cowboy story, we'd go live and mobile, taking the show to the kids by broadcasting from one of three locations: the Durocher Centre in Lower Town, La Canardière Centre in Limoilou, or a Knights of Columbus Hall in Ste-Foy, near Laval University. It was amateur radio at its best, and our weekly draws for ice-cream products, hockey sticks, and tickets to Citadels or Senior-league Quebec Aces games were wildly popular. The first week, two hundred kids came by to watch; four weeks later, we had an audience of more than a thousand.

Later still, my popularity with the younger generation of Quebec hockey fans reached record heights when I became the Laval Ice-Cream Man. The dairy built a cooler to fit into the trunk of my car and filled it with all sorts of goodies. My duties were simple: whenever I came across a group of kids, I'd pull over to the curb, open the trunk, and pass out free ice cream. The 1950s were a far more innocent time, obviously. Anyone who did this today might risk arrest.

Of course, these activities were rudimentary meet-the-public techniques. But you have to start somewhere. I was always—and I suppose still am—an introvert, a trait inherited from my mother. The idea of making a speech had always unnerved me. But when you're introduced to an audience of five hundred people who have gathered to hear you say something and the microphone is shoved into your hand, you learn quickly enough. It's a form of shock therapy for the habitually shy.

At least Laval Dairy was a family business, and they treated me like family. It was owned by two brothers, Jules and Paul Côté. Jules enjoyed our Saturday radio show so much that he'd often get up and start dancing. Paul was more reserved, but he always came to the broadcasts, too. Each of them had a son: Pierre and Jacques, respectively. Jacques and I became particularly close. The two elder Côtés were ideally matched in temperament to run the company together, as were their sons later on, when Jacques took over the production side while Pierre handled administration.

What began as a professional relationship quickly became a series of lasting, enriching friendships. The Côtés were dedicated family men, and when Paul's wife passed away, he was desolate. I was playing in Montreal at the time, and I remember Jacques called me from Quebec City.

"Jean, we have to do something for my father. He's completely lost without my mother and we need something to pick him up and get him going," he said. I managed to find a pair of Canadiens' season tickets, and for years after, Paul never missed a game. In August, when the upcoming season's schedule was published, he'd make an entire season's worth of reservations on the Quebec-to-Montreal train, as well as room reservations at the Queen Elizabeth Hotel if he had to stay overnight.

That first year, the only two season tickets I could secure were down at one end of the rink. In those days the height of the protective glass was somewhat lower, and one night a puck flew over the net, giving Paul just enough time to raise his arm. For weeks afterward, he brandished the broken wrist in a cast and happily bragged to friends and acquaintances, "I got hit by a puck in the Forum."

One of the saddest moments of my life was the day in 1971 when news arrived that Jacques Côté had died in the same plane crash that claimed the life of Roger White, the harness-racing driver. Jacques had owned several pacers, and the two men were en route to southern New York from a Fort Erie racetrack when their plane went down.

While I may have been a star hockey player and a budding media personality, Quebec City in 1950 was a simpler, gentler place. I never thought to demand a luxury penthouse as a signing bonus. That second season I roomed in a boardinghouse run by three older ladies, the McKenna sisters. One of them worked for the Red Cross, the second for Anglo-Canadian Pulp and Paper, and the third managed the boardinghouse. I had a small room on the third floor and another opportunity to practice my English, although all three sisters were perfectly fluent in French.

Many of my friends and acquaintances in the neighborhood had become familiar with my daily jaunts all over the *quartier*, and I think some of them despaired of a tall, young man whose only pursuits seemed to be hockey and books. Among them were the Gagnon family, who lived around the corner on des Érables. They were regulars at our games and I often met them on my walks.

One Wednesday night, a few days before the next scheduled game, they invited me to join them for a night out. "We have a nice girl we'd like you to meet." They wouldn't take no for an answer and soon after we were on our way to the Manoir St. Castin at Lac Beauport, north of the city, in a party of ten or eleven. (It's a small world: forty years later, the Manoir was bought by a group of Quebec City investors that included Marc Tardif, my teammate with the Canadiens in 1970 and 1971.)

I met Élise Couture that evening. What impressed me the most about the pretty, bilingual blonde was that she knew absolutely nothing about hockey. She'd never been to a game and had no idea what all the fuss was about. It would be several months before she dared to tell her mother that we were dating. Mrs. Couture, whose maiden name, Mahon, reflected her Irish ancestry, had little confidence in hockey players.

Élise and I didn't dance much, because I'd never really learned how, but we did spend a lot of time talking. Before long I realized that this was a strong-willed young woman, one with clear convictions and opinions, and that I would like to get to know her better. That winter, as our relationship slowly developed, she taught me how to drive her family's Studebaker—a timely lesson, as I would soon appreciate.

On the ice, my career was accelerating at a breakneck pace, so much so that in one three-week period in late November and early December of 1950, I played games at three different levels of hockey. In addition to the regularly scheduled games of the junior-league Citadels during those weeks, I joined the Quebec Aces of the senior league for a game on November 26 at the Colisée against my former coach Roland Hébert and his Chicoutimi Saguenéens. I played on a line with Dick Gamble, who would join the Canadiens before the season was out, and we both scored a pair of goals in a 4–4 tie.

Twenty days later, Bernie "Boom Boom" Geoffrion of the Nationals and I made our National Hockey League regular-season debuts with the Canadiens in a 1–1 tie against Boston. Boom Boom scored Montreal's only goal, but I had nine shots on net, earning me the game's first star and scaring the heck out of Frank Byrne, who remained skittish at the possibility of my deserting the Citadels. As one Montreal columnist wrote the following week, "Mr. Byrne was here to watch the boy make his debut in National League company, sharing the Selke box for the occasion. He declined Selke's invitation to visit the directors' room for a sandwich and a cup of coffee after the game. 'I can't say I blame him,' said Selke. 'He must have suspected he'd be under a lot of pressure if he'd come in here.'"

Six weeks later, with both Billy Reay and Maurice Richard ailing, Boom Boom and I joined the Canadiens once again, along with Dick Gamble of the Aces and Hugh Currie of the Buffalo Bisons. Teamed with left-winger Claude Robert, Boom and I each scored a goal and an assist against veteran netminder Harry Lumley in a 4–2 win over Chicago, a team that had gone winless in nineteen games. Another two weeks later, I played for the Aces in a special exhibition game against the Detroit Red Wings in Quebec City, but that would be the last NHL competition I would enjoy until late in 1952.

As it turned out, this hiatus did not bother me in the least, because the Citadels were firmly atop the league standings. I was enjoying my most productive season ever, locked in a struggle for the scoring championship with Boom Boom and his Nationals linemate, Skippy Burchell. Late in the season, Boom was summoned by the injury-riddled Canadiens and left the Nationals, having achieved ninety-six points, ten more than his league-leading eighty-six the previous season. It was an amazing figure, considering that he'd played only thirty-six games. As luck would have it, Burchell and I came down to the last game tied at 122 points each, an all-time junior-league record.

In the final, the Nationals jumped on us quickly, taking a 4–0 lead on a pair of goals by Burchell and Bert Scullion, but we got two back before the end of the period when Gordie Haworth scored at 15:40 on a pass from Camille Henry and I racked up my sixtieth of the season on a penalty shot. Gordie made it 4–3 midway through the second period and Ray Goyette added still another. As the minutes passed, it appeared likely that both the Nationals' lead and Burchell's scoring championship were safe, especially after Pete Larocque collided with me in the second period and I went off with a charley horse, seemingly finished for the night. I sat in the dressing room for the rest of the period and into the intermission. A large ice-pack did very little to relieve the physical pain and nothing to ease my emotional anguish. The scoring title had eluded me. We had beaten the Nationals in seven of nine previous games and clinched first place much earlier in the season, so only my personal satisfaction was at stake. Or so I thought.

Pete Martin and special adviser Kilby Macdonald filed in with the rest of the team during intermission. Outside, the fans were despondent. The Citadels were losing, but for them this seemed secondary. The local star had fallen behind his Montreal rival in the scoring race and was condemned to finish second for the second straight year.

"Nobody in this room will think you selfish if you go out there and try to tie Burchell," Martin said to me. "I don't have to tell you how everybody feels about Larocque's hit, either." In fact, I hadn't thought that Larocque had caught me with a bad hit, but every subsequent whistle from referees Déziel and Saint-Armand had been greeted by a chorus of boos.

There was a tremendous cheer when I came out for the third period, limping noticeably. Camille Henry joined Rainer Makila and me for the final period, replacing Bernard Guay on left wing. That added offensive punch to our line and gave the Nationals something else to worry about. During the entire third period, two games were being played, neither of which had anything to do with the score. Our checkers were doing their utmost to shut down Burchell whenever he was on the ice, while the Nationals' checkers did the same to contain Camille, Rainer, and me.

Even though the Nationals won the game, 5–4, our side won the scoring joust. With the teams playing four a side, Makila broke out of our zone, one-on-one with a Nationals defenseman, with me trailing. He drew the Montreal defender to him and laid a perfect pass onto my stick. I had plenty of net to shoot at and so took my first scoring championship, albeit a shared one.

After the game, an army of photographers gathered around Skippy Burchell and myself as we posed for a study in contrasts—his five-foot, seven-inch David to my six-foot, three-inch Goliath. We'd both wound up with 124 points, mine on a league-leading sixty-one goals and sixty-three assists, Burchell's on forty-nine goals and a league-leading seventy-five assists.

We would meet the second-place Junior Habs in a best-of-nine semifinal, while the Nationals, Verdun, and Trois-Rivières would play a six-game round-robin to determine the other finalist. This format made little sense, but we were grateful for an opportunity to avenge our 1950 loss to Montreal. The 1951 edition remained a formidable group, with Moore, Sinnett, English, McCready, Nadon, and Marchesseault returning from the previous year and joined by two promising newcomers, forward Scotty Bowman and goalie Charlie Hodge. We had come out ahead in our ten-game season series by the narrowest of margins with our 6–4 tally, and the nine-game play-off promised more of the same.

I went into the play-off opener hoping that my charley horse had cleared up. I scored two goals and an assist, while Makila popped two and added three assists; we took the opener 5–3. After four games, with the series tied, I had a double charley horse and wasn't feeling so well. I'd been out for a week, missing the third and fourth games, when Frank Byrne and Sam Pollock began a spat over the scheduling and site of the fifth game. The fourth game had been played at the Forum on Sunday night; the next was slated for the Colisée on Tuesday. For some reason or other, the Colisée was unavailable that day, and Buster Horwood, the league president, ordered that the game be transferred back to Montreal.

"We are obliged to finish our Quebec play-offs by April 1, so the winner can go on to the next level," he said. "We cannot have four-day breaks between series games if the championship is to be completed in time."

Frank Byrne got his Irish up and kept the Citadels in Quebec that night, claiming that we'd won home-ice advantage throughout an arduous season and would not yield it at a bureaucrat's whim. Horwood threatened suspension, forfeit, and fine, but when he saw that Byrne was determined, he relented, scheduling a Thursday night encounter in Quebec, followed by a sixth game in Montreal on Sunday.

At the same time, Horwood could not resist a parting shot at what he thought was Byrne's real reason for not playing in Montreal. In an official statement released by his office, the president stated, "It is most probable that the Citadels are acting this way to give Jean Béliveau time to recover from an injury."

Whatever the reason, we won the fifth game 4–0, and went on to win the series, too—but not before Dickie Moore became embroiled in a penalty-box scuffle with two Quebec City police officers, which prompted his teammates to swarm over the boards when the fighting spread into the nearby stands.

A week later, with a four-game sweep of the Trois-Rivières Reds under our belts, we patiently awaited the representatives of the Ottawa and District Hockey League. One day after practice, Roland Mercier mentioned that the team wanted to express their gratitude to me with a special presentation before an upcoming home play-off game. Would I mind? Figuring that I was in line for a nice watch and a couple of well-wishing speeches, I agreed and thought no more about it. We were busy defusing the Inkerman Rockets, 9–0 and 16–4, in the first two games of our best-of-five eastern Canadian series.

On Tuesday, April 10, immediately after dignitaries from three levels of government had saluted the teams in a pregame ceremony, a 1951 Nash Canadian Statesman de Luxe was driven onto the ice. The license plate was 99-B, in honor of my number 9 jersey. Flabbergasted, I took possession of the keys and tried hard not to fall down on the spot. My teammates and I were so dazzled by this remarkable show of appreciation that we went on to demolish the hapless Rockets 13–0 and to sweep the series in three straight games.

Up next were the semifinals and the Barrie Flyers of the Ontario Hockey League, a powerhouse coached by the venerable Leighton "Hap" Emms with five future NHL stalwarts in its ranks: Jim Morrison, Leo Labine, Réal Chevrefils, Jerry Toppazzini, and Doug Mohns, the last a Junior B call-up for the series.

The Toronto newspapers began to promote the series as Béliveau versus the world. After we lost the first two games at a sold-out Maple Leaf Gardens 6–2 and 6–4, the press shifted gears, writing off Béliveau and the Citadels as the stuff of an inferior league. We weren't convinced. Returning home, we promptly tied the series with 7–2 and 4–2 wins. Then yet another dispute over venues broke loose.

Many people will be surprised to learn that it was Frank Selke who would bear much of the responsibility for our failure to win the Memorial Cup that year. In those days, a junior team competing for the cup could pick up one or two last-minute star players from other teams that had been eliminated in earlier rounds. That year, Frank Byrne had asked Dickie Moore if he would join the Citadels, and Dickie had said he'd be happy to oblige.

Much later, Dickie told me what happened. "I was a Quebecker and I would have loved to stop an Ontario team for a third straight year," he said. By this he meant that he'd helped win the two previous cups, first with the Montreal Royals, then with the Junior Canadiens.

"But Frank Selke stepped in. The year before, he'd broken up the Royals and directed most of their talent to the Nationals. I went and signed with Sammy Pollock and the Junior Canadiens, which didn't please Selke one bit. When I told him I wanted to play for the Citadels in the Memorial Cup, he said, 'Over my dead body.'"

Hap Emms had heard a rumor that Moore would join the Citadels for the Flyers series. He thought the gossip might be true when he ran into Dickie at the Colisée early on the day of game 3.

"What are you doing here?" Hap asked.

Dickie laughed at Hap's discomfort. "I'm playing for Quebec, if we can find a way to kill Frank Selke."

Selke lived, however, and Dickie wasn't able to supply us with his awesome competitive skills.

Prior to the series, the Barrie Flyers had argued long and loud that at least one game should be played in their home rink fifty-five miles north of Toronto, a tiny little bandbox with very few seats and very little on-ice room to maneuver, especially for visitors who were unfamiliar with its nuances. We'd argued just as long and loud against this unwelcome scheme. It was accepted practice in those pretelevision days for Memorial Cup games to be played only in large-capacity arenas, such as Maple Leaf Gardens, the Forum, or the Colisée. Furthermore, smaller towns such as Barrie were not readily accessible by train or plane, making the back-and-forth travel of a seven-game series tiring and time consuming.

Unfortunately, we lost the argument and prior to game 5 left Quebec City on a Rimouski Air Lines flight at four thirty in the afternoon, flew to the Camp Borden army base, then caught a bus to Barrie. We walked into the Barrie arena at 9 PM and took the opening face-off thirty-two minutes later. The Flyers were waiting for us. They scored four power-play goals in the first thirteen minutes, and we took a 10–1 shellacking. We tied the series back in Quebec City, but lost 8–3 in game 7 at Maple Leaf Gardens, having survived yet another adventure in early Canadian passenger aviation. It was only fitting that a team named "Flyers" won that series. To give them their due, they played well and were very well coached. In fact, they went on to defeat the Winnipeg Monarchs for the Memorial Cup.

With that, my first two years with the Citadels came to an end. Summer would be decision time. Where would I play that fall: Quebec City or Montreal?

4

THE TUG-OF-WAR

IN 1991, ERIC LINDROS shocked the National Hockey League hierarchy and most of the population of Quebec when he refused to report as ordered to the Quebec Nordiques. This highly talented six-foot, five-inch center, who weighed in at 235 pounds, had been designated "the next one" in his early teens. His progress through the ranks of minor hockey had been closely monitored by the media, just as they had earlier kept a breathless watch on Bobby Orr, Wayne Gretzky, and Mario Lemieux. There's always a "next one" in the wings, keeping the sports press busy.

I watched every episode of this soap opera, as it unfolded over the following two years, with more than passing interest and a little sympathy. Despite our superficial similarities, Lindros's situation and mine were curiously reversed. If he was the sensation of the 1990s who wouldn't go to Quebec City, I was the rising star of the 1950s who seemingly wouldn't leave.

With the 1951–52 season approaching, Frank Selke was determined to sign me to a professional contract and as quickly as possible. My two games with the Canadiens in the previous season had whetted the appetites of Montreal fans, the city's media, and the club's management. Having not won a Stanley Cup since 1946, they believed that they simply had to have me.

Why did I stay in Quebec? Let me list just a few of the reasons: Élise Couture, the Côtés, Roland Mercier, a 1951 Nash, the Château Frontenac, the McKenna sisters, and St. Cyrille Quartier. In addition, I was barely twenty years old, and Quebec City had come to feel like home.

The first time I thought seriously of staying was the afternoon of our third game against the Inkerman Rockets, when the Citadels presented me with my first car, that beautiful Nash sedan. I felt an overwhelming obligation to the people of Quebec City that day. Shortly after our play-off loss to the Barrie Flyers, I expressed my feelings to Élise and Roland Mercier. "What can I do to thank the fans and the city for these two great years? I was treated like a king here." The answer came to me at once. The best way to show my appreciation was to play another year.

In deciding to remain, I also decided to take a step up from the junior ranks to the Quebec Aces of the semiprofessional Quebec Senior Hockey League (QSHL). If Frank Selke was disappointed by his inability to sign me after my first year with the Citadels, he must have been thoroughly frustrated on June 8, 1951, when my father and I worked out an agreement with Aces coach George "Punch" Imlach and club treasurer Charlie Smith, who came to Victoriaville to finalize the contract. A couple of weeks later, the news was made public, but then yet another stumbling block appeared.

The NHL and the Canadian Amateur Hockey Association (CAHA) had reached a tentative agreement that, if confirmed, would bring about two major changes in the conduct of the game and the movement of players. The on-ice change concerned games played at the senior level; it replaced the two-referee system with one referee and two linesmen. The second change became known as the "Béliveau Rule," because it seemed specifically targeted at me.

In essence, it stipulated that every player whose name appeared on an NHL team's negotiating list had to sign a contract to play with that team before he would be eligible to play in the Quebec Senior Hockey League. For example, if I wanted to play with the Aces, I'd have to sign with the Canadiens first. They would then assign me to the Aces, but only if both parties agreed to the deal. If the Canadiens wanted me in Montreal, I would have to play there.

Not surprisingly, Jack Latter, the owner of the Aces, was against this rule, but he was in the minority. Ratification at a future CAHA meeting looked inevitable. I don't know to this day precisely what happened next, but apparently telephone calls were made by highly placed persons to NHL headquarters in Montreal. The rule was never ratified, and I spent the next two years in an Aces uniform.

The extreme rivalry that then existed between Quebec City and Montreal will be familiar to longtime fans. But some will have a hard time grasping the way that Quebec politics and business concerns intruded into sports in the 1950s. Let me explain that by dealing first with the subject of money.

Perhaps the major difference between Eric Lindros's situation and mine was that the 1991 Quebec Nordiques, then a full-scale NHL franchise, could not successfully compete for his services against other teams in larger, wealthier, American markets. In my case, the Aces were comparatively "backwoods" as part of the semipro QSHL. Logically, they should have been out of the bidding for my services when the Canadiens came calling. But they weren't.

I wanted to stay in Quebec for personal reasons and would have considered any offer that the Aces happened to present. Further, they could match or better any Canadiens offer because they were owned by a large company, Anglo-Canadian Pulp and Paper. (The name "Aces" was an acronym of Anglo-Canadian Employees Association. Later, when nationalist sentiments were on the rise in the province, the team name was changed to the As de Québec.) Just as the Citadels had been determined to outbid the Junior Habs, the Aces had money in the till to trump the Canadiens. They knew they'd make money, too: in Quebec, senior hockey didn't take a back seat to the professional ranks. The Colisée was filled to capacity night after night.

Financially, at least, I had nothing to lose by staying in Quebec City. In my first year with the Aces, the 1951–52 season, I was paid $10,000. The going rate in the NHL at the time was $100 a game, or $7,000 a year, for a seventy-game season. In September, when I left to attend the Canadiens' training camp once again, the Aces offered to meet whatever figure Frank Selke might come up with, just as the Citadels had done.

How serious were they about keeping me in the Aces uniform? I found out when it came time to sign my next contract with them, for the 1952–53 season. This time other figures became directly involved. You may remember that Premier Maurice Duplessis—*le Chef*—ruled Quebec with an iron fist between 1936 and 1939 and again from 1944 until his death in 1959. His right-hand man, the man with his fingers on the purse strings, was Gérald Martineau. Martineau had two favorite sports, politics and hockey, and he was long involved with the Quebec Frontenacs junior team.

In preparation for my second season with the Aces, I met owner Jack Latter and treasurer Charlie Smith and agreed to a raise to $15,000—not bad by NHL standards. The day before I was to sign, I got a call from Latter.

"Jean, would you mind if we go to Mr. Martineau's office to sign the contract, instead of meeting at Anglo-Canadian?"

I was somewhat mystified by this, but told him it didn't matter to me.

The following day, at eleven o'clock, we went to Martineau's office and found the contract on the meeting room table. As I moved toward it, Martineau said to Latter, "Jack, you're making money with Jean. Give him $5,000 more."

Martineau was the bagman for Maurice Duplessis. Anglo-Canadian Pulp had lumber concessions in Forestville. Latter had to go through Martineau to get them. In other words, Martineau's comment wasn't a suggestion, it was an order.

I sat there, my eyes widening, as Jack Latter, one of Quebec City's top executives, meekly agreed that Mr. Martineau was "probably right." Which is how twenty-year-old Jean Béliveau became a $20,000-a-year semipro hockey man at a time when the NHL base rate was barely a third as much. Indeed, for a short time, I was making more than Gordie Howe or Maurice Richard. That being said, it wasn't the money that kept me in Quebec City, even though by staying I was conducting a rather subtle negotiation with the Canadiens, whether I fully realized it or not.

In Montreal, meanwhile, the media were forever speculating that I was remaining in Quebec because I had a fragile psyche and lacked the confidence to make it in the big time. After all, Bernard Geoffrion had gone straight to the NHL from junior, they argued. Dickie Moore had spent a half-season in senior before moving up to the Canadiens. And here was Béliveau, hiding out in Quebec City while the world passed him by.

It goes without saying that these commentators didn't know me. My decision was only partially about hockey. I stayed in Quebec City, first and foremost, out of a sense of obligation to its people. As for Boom Boom and Dickie, they were city boys born and bred, whereas I came from a small town. The extra time in Quebec helped me acclimatize to the demands of city life and to grow up gradually, more normally, than I would have had I been a twenty-year-old Montreal Canadien.

It was perhaps the wisest course to choose. I've seen the almost insane demands that were placed on Lindros, Gretzky, Lemieux, and Guy Lafleur while they were still teenagers. I didn't envy them the sudden loss of their youth. By contrast, I was able to mature both on and off the ice, at more or less my own pace, surrounded by what we'd call today a support network of close and reliable friends. As a result, the Jean Béliveau who finally did sign with Montreal in 1953 was much better prepared for the pressures of NHL stardom.

Quebec City was an idyllic place in the early 1950s, especially for a young francophone hockey player who was making excellent money and who had met the lady of his life. It was still the pretelevision era, and we made our own fun in the many *boîtes*, bistros, clubs, and restaurants in and around the city.

What follows might appear to be a dated travelogue of the city, the equivalent of showing slides of your vacation to a captive audience. But this period shaped who I was and who I was to become. Many people have complimented me on my comportment during my career with the Montreal Canadiens. I'm flattered, but if I behaved well, it stemmed from lessons learned in *la vieille capitale*.

I plunged into the social whirl of a vibrant provincial capital with a large group of people my age and slightly older who frequented places like Chez Gérard and La Porte St. Jean, two nightclubs run by the very convivial Gérard Thibault. Artists from both Quebec and France were regulars in the clubs, among them Patachou, Charles Trenet, and Carlos Ramirez. We enjoyed live entertainment, inexpensive and accessible, and I gradually developed social skills and conversational ease. I started to come out of my shell.

Roland Mercier introduced Élise and me to the club scene; he worked for the federal revenue department, ensuring that foreign artists paid tax on revenue earned in this country. Gérard Thibault was a Quebec City institution, the subject of a fascinating biography.

He brought Charles Trenet to Canada, and I remember the famous *chansonnier* sitting on the wharf near the Lévis ferry writing songs. Élise and I had a regular table at La Porte St. Jean and the use of a semiprivate entrance through the side door.

Another regular haunt was a famous restaurant on St. Joseph Street in Lower Town called Le Baril d'Huîtres—The Oyster Barrel—owned by Adrien Demers and Raymond Comeau. The Baril gang and some young Jewish boys whose families owned stores on St. Joseph Street used to play pickup hockey games at the old Colisée on Monday nights; I and Phil Renaud, a teammate on the Aces, would referee. After the games, both teams retired to the Baril for oysters and beer. It and Pat Mercier's Tavern on Dorchester were the closest things we had to sports bars in those days.

The crowds from both places were fanatical Aces fans and would follow us all over the league, especially to games in Chicoutimi, a 150-mile drive. Every time we played the Saguenéens, a convoy of thirty cars or more formed behind our team bus. After the game, we'd all turn around and come back home again, stopping at L'Étape, a restaurant and gas station complex in the middle of Parc des Laurentides that provided both good food and the only restrooms that were open at that hour of the night.

Sometimes we'd crawl along the highway in the midst of a terrible snowstorm, barely making it to L'Étape for beans and *tourtières* at three in the morning. We continued on our way when daylight broke and we could follow a snowplow. One night the bus's fuel pump failed in twenty-five-below-zero-Fahrenheit weather. The police came out to rescue us and ferried us to L'Étape in their cruisers.

By this time, Élise was attending hockey games. Once she accompanied Jacques Côté and his wife Claire to see me play in Chicoutimi. Having noticed fans at other games ring bells in the stands, she took along a little dinner bell from her mother's silverware set. We played well that night, and the tiny bell got a real workout—until a disgruntled Chicoutimi fan grabbed it and disappeared out the nearest exit.

As mentioned earlier, Élise's mother did not have a high opinion of hockey players. "How am I going to tell her that the bell is gone?" Élise moaned after the game.

"Well," I said, "you'll start by forgetting to mention the circumstances under which it disappeared."

Chicoutimi was well and good, but perhaps the best trips were to Montreal, where the QSHL staged those memorable Sunday afternoon contests at the Forum. In later years, Camil Des Roches, then the Canadiens' public relations guru, and I would often recall them. He'd have to march out onto St. Catherine Street and tell people to go home because the Forum was sold out.

"I never did that for Canadiens games," he said. "Only for senior-league games and especially when the Aces came to town to play the Royals." Busloads and trainloads of Quebec City faithful would travel to Montreal for those games, and it wasn't unusual to have 50 or 60 percent of the crowd cheering for Quebec.

There was one other special trip, in December 1952. I was called up by the Canadiens for another three-game trial, my first return to the NHL in more than a year. I would play in Montreal Thursday night against the New York Rangers, and follow that with a home-and-home series with the Boston Bruins at the Forum on Saturday night and in Boston on Sunday.

The gang at the Baril d'Huîtres was crazed with excitement. They quickly organized a private car on the two o'clock train to Montreal on Thursday afternoon, and one of the guys went ahead on Wednesday to scare up some tickets. When the train pulled into the station, he was waiting with enough seats for everybody. He'd gone all over town, picking up pairs wherever he could find them in factories, restaurants, offices, and hotels. I don't think he'd had the luxury of too much sleep. That night I scored three goals, and the Baril boys hooked up their private car to the midnight train and celebrated all the way home. With fans like that, you can see why I was more than happy to remain in Quebec City.

I have to credit one more person who helped convince me to stay. His name was Émile Couture. Everyone assumed, once I began going out with Élise, that she and he were sister and brother. In fact, they weren't related in any way.

Émile worked for Calvert's Distillery, which at one time awarded a trophy to the junior league's most valuable player. He was a happy-go-lucky *boulevardier* who loved the good life and knew the best spots in town. He also knew people in the Aces organization and acted as a sort of intermediary between myself and the club. He came to all the hockey games, and I was always pleased to see him, since I'd known him back in Victoriaville. His family owned a restaurant and hotel in Laurierville called La Maison Blanche, where all the professional wrestlers on the circuit stopped in on their trips between Montreal and Quebec City. Few people knew that Émile's name was also recognized around the world—at least, by a select group of international military personnel.

During the Second World War, British prime minister Winston Churchill, American president Franklin Roosevelt, and Canadian prime minister William Lyon Mackenzie King met in Quebec City in 1943 to discuss plans for the European theater of operations the following year. Destroyers and minesweepers patrolled the St. Lawrence River below Cap Diamant, warplanes of three nations flew overhead, and heavily armed soldiers cordoned off most of the city center, erecting checkpoints on all the major roads and at the railway station. The most secure place in town was the Château Frontenac, where the three leaders stayed and held their meetings. And yet Émile Couture managed to walk out of that building with plans for Operation Overlord—the Normandy invasion—tucked under his arm.

Émile at that time was a sergeant in the Royal 22nd Regiment of

Quebec, on quartermaster duty. It was his task to provide the stationery for each session. He also had strict orders to destroy anything that was left on the tables after the meetings ended each night. On the second-last day of the conference, he was asked to remove the desks of several participants who'd completed their presentations. He did just that, but when he looked inside one of the desk drawers, he found a sheaf of papers in a red binder. If he'd stopped to think, he'd have destroyed it then and there. But he didn't. Instead, he returned to his quarters at Lac Beauport. Later that night, out of idle curiosity, he took out the binder and began to read.

In his hands were plans for the 1944 Allied invasion of occupied France—who, what, when, and where; how many planes, ships, and men. He read some more, then tried to go to sleep, but he couldn't. At dawn, he returned to the Château, where the belated discovery that the binder was missing had headquarters in an uproar. Émile tried to report his find discreetly to a succession of top brass, all of whom were too panicked to pay attention to him.

Finally, after several hours had passed, he prevailed upon the commander of the military district to listen to his story. Within minutes, Émile was surrounded by military investigators. After the authorities were convinced—to their relief—that the binder hadn't fallen into enemy hands, the question became what to do with Sergeant Couture.

His background was impeccable, his military record spotless, and they couldn't very well lock him up. He'd returned the materials of his own volition, and a jail sentence might arouse suspicion within the community—the Coutures were widely known—which in turn might somehow alert the enemy.

For months, Émile was kept under strict surveillance. Finally, after the invasion had taken place on June 6, 1944, he was off the hook on the condition that he wouldn't publish the story without permission. *Life* magazine approached him at least once, but, as far as I know, his tale never appeared in print. I learned about it only because he and I were so close; Émile never really liked to talk about it. After the war, however, he was awarded the British Empire Medal, a very important decoration. When people asked him about the BEM, Émile would smile innocently and reply, "Who knows why they give out these things?"

It was with such interesting companions that I spent life off the ice. On the ice, I'd moved up into faster company, in every sense of the phrase, the minute I put on an Aces uniform. The QSHL was the stomping ground of former NHL and American Hockey League (AHL) players who had been looking for a congenial environment in which to spend the latter stages of their careers. They were shrewd and experienced, and they taught me a great deal.

In my first year with the Aces, one of my linemates was Gaye Stewart, recipient of the Calder Trophy as NHL rookie of the year with the Maple Leafs in 1942. Jack Gélineau, our goalie, had won this honor with Boston in 1950. Other veterans included Ludger Tremblay, Gilles' older brother; the infamous Frank "Yogi" Kraiger; Joe Crozier, formerly of the AHL Cleveland Barons; Claude Robert (my linemate on my first call-up with the Canadiens in 1950); Jackie Leclair, another former Canadien, and Marcel Bonin, who would travel with me to Montreal via a circuitous route.

Yogi Kraiger deserves a book of his own. He was as tough as nails when he wasn't into the sauce. When he was, he was truly spectacular. Sometimes he would get so inebriated that he'd forget where he'd left his car and have to ride all over town on Quebec City Transit buses, looking for it.

During my first November with the Aces, we had a light schedule and five or six days off. Our coach, Punch Imlach, hated the idea of us growing stale, so he organized an exhibition game in Cornwall. We returned the next morning by bus up Highway 2, the main link between Montreal and Toronto before the construction of

Highway 401. We'd just reached the old Soulanges Canal, and our conversation turned to swimming.

Yogi wasn't the retiring type, even when sober, and on this occasion he'd found a source of liquid inspiration in Cornwall. We'd become accustomed to his shameless self-promotions; simply put, Yogi was the finest athlete ever, in every sport, and as it happened swimming was his personal best. If you were foolhardy enough to question his aquatic talents, Yogi was bound to take exception. This could be dangerous. Yogi was an impressive physical specimen whose idea of a limbering-up exercise was doing chin-ups by his fingertips off the top of a door frame.

Yogi had made a career of upsetting Punch Imlach, and by the time we arrived at the canal that day, Punch was on the boil.

"I've heard enough of this B.S.," he announced to the team in a loud voice. Then he turned to the driver. "Next bridge we come to, stop the bus. All this nonsense about swimming for miles in Lake Superior is crap, pure and simple, and I'm going to prove it. I'm bettin' fifty bucks he can't swim across the canal."

Have I mentioned that it was late November and that chunks of ice floated near the canal shores?

"For fifty bucks, I'll do it," Yogi replied. As usual, he was dead broke, but a plea to his teammates yielded instant results. Dollar bills rained into his hands, and the action in side bets demonstrated team unity at its best. Per instructions, the driver stopped the bus at a convenient bridge, and team trainer Ralph McNaughton fetched a couple of blankets for our Polar Bear Club inductee.

Everybody hopped off the bus to admire Yogi's striptease down to his boxer shorts. With barely a pause, he dived into the canal, losing his shorts in midair. He then proceeded to swim the canal buck naked, as Ralph walked along the opposite bank, blanket at the ready.

The sight of twenty or so young men peering anxiously into the frigid, stagnant canal was a red flag for passing traffic. Cars and trucks came to a screeching halt and a crowd gathered to gawk at what they assumed was an awful accident.

Instead, they were greeted by the sight of Yogi climbing onto the opposite bank, wearing not a stitch. Ralph wrapped him up and they quick-stepped back across the bridge and onto the bus. The team followed, and we continued on our way. Naturally, all this exercise had aroused a powerful thirst in Yogi Bare. When we hit the outskirts of Montreal, near Vaudreuil, he told Punch, "You'd better get me a gin to warm up, or I'll have a cold for the rest of the winter."

Once again Punch stopped the bus, and we all trooped into the Vaudreuil Inn at eight o'clock in the morning so Yogi could have his gin. We never did recover his boxer shorts.

Punch, of course, was dumb like a fox. For $50, Yogi's morning dip was a bargain in building team morale and harmony.

Another famous character on the Aces was Marcel Bonin, whom I'd played against in junior and would meet again in Montreal in the late 1950s. Marcel frequently appeared for practice in November in his hunting outfit, two or three rifles or shotguns on his arm.

"Hey, Punch, make it a short practice today," he'd say. "Marcel is going hunting in Dorchester County, and the light goes early at this time of the year."

Punch knew better than to quibble with an armed man, especially a marksman like Bonin. Besides, thanks to Marcel, the Aces had acquired a taste for venison.

Marcel was a tough guy, like Yogi. He made his way into the NHL thanks to an exhibition game we played against the Detroit Red Wings in February 1952 on behalf of the Federated Charities. He got into a scrap with "Terrible" Ted Lindsay and raised eyebrows by holding his own. Then, and I can't recall how it happened, he ended up in a penalty-box brawl with Vic Stasiuk. Somehow, Marcel's thumb became wedged in Vic's mouth, and Marcel used it as leverage to lift Stasiuk and repeatedly bang his head on the concrete wall at the back of the box. Stasiuk was biting down to save his life, but nothing could stop Marcel from pounding him senseless.

People said that Marcel used to wrestle bears for a living, and perhaps it's true. In any case, the Red Wings were impressed by his fisticuffs. Not long afterward, they purchased Bonin, and he went on to terrorize the opposition in a similar fashion before joining the Canadiens in 1957–58.

I noted earlier that Claude Robert had played with me in my very first call-up with the Canadiens. When I joined the Aces, he was already with the team. He was a burly man, very strong, who eventually joined the Montreal police. He had a high tolerance for pain, too, as he proved to Punch the day we played, and defeated, the AHL's Providence Reds in an exhibition game in Grand'Mère.

During the contest, Claude took a major-league body check in the corner along the boards and flew into the air, landing awkwardly. He limped back to our bench, went right through the door, and on to the dressing room. When Punch and the trainer caught up with him, Claude said he was injured and didn't think he could continue play. In those days you played with pain, a lot of it; coaches did anything they could to get you back on the ice.

Imlach turned to Ralph. "Guess we'll have to freeze the leg. Get the needle."

As tough as Claude was, he was scared to death of needles. He would run a mile to avoid hearing the word.

"Uh, I'm okay, I can play," he said over his shoulder as he scurried out of the room and back to work.

Claude played in all our games for the next three weeks but complained that the leg still bothered him. Finally, Punch relented and sent him to hospital to have it checked. X-rays showed a clean break.

Years later, when the media made a fuss about Bobby Baun playing on a hairline fracture for one game during the 1964 play-offs against Detroit, I immediately thought of Claude. It might be nothing more than coincidence, but Baun's coach that season was none other than Punch Imlach.

For all his grit, Claude was a natty dresser. He always looked good, in part because he managed his finances well and his money went a long way. Marcel Bonin, equally hardened, spent his money like water, especially on the necessities of his favorite pastime, hunting.

One evening, I came upon them in the dressing room. Claude was coaching Marcel on fashion and budgeting. "Marcel, you could end up in the NHL one day, and they aren't going to let you wear lumberjack shirts or hip waders. You'll need a shirt and tie and a suit," he said. Claude's locker looked like a rack from a high-end men's clothier. Extra suits in dry cleaner's plastic hung in a row. Shirts in their packages were stacked neatly on a shelf. There was even a tie rack, filled with the latest looks.

"But," Bonin protested, "I don't have that kind of money."

"Yes, you do, Marcel, but every time you get a dollar you spend it on another gun."

I left them deep in their conversation, convinced that Claude would have an uphill battle if he hoped to make over Marcel.

At the next home game, we were amazed to see a spiffy Marcel Bonin strut into the room wearing a suit, dress shirt, and tie. Claude was the most surprised of all. "Marcel, those are my clothes!" he declared.

"I know," Bonin answered, proudly. "How do you like my budgeting?"

THE QUEBEC SENIOR HOCKEY League was a remarkable training ground for me and for others. I played with and learned a great deal from men such as Ludger Tremblay and Gaye Stewart. After his rookie year with Toronto, Gaye ended up playing with every other NHL team but one, Boston. He turned in 510 NHL games over nine seasons in the twelve-year period between the 1941–42 and 1953–54 seasons and finished up with 185 goals and 159 assists. Today's junior graduates will never have the opportunity to play with someone with that kind of experience, prior to moving up to the NHL.

The QSHL had a host of veteran forwards and defensemen, as well as up-and-coming stars like Dickie Moore, Bob Fryday, Bob Frampton, Les Douglas, and Jacques Plante, all of whom played for Frank Carlin's Montreal Royals. Tommy Gorman's Ottawa Senators played out of the old Ottawa Auditorium and featured Neil Tremblay and Al Kuntz up front, Frank "Butch" Stahan on defense, and the legendary William "Legs" Fraser in nets. Valleyfield was coached by Toe Blake and included players such as my former junior teammates Gordie Haworth and Bruce Cline, André Corriveau, Jacques Deslauriers, and Larry Kwong. Sherbrooke stars included Tod Campeau, Jimmy Planche, Bobby Pepin, and Jacques Locas. In Chicoutimi, they had Lou and Stan Smrke, Pete Tkachuk, Ralph Buchanan, Sherman White, Gerry Glaude, Marcel Pelletier in nets, and Georges Roy and Jean Lamirande on defense. They were coached by Roland Hébert, my former junior mentor in Victoriaville. Last but not least, the Shawinigan Cataracts rallied behind star netminder Al Millar, and included Jack Taylor, Erwin Grosse, Roger Bédard, and Spike Laliberté.

The QSHL was also home to many players who, for various reasons, never would make it to the NHL. One such player was Herbie Carnegie, a smooth-skating playmaker equally adept at center and on a wing. Herbie was black, or "colored" as the expression went back then. When I was a youngster in Victoriaville, Herbie, his brother Ozzie, and a third black, Matty McIntyre, all played with Sherbrooke in the Quebec Provincial League. Herbie made it up one rung on the hockey ladder but no farther.

It's my belief that Herbie was excluded from the NHL because of his color. He certainly had the talent and was very popular with the fans, who would reward his great playmaking with prolonged standing ovations, both at home and on the road. Perhaps they suspected that race was an issue for the NHL, but it certainly wasn't for them. I followed Herbie from a distance over the years. He did very well with Investors Syndicate, as I could see as a board member with the company. Mutual acquaintances told me that he was a major contributor to public service in the Toronto suburb of North York.

The Aces had their share of excellent players, too, forwards like Armand Gaudreault, Martial Pruneau, Jackie Leclair, Copper Leyte, Bob Hayes, and Murdo Mackay. Our captain, Phil Renaud, anchored a defense that included Joe Crozier, Yogi Kraiger, Jean-Guy Talbot, and Joseph "Butch" Houle. We had the speed, quick hands, toughness, and determination that enabled us to defeat Chicoutimi in our own league final and then John "Peanuts" O'Flaherty's Saint John Beavers, to capture the 1953 Alexander Cup, emblematic of the senior hockey championship of eastern Canada.

In my two seasons with the Aces, I won the QSHL scoring championship both years. Not surprisingly, this helped intensify the pressure in Montreal for me to sign with the Canadiens. The "man who stayed away" story made the rounds, kept fresh in the public mind by hockey commentators throughout the NHL.

The *Toronto Star* went so far as to run a wanted poster on me. "Jean Béliveau. Age 20. 6′2″. 195 lbs. Wanted by Canadiens to play NHL hockey. Reward $15,000 a season... and he turns it down. There's a reason. Jean Béliveau, star of the Quebec Aces, is hockey's highest paid 'amateur.' In addition, he picks up a few odd thousand a year as a public relations man and doing a daily radio broadcast." And so forth. A couple of months later, the same poster ran in the French press, but by then it was out of date. I stood six foot, three inches and weighed 205.

Rumor and speculation ran rampant in Canada and in the United States. Read one report from New York, "If Béliveau doesn't sign by his birthday (August 31), he will be removed from the Canadiens' negotiation list and then claimed by the team in the NHL basement (the New York Rangers)." Another version had me headed for Chicago for a preposterous sum of money.

Meanwhile, it seemed every sports columnist in eastern Canada was negotiating a deal with the Canadiens for me. The most bandied-about offer was Frank Selke's opener: $53,000 over three years, comprising $20,000 as a signing bonus plus salaries of $10,000, $11,000, and $12,000 per annum over the length of the contract. Of course, we had turned that down. Thanks to Gérald Martineau, I was making $20,000 annually, not $15,000, with the Aces.

Naturally, it wasn't my long-term ambition to remain in Quebec City forever, making more and more money every year. As my second season with the Aces unfolded, I sensed it was time to move on, to test myself at the next plateau. Besides, if I'd stayed much longer, I might have started to pose a threat to Premier Duplessis, who remarked on my popularity when he himself fell victim to it.

At that time, Quebec's leading radio personality was Saint-Georges Côté of CHRC, who frequently invited me to join him on his morning show. In 1952, he bought a well-known restaurant on Boulevard Ste-Anne called La Dame Blanche, and he staged a grand opening complete with foot-long hot dogs and two guest "celebrities," Élise and myself. That same day, Premier Duplessis and a host of political dignitaries were busy opening a new highway over the Pont de Québec; very few citizens turned out. On Boulevard Ste-Anne, Élise and I were swamped by a crowd of seven thousand hot-dog lovers.

Élise and I had become engaged at Christmas 1952, and we started to consider seriously what our lives might hold in the future. "This will be my last year in Quebec City," I told her. "I've always intended to play for the Canadiens, and next season will be the right time for me. After we're married in June, we'll head to Montreal and scout out a place to live."

Élise was the first to hear of my plan. I was in no rush to let Frank Selke know. I wanted to keep my bargaining power as high as possible. Two scoring championships, an Alexander Cup victory, and full houses throughout the QSHL and in the Forum added to my credit column. But the negotiations could wait. On June 27, 1953, at a little after eleven o'clock in the morning, the only woman in my life became Mrs. Jean Béliveau at St. Patrick's Church in Quebec City.

While we were on our honeymoon, the QSHL franchises met in Montreal to debate whether or not the semipro league would turn fully professional. Punch Imlach (who didn't know of my intentions, either) was not in favor, but when he arrived at the meeting, all of the other owners were lined up against him.

Punch began by reminding them that Jean Béliveau had filled their buildings over the past two seasons. Forrest Keene of Sherbrooke said that this wasn't entirely the case. Tommy Gorman of Ottawa answered that by going professional, he'd be better able to control the destiny of his franchise, rather than having to depend on NHL and AHL teams to assign players to him each September. (As it turned out, Sherbrooke dropped out of the QSHL shortly before the 1953–54 season began, and Gorman's Ottawa Senators folded just before Christmas.)

With the wisdom of foresight, Punch said that while both owners' points were debatable, only one thing was certain: if the QSHL went professional, I belonged to the Canadiens, who would claim me in five seconds flat.

Punch lost the vote, and I was on my way to the NHL.

left — The processional at Maurice Richard's funeral on May 31, 2000.

above — Aerial wide-angle view of crowds winding around Windsor Station and the Molson Centre, where Rocket Richard lay in state.

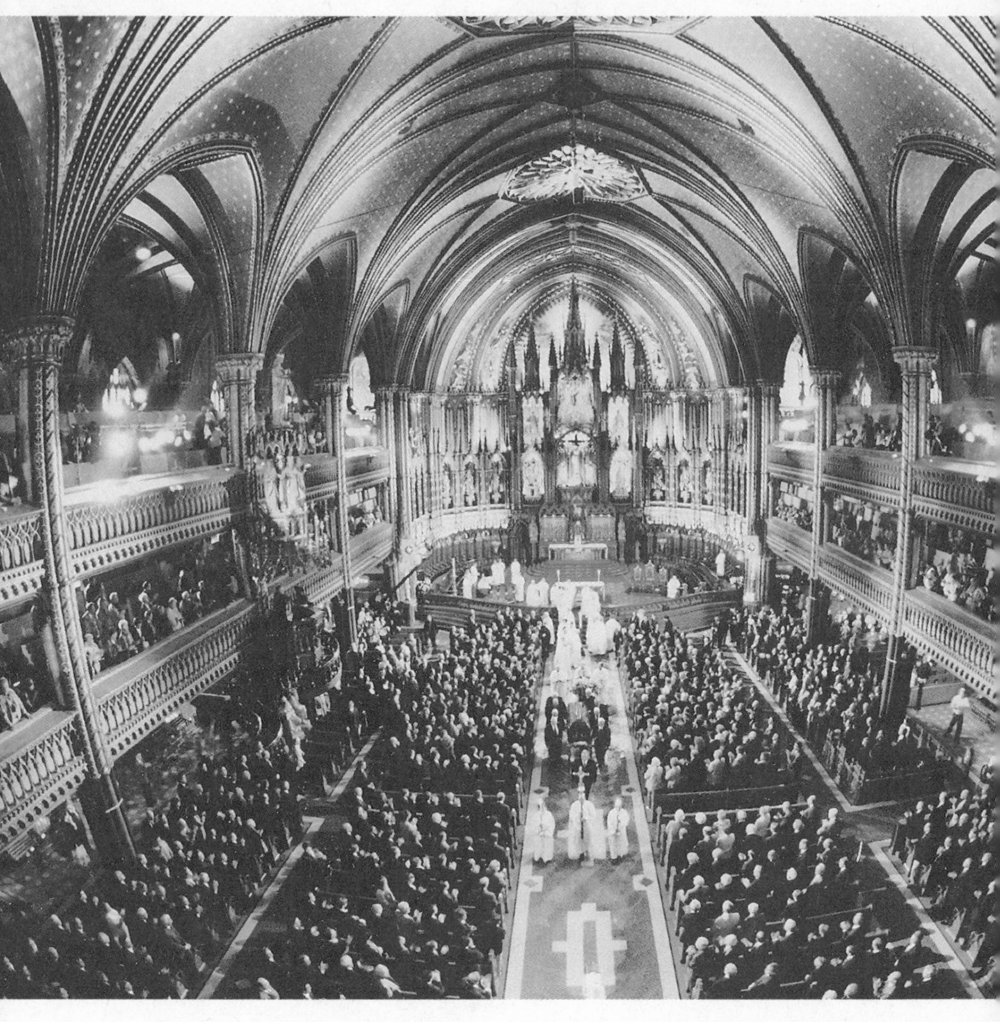

above — Panoramic photo of Maurice Richard's funeral at Notre-Dame Cathedral.

top right — Maurice Richard's teammates carry his coffin.

bottom right — Rocket Richard's pallbearers and teammates sit in the front pew at his funeral.

THE SMILING BOYS ABOVE WON FOUR OF THE NATIONAL HOCKEY LEAGUE'S SIX INDIVIDUAL AWARDS IN 1955-56, AN UNUSUAL AND REMARKABLE ACHIEVEMENT. ON THE LEFT IS DOUG HARVEY WITH THE JAMES NORRIS MEMORIAL TROPHY, JEAN BELIVEAU IS IN THE CENTRE WITH THE ART ROSS TROPHY AND THE HART TROPHY WHILE JACQUES PLANTE ON THE RIGHT STANDS WITH HIS AWARD, THE VEZINA TROPHY.

top left — Entering Notre-Dame Cathedral to attend Maurice Richard's funeral are Quebec premier Lucien Bouchard (center), Canadian prime minister Jean Chrétien (looking back, just ahead of Bouchard and to his left), former Quebec premier Jacques Parizeau (two behind Bouchard on left), and federal Opposition leader Jean Charest (top left, one person down from back row).

left — Doug Harvey, Jean Béliveau, and Jacques Plante with a huge trophy haul in 1955–56.

above — To honor Jean Béliveau's fiftieth anniversary in the NHL, this painting shows all Canadiens players wearing his #4 on their sweaters during pre-game ceremonies.

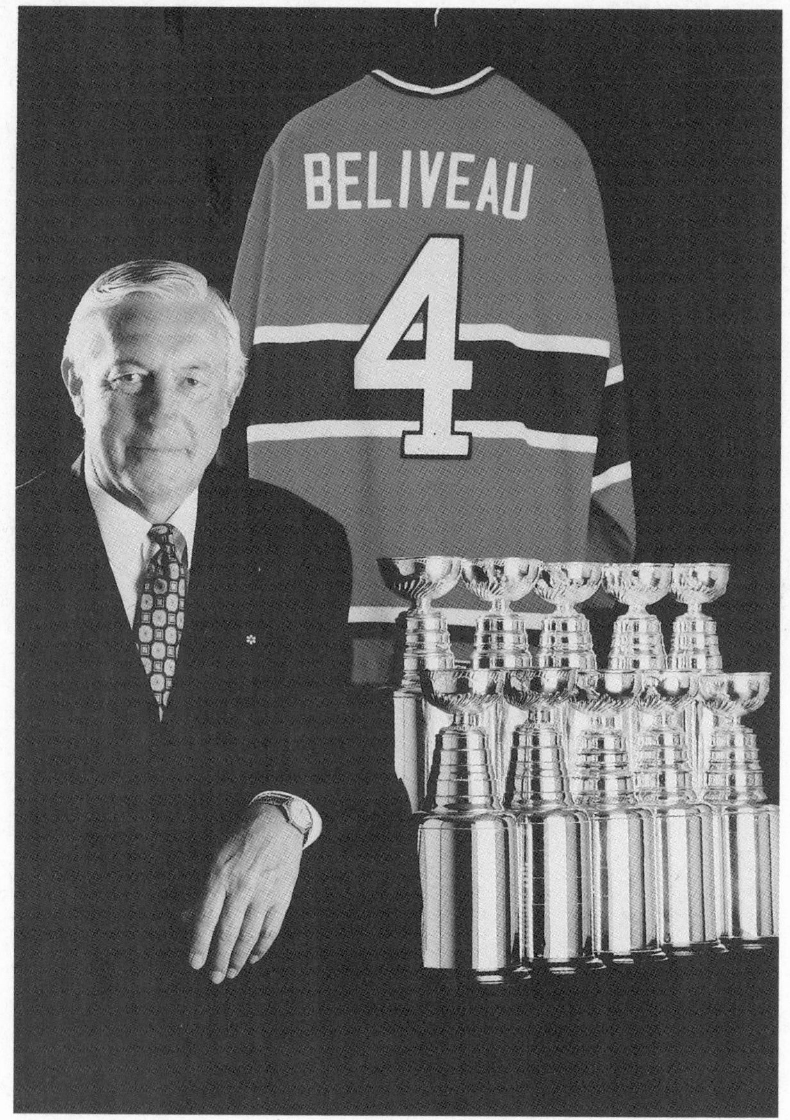
BELIVEAU
4

left—Jean and his ten Stanley Cups won as a player.

above—Former teammates join Jean at the launch of the first edition of this book in October 1994. J.-C. Tremblay (third from right, top row) left hospital to attend, and it was his last public appearance; he returned to hospital shortly after this picture was taken and died of cancer a month later.

5

THE FANTASTIC FIFTIES

AN AUTOBIOGRAPHY MUST by definition be written in the first person, but the "first person" was never what my career was about, on or off the ice. Everything I achieved and all the rewards that followed came as the result of team effort. If they say anything about me when I'm gone, let them say that I was a team man. To me, there is no higher compliment.

I had the God-given talent and immense good fortune to become a star on a team of stars—the Montreal Canadiens, circa the late 1950s—who set a record that may stand forever. That record, of course, was five straight Stanley Cup wins. It seems doubtful that any team now or in the foreseeable future will be able to approach, match, or surpass this feat. Professional hockey has changed so much since then—we've seen the expansions, the use of entry drafts to disperse talent among the neediest franchises, and the rise in player salaries—that it's unlikely any general manager or coach, no matter how savvy, will ever again assemble a bona fide dynasty team.

That's why I'd like to tell you about my team, my equally talented teammates, and the reasons why the Montreal Canadiens surged ahead of the rest of the NHL in the late fifties and have stayed competitive ever since, even though the Cup victories are fewer and farther apart.

Let's look first at the pure numbers before meeting the many individuals who contributed to these remarkable statistics. In 1955–56, we finished first with one hundred points on forty-five wins, fifteen losses and ten ties, twenty-four points ahead of second-place Detroit. We won the Cup with 4–1 series victories over both the Rangers and the Red Wings.

In 1956–57, we were in a three-team race during the regular season with Detroit and Boston. Detroit surged ahead at the end, finishing first with eighty-eight points, to our eighty-two and the Bruins' eighty. But we defeated the Rangers and Bruins 4–1 in both series to win the Cup again.

In 1957–58, we left the opposition far behind, ending the season with ninety-six points, nineteen better than the Rangers. We then swept the Red Wings in the semifinal and defeated Boston 4–2 in a six-game final.

In 1958–59, we once again won the Prince of Wales Trophy for finishing first in the league, twenty-one points ahead of runner-up Boston. We downed the Chicago Black Hawks in six games in the semifinal and Toronto in five in the final, for our fourth Cup.

In 1959–60, we won our fourth regular-season title in five years, earning ninety-two points to Toronto's seventy-nine. We improved on the previous year's play-offs by sweeping the Hawks, then the Leafs in eight straight games for our fifth consecutive Stanley Cup win.

This fabulous run began for me when I signed my first contract with Montreal on October 3, 1953. Frank Selke was there, of course, sporting the biggest of smiles, as was Dick Irvin, the team's coach.

Later that same day, I played my first official game as a Montreal Canadien in the season opener against the NHL All-Stars.

Between 1947 and 1965, it was traditional for the reigning Stanley Cup winner to play host to a collection of the best players from the five other so-called Original Six NHL teams. That evening I found myself on the ice with Gordie Howe, Ted Lindsay, Leonard "Red" Kelly, Alex Delvecchio, and Terry Sawchuk of Detroit; Fleming Mackell and Bill Quackenbush of Boston, and Bill Gadsby of Chicago, among other intimidating hockey greats. We had our own all-stars in our lineup, of course, including Doug Harvey (a first-team selection), and second-teamers Gerry McNeil, Maurice Richard, and Bert Olmstead. We lost 3–1, but, to be honest, I didn't feel out of place.

There was plenty of excitement at the Forum that night for several reasons. Since the Canadiens were the defending champions, the crowd was eager to see if they would maintain their supremacy. Moreover, everyone could sense that Frank Selke's patient cultivation of the rich soil of Quebec junior and senior hockey was about to produce the first of many bumper crops.

No other NHL franchise had a list of young stars as talented as those who had toiled in the minors for Montreal. Boom Boom Geoffrion, Dickie Moore, and myself were the leaders of three successful junior teams, and all three of us had excelled in our NHL call-up games while still of junior age. Now we were finally in the Canadiens' lineup as full-time players, along with Jacques Plante. At the same time, the fans knew that Jean-Guy Talbot, Don Marshall, Phil Goyette, André Pronovost, Henri Richard, Charlie Hodge, Ralph Backstrom, and Claude Provost would join our ranks sooner or later. There was great potential waiting in the wings out west, as well, in players like Bob Turner, Ab McDonald, and Billy Hicke.

If every year Montreal could add one or two of these up-and-comers to a Stanley Cup team that already featured Doug Harvey, the league's premier defenseman, Maurice Richard, its top scorer and most exciting player, and veterans such as Tom Johnson, Bert Olmstead, Dollard St. Laurent, Floyd Curry, Gerry McNeil, and Ken Mosdell, then the Canadiens should be at or near the top of the NHL standings for a generation. All of which did come to pass, pretty much according to Frank Selke's plan, even though we'd have to wait two years after my arrival for our next Stanley Cup victory.

One reason for the delay was the presence of yet another dynasty, Jack Adams's Red Wings. Between 1947 and 1954, the Wings finished first in the regular season for seven consecutive years and brought four Stanley Cups to the Motor City. Another contributing factor was one of the most notorious incidents in the history of NHL hockey, the "Richard Riot" of 1955.

The Canadiens may have been managed by Frank Selke, but they were really Joseph Henri Maurice Richard's team. The Rocket was the heart and soul of the Canadiens, an inspiration to us all and especially to younger French Canadians who were rising through the ranks. He was man and myth, larger than life in some ways, yet most ordinarily human in others.

Maurice was not only first in the hearts of French Canadians, he was the first among his NHL peers: the first to break Nels Stewart's NHL scoring record with his 325th goal; the first to reach the 400- and 500-goal plateaus; the first to score fifty and then seventy-five play-off goals. Moreover, the timing of his accomplishments, from the war years through to 1960, coincided with that period in Quebec when a tidal wave of social change was sweeping aside more than three hundred years of history. He became a cultural icon.

As players, we saw Maurice in simpler, more immediate terms. He embodied a force, an energy, something that rubbed off on many of his teammates and carried us to five straight championships by the end of the decade. Maurice Richard hated to lose, with every fiber of his being, and his fever was infectious. Everyone picked it up—his teammates, his opponents, the media, and the hockey public at large.

Headline writers in the United States borrowed from their national anthem to celebrate "the Rocket's red glare." North of the border, in a country that had been forged by steel rails, another metaphor held sway: Maurice was often described as a runaway locomotive with a Cyclopian eye that rooted helpless goalies to the ice, like deer caught in the headlights.

For me, the best description of Maurice Richard was penned by a winner of the Nobel Prize for Literature, the American novelist William Faulkner. This Southerner, who knew very little about the game, was commissioned to write a story on hockey for *Sports Illustrated* magazine in 1955. He covered a match between the Canadiens and the Rangers at Madison Square Garden and was immediately captivated, writing that Maurice had the "passionate, glittering, fatal alien quality of snakes." Indeed, the last thing a goalie would see were those mesmerizing cobra-like eyes, microseconds before Maurice struck.

Maurice Richard would be the first to admit that he was not the greatest skater in the world. Nor was he the best shot, stickhandler, or passer on our team, let alone in the entire league. What made him unique was the way he channeled his incredible, virtually unstoppable will to win into an explosive charge from the opposition's blue line all the way to their net. This awesome concentration of firepower was his trademark.

Every star has his critics, and Maurice was not immune. It was said that he was a lousy back checker, that he had little interest in the defensive game, and that this shortcoming drove his coaches to distraction. It was baloney, of course.

Admittedly, the kind of all-out attack that Maurice launched at the opponent's net usually ended with him sprawled in front of the crease or over in the corner. He wouldn't be able to rejoin the play right away, especially if the other team made a rapid transition to offense. Even when he scored, he'd always have one or two defenders on top of him. The puck was in the net and Maurice was flat on his back.

Although truly spectacular to watch, the Rocket had to make sacrifices to play that way. He was a highly tuned, highly specialized hockey instrument, not a well-balanced all-round player. The other elements of his game were there, all right, but perhaps they suffered by comparison.

His charges were doubly dramatic because he was a left-handed shot playing on the right wing. This allowed him to take the puck on his forehand and break straight for the goal, letting the puck go off-stride and catching many netminders napping. Add to this a lethal backhand off a straight blade and you'll understand why a common reaction to one of the Rocket's goals was, "I didn't see it coming."

Maurice was much more than a hockey player. He was a hero who defined a people emerging from an agrarian society in the post-war era and moving to the cities to seek their fortunes. I was just one of thousands of adolescent hockey players who sat rapt by the family radio on Saturday nights, letting my imagination magnify the Rocket's epic feats on *La Soirée du Hockey*, then mimicking those same moves at the local rink on crisp Sunday mornings after Mass.

Later, as his teammate, my sense of awe remained. The realization that Maurice had opened up the game for us—built a foundation for us—was almost overwhelming. Even more impressive was the fact that he was rather shy and very modest about his exploits. In 1952, when I scored three goals against New York in a call-up game, it was Maurice who assisted on all of them, twice putting me in alone on goalie Claude "Chuck" Rayner with perfect passes.

After that, about the only time we played together was on the lethal Montreal power play that changed the rules of hockey.

Nowadays, when a power-play goal is scored, the penalized player can leave the penalty box. This wasn't always the case. A player used to serve his full two or five minutes, no matter what happened while he was off. The NHL was forced to change that rule because the Canadiens would habitually rack up two, three, or sometimes four goals while the other team was short-handed.

Since the inception of the National Hockey League, players have scored a grand total of well over one hundred thousand goals, but to my mind they're all eclipsed by Rocket's goal in the 1952 play-offs. It was the stuff of legend.

The Canadiens were expected to win the Stanley Cup semifinal that year against the Bruins but went into Boston trailing three games to two on Sunday, April 6. The Canadiens were saved by an overtime score from Paul Masnick, one of Frank Selke's Saskatchewan boys, and tied the series. The teams returned to Montreal for the deciding game two nights later.

Early in the second period of a 1–1 contest, the Rocket was knocked unconscious in the course of one of his spectacular rushes. Maurice had swept past defenseman Hal Laycoe when Bruins winger Leo Labine moved across, using his teammate as a screen. Labine went low and Rocket saw him at the last second. He tried to jump over the check, but it was too late. Labine caught him on the shins, Richard's legs were knocked straight up in the air, and he crashed to the ice head-first.

You could literally have heard a pin drop as Rocket lay unconscious in an expanding pool of blood from an ugly gash over his left eye. Trainers Bill Head and Hector Dubois brought him around with smelling salts, but when Rocket was escorted to the Forum clinic, not a soul among the 15,100 fans that night believed he would return. Passing in and out of consciousness, Maurice stayed in the clinic for almost an hour, occasionally asking the medical attendant to update him on the score.

With five minutes remaining in the third period and the game still tied at 1–1, Rocket made his way to the bench and sat down alongside his teammates. After checking Maurice's condition, coach Dick Irvin sent him over the boards with Bert Olmstead and Elmer Lach at around the sixteen-minute mark. Every eye in the Forum was on number 9, who leaned over with head down, waiting for the puck to drop at the face-off.

The puck went deep into the Montreal end, but Butch Bouchard got to it behind the net and passed it quickly across to Rocket, who was already building up a head of steam. Rocket flew up the right-wing boards and cut in toward defenseman Bill Quackenbush. Holding him off with one arm, Maurice stormed toward "Sugar Jim" Henry in the Boston goal and jammed the puck into the net from the edge of the crease. The Forum exploded.

Afterward, a dazed and bloodied Richard shook hands with Henry, who had two black eyes of his own from earlier action in the series.

Three years later, Boston defenseman Hal Laycoe was involved with the Rocket in another spectacular incident, the altercation that would culminate in the infamous Richard Riot. The bespectacled Laycoe, who had played with the Canadiens for four seasons between 1947 and 1951, was not a dirty player. Far from it: he had been Rocket's tennis partner in the off-season and bore him no grudge.

Before I describe the events of March 1955, I must stress that although he was arguably the game's greatest star at that time, Maurice Richard had been forced to spend his entire career battling extremely tough and hardened players. His fights were almost as spectacular as his goals. He went the distance with Detroit's "Terrible" Ted Lindsay in a string of memorable brawls, pummeled Boston strongman Fernie Flaman, and KO'd the Rangers' Bob "Killer" Dill at Madison Square Garden.

The same held true for Gordie Howe and other fifties superstars. The team "policeman" had yet to make his appearance in the NHL, and you were expected to take care of yourself, no matter where you stood in the scoring statistics. Fortunately, Maurice was gifted with his fists, and he had the temperament of a live grenade when aroused.

Several episodes earlier in the 1954–55 season paved the way for the riot. In a game in Toronto during the Christmas holidays, Maurice became embroiled in a fight with Leafs defenseman Bob Bailey. It was broken up, and the combatants were escorted to their respective dressing rooms. As Maurice approached our bench, Dick Irvin leaned over the boards and said something to the Rocket, who turned and charged after Bailey for a second time. During this rematch, Maurice manhandled the linesman, George Hayes, but referee Red Storey did not assess an extra penalty, nor did he write up the incident in his game report. Later, the newspapers speculated that Maurice was incensed because he believed that Bailey had been trying to gouge his eyes during the original fight. As it happened, the Leafs had filmed both the fight and Irvin's intervention, and they sent the footage to league president Clarence Campbell.

No suspension resulted, but Maurice and Frank Selke received a severe tongue lashing at NHL headquarters and the league decided to initiate a crackdown on violence. Later that season, when Ted Lindsay attacked a fan in Toronto, he was suspended for ten days, a signal that any further altercations involving officials or onlookers would be dealt with harshly.

On Sunday, March 13, we were in Boston, getting whipped 4–2 by the Bruins. The score was not sitting well with us, because we were involved in a close race with Detroit for first place, and a loss to the fourth-place Bruins would be frustrating in the extreme. Late in the game, I faced off with Olmstead and Richard on my wings and we moved down the ice. Maurice closed in on Hal Laycoe at the blue line; Laycoe got his stick up and cut him. I was standing only a few feet away and saw Maurice take off his glove. He passed his hand over the gash and it came away covered with blood.

Maurice immediately went after Laycoe, and everybody else on the ice dropped their gloves and paired off. I took Fleming Mackell up against the glass, trying to follow the growing melee out of the corner of my eye. Apparently, when Rocket charged Laycoe, referee Frank Udvari and linesman Cliff Thompson got in his way. One version of the story is that Maurice was well under the control of the linesman, but Doug Harvey broke free of Fern Flaman and pulled the official away. Maurice got free, as well, then cracked his stick across Laycoe's back. He was still going after him when Thompson intervened once more. Maurice later said that when Thompson grabbed him the second time, Laycoe was able to punch him unimpeded. After warning Thompson three times to let him go, Richard turned and pushed the linesman hard and was assessed a match penalty by Udvari.

Dick Irvin was quoted in the papers to the effect that Maurice was so mad he was in a trance. "At this point, it was almost as if he'd just discovered the presence of the linesman. I still don't know whether Rocket recognized who he was." According to yet another story, Irvin himself handed Maurice a stick so he could go after Laycoe yet again.

This sort of display was not about to pass unnoticed. The expectation was that Rocket would be suspended for the three games remaining in the regular season, thereby losing his chance of winning the scoring title. Nobody thought that he'd get off with impunity. However, when Clarence Campbell suspended him for the rest of the year, play-offs included, the penalty struck most observers as far too punitive, both for Maurice and for the Canadiens.

I was sure that Campbell hadn't made this decision alone. To my mind, the other five teams had ganged up on the Canadiens. Frank Selke was quick to describe the rancor of his fellow managers: "All these gentlemen demanded that something be done to curb Maurice

Richard, whose greatest fault was defeating their teams and filling their arenas to capacity."

French-speaking Montrealers were likewise resentful of Rocket's suspension. For them, it was simply another opportunity to humiliate French Canadians by excessively punishing their favorite. Death threats and bomb threats streamed into NHL headquarters, and Montreal's mayor, Camillien Houde, suggested that Campbell would be prudent to avoid the upcoming game on Saturday against the Red Wings. Campbell, who had been a prosecutor at the Nuremberg trials of Nazi war criminals, said he would not back down in the face of threats from any quarter and promised to be at the Forum in his regular seat.

Despite the loss to Boston and Rocket's suspension, our fight for first place with the Wings was still on. A win that Thursday would put us out in front. But the suspension had unsettled us and Detroit took advantage, going ahead 4–1 in the first period. Toward the end of the period, a young fan went up to Campbell and threw a punch at him. Others in the crowd hurled tomatoes, eggs, and sundry debris in Campbell's direction. The action in the stands was heavier than on the ice.

We were craning our necks to see what was happening as we filed out to our dressing room at period's end. Even there, we could hear the mounting clamor. Just at the moment the racket outside reached its loudest, Frank Selke came into the room. "Get dressed, boys," he said. "The fire commissioner has ordered us to empty the Forum." We showered, dressed, and emerged into a downtown battle zone.

Over my many years in the league, I came to appreciate and respect Clarence Campbell as a fair-minded individual who always had the NHL's best interests at heart. Still, I could not agree with Rocket's suspension, particularly since it smacked of a deal worked out among the board of governors. Nor did I think that Campbell was wise to make an appearance at the game.

On the other hand, what could he do? As league president, he couldn't appear to be hiding, especially with NHL headquarters a short drive away. Maybe pride was a factor; maybe he felt he had to make a statement by attending. Besides, his absence might not have made any difference.

Whatever the case, Campbell hurt both Maurice, who lost the scoring title, and the team, which lost first place in the final week of the season and went down to defeat in seven games in the Stanley Cup play-offs against the Red Wings. I would have liked our chances against them had Rocket been in the lineup. Maurice rose to the occasion during any play-off and scored many critical goals.

His suspension also affected the league scoring race, which continued without him. Boom Geoffrion and I were right behind him in second and third place respectively, and the idea of adding to our tallies while he couldn't play was not appealing to either of us. The team had to finish ahead of the Red Wings to secure home-ice advantage for the duration of the play-offs, but Boom was worried. For all his laughter and shenanigans, he was a sensitive guy, concerned about his image and eager to be liked by the fans.

"If we go ahead of the Rocket, those people out there are going to come down on us as traitors," he said to me just prior to our final regular-season game against the Red Wings at the Forum.

Doug Harvey was sitting nearby. "We're goin' for first, Boom," he said, with the finality of a field general who would have your stripes if you weren't giving your best. "There's no question of shootin' wide of the net."

I agreed with Doug. "Boom, if it's there, you have to score. The fans will understand."

I was wrong and Boom was right. The team wound up in second place, two points out of first. Boom scored one more point than the Rocket and two more than me, as we finished one-two-three atop the scoring list. I hit the post twice in that final regular-season game.

A few days later, just before our first home game against Boston in the semifinals, Maurice was introduced to the crowd, prompting a prolonged standing ovation. Minutes later, when Boom was presented with the Art Ross Trophy for winning the scoring race, the fans booed him for almost as long as they had cheered the Rocket. Boom Boom remembered this episode for a long time. Try as we might to convince him that the crowd's reaction had everything to do with Maurice and nothing to do with him, Boomer was inconsolable. Still, he and I each managed to score a goal in a 2–0 win that night, and he was our leading scorer with eight goals and five assists in twelve games as we took Detroit to seven before finally losing the Cup.

WHILE I WAS STILL in my first year with the Aces, Elmer Lach was quoted by a Montreal paper as saying that when Béliveau got to town, it would signal his swan song with the Canadiens. This was a strange comment coming from a man who continued to display great strength at his position even in his later years. For four seasons, he'd teamed up with the dependable strength of Toe Blake and the spectacular scoring of the Rocket to form the Punch Line, one of the league's top trios. When Toe broke his leg and retired, Elmer carried on with the Rocket and a succession of left-wingers, including Bert Olmstead, a player who was similar to Toe in the corners.

When I joined the Canadiens in 1953, Elmer was still there, contributing both on the ice and off. Just as Punch Imlach had tried to improve my quickness by having me work out with veteran teammates on the Aces, Dick Irvin assigned Elmer as my tutor during my first season with Montreal. He was especially skilled at face-offs, and I picked up a number of useful tricks. I'd always tried to put my stick down just as the puck hit the ice, but Elmer told me not to wait, to be in motion as the puck was dropped. That split second gained meant a lot of face-offs won, and winning face-offs has always been a significant factor in winning games.

Elmer was also one of the finest passers in the league. He could give you a quick, soft pass that would nestle on your stick; it just seemed to settle on the blade without a bounce. In addition, he was a very smooth and shifty skater. Although his shot wasn't particularly heavy, his quick release made him dangerous. He would use a defenseman to screen the goalie, especially when he got to within fifteen or twenty feet of the net. If Maurice and Toe were covered, Elmer could take the netminder by surprise. If a goalie tried to look around his defensemen for Elmer's shot, that wonderful passing ability would come into play, and one of the wingers would find himself with an easy score after the puck appeared as if by magic on his blade. I knew I would have a long career in the NHL if I could learn to pass half as well as Elmer.

Another veteran who shaped my game in my first years with Montreal was Bert Olmstead, the hard-rock left-winger who could hammer an opponent senseless and seconds later chew you out on the bench because you were three inches out of position on a play. The best years Boom and I ever had—and remember that we won back-to-back scoring championships in 1955 and 1956—was when Bert was on our line. He never let us relax or gave us a minute's rest. He was always after us, pushing, pushing.

Often, Bert would be banging away in the corner with two or three opponents draped over him, while I waited out in front of the net. Instinctively, I might drift over to help him, but he'd scream, "Get the hell out of here! Get back in front, and stay there!" More often than not, he'd come up with the puck, Boom or I would receive the pass, and we'd find ourselves staring down the goalie, unopposed.

Pity the defensemen who faced us in those days. If you played on the right side, Dickie Moore and Bert Olmstead would be pounding on you shift after shift. If you were on the left, you had Boom Boom and the Rocket to contend with.

When I joined the Canadiens, Émile "Butch" Bouchard was on his last legs, both at our blue line and as our team captain. I played with Émile for only two years, and in the last year he didn't play all that much. Still, he was well respected throughout the league for his tenacity. One night, a fracas started in Detroit and he went right to the Red Wings' bench, opened the door, and chased a player behind the boards—unheard-of behavior then as now. Nobody on the Detroit team dared to retaliate, and they certainly had their share of tough customers. The only other defenseman of that era who matched Butch in physical power was the late, great Tim Horton of Toronto.

Butch lived in Longueuil, not far from me, and in his final season we often drove to the Forum together. Like many large, strong men, he was somewhat reluctant to demonstrate his professional prowess off the ice, believing that a kind word and a smile went a lot farther than brute force. As a captain, Butch took great pains to listen to everyone's opinion on any issue, and he served as a model for my stint as team captain in the 1960s.

Butch held another interesting distinction. Although I played with several sets of brothers—the Richards, the Mahovlichs, the Rousseaus, and the Plantes—Butch was the only player whose son would become a teammate in later years—in my last season, in fact. Pierre Bouchard, "Butch Junior" to his friends, had his father's strength and easy laugh. Unlike many hockey fathers, however, Butch Senior didn't bring his son to the Forum very often. Pierre must have learned his lessons at home.

Besides Bouchard, the other influential veteran on the Canadiens when I joined them was Doug Harvey. Doug was a one-man Welcome Wagon. If a rookie needed anything, he could go to Doug. He was a team man on the ice, in the dressing room, and on the road. Oh, and Doug Harvey was also the best NHL defenseman who ever lived. No exceptions. Offensively, of course, Bobby Orr was his better. Orr was so fast that he could take chances in an opponent's zone, then rush back to his blue line if his sortie didn't work out. That said, Bobby Orr could not do everything Doug Harvey could—a judgment shared by Doug's teammates, his opponents, and anyone who had the good fortune to marvel at his on-ice abilities.

Defensively, Harvey was far superior to Orr and thus to anybody he faced. As described earlier, he was probably the finest natural athlete ever to play our game. Scouts, managers and sportswriters argued endlessly about his equal abilities in baseball, football, and hockey. His stamina was a marvel to behold. If the Canadiens had lost two or more players to injury, especially in the middle of a road trip, Doug would play all night. If he needed a rest, or thought the game was getting too frisky for his liking, he'd simply slow it down.

How could a single player dictate the tempo of a game? Simply by controlling the puck and defying any and all comers to take it from him. Forecheckers were reluctant to challenge him because he could easily handle them physically or embarrass them with a sudden move. When an opponent got careless, Doug would let go with a long pass that would spring a teammate into the open for a breakaway. Even at the end of his career, when he came up with St. Louis for the 1968 play-offs thirty pounds overweight and barely able to skate, he was still directing the game in subtle ways.

When Doug was on the ice, you played his way or you didn't play at all. Many sports fans like to indulge in "what if" speculations, wondering how players from my era would fare if they time-traveled to today's NHL. Doug Harvey would fare very well, especially when up against a number of today's wingers who have the habit of hanging around the boards at their own blue lines, waiting for the breakout pass from a defenseman.

Doug used to tell our forwards, "I won't give you the puck if you're not skating. If you're standing still, if you park yourself near the boards and wait for a pass from me, it won't come. You'll die of old age standing there. If you want the puck, you'll get it on the fly."

We skated, and he got us the puck. For his efforts, Doug won every Norris Trophy as top defenseman between 1955 and 1962, save 1959 when it went to his teammate, Tom Johnson. Only Orr, with eight trophies, has surpassed Doug's magnificent record.

I well remember one occasion when Doug literally called his shot. We were going for our fifth straight Cup in March 1960 and had opened the series against Chicago with a 4–3 win at home. It had been a surprisingly hard-fought contest, given that the Hawks were without Stan Mikita and Bobby Hull. Two nights later, we were sitting on a slim 3–2 lead when Billy Hay stole the puck from Doug at our blue line and scored with a minute to go in the third period. We sat in the dressing room glumly contemplating overtime.

"Well, boys, I owe you one," Doug said, very matter-of-factly. And at 8:38 of the fourth period, he walked in on Glenn Hall to keep his promise. Nor did he relax his vigilance in subsequent games. The Hawks never scored again in the series, as we dumped them 4–0 and 2–0 back in Chicago to advance to the final. Jacques Plante received much of the credit for those back-to-back shutouts, but it was Doug's inspired play that made the goalie's work that much easier.

That Chicago series was one of the few times when I didn't see Doug displaying his almost perpetual grin. He was a nonstop joker, a happy-go-lucky guy who could always be counted on to lighten the tension during a vital game. When a game didn't count for much in the standings, he'd keep us all in stitches. Once, at an exhibition match in Sudbury against the Wolves of the Ontario Senior Hockey League, he went right over the top.

Hector "Toe" Blake had succeeded Dick Irvin as coach by then. Sudbury was Toe's hometown, and he wanted his homecoming to be a memorable one. We were leading 5–0 in the third period, just coasting along, when the Wolves suddenly managed to score.

Whenever the local team put the puck in the net, an effigy of a wolf flew out from behind a curtain at one end of the rink and floated above the ice surface on a guy wire. A taped recording of a howling wolf filled the air. Naturally, the crowd would start to howl along, and soon the whole arena would sound like a reunion of the world's largest wolf pack.

Doug was so taken with this that several minutes later, he accidentally-on-purpose put the puck past a flabbergasted Jacques Plante. When Doug returned to our bench, Blake was howling mad. "Are you nuts? This isn't a practice where you can fool around, this is a game!" His face was tomato-red and a vein throbbed alarmingly on his temple.

Doug flashed his trademark Little Rascals grin. "Sorry, Toe, but seein' that wolf again was worth it."

Earlier I referred to Doug's other side—the drinking and carousing that colored his post-Canadiens career and diminished him in some people's eyes, though never in mine. The fact is that Doug had come out of a hard-drinking, harder-working blue-collar neighborhood in the 1940s. That background, and the Snowdon Tavern, never left him.

I have been asked many times, "What could you have done to help him? Did you as players see him heading in this direction?" In truth, there was very little we could have done. It wasn't our place to dictate his behavior. Doug was older than us, one of our leaders. Besides, his drinking didn't affect his play. He never showed up for a game the worse for wear.

Yes, the weekends were rough, and Doug would celebrate a victory or drown the sorrow of a loss. But he wasn't alone in this, by any means. Just like players today, we'd all have beers after a game. You could lose four to five pounds over three periods of play, and your first priority afterward was to replace the lost fluids. A player isn't hungry at eleven o'clock, just thirsty. And what's open at eleven o'clock at night, especially on the road?

Doug enjoyed his parties, but he never hurt anyone, with the possible exception of himself. On the contrary, he was always eager to help. Once, after his playing days were over, he called me at the Forum from a charitable organization's summer camp, somewhere in the Eastern Townships, where he was building a walk-in freezer.

"We're running short on wood, Jean. Is your foundation able to help?" He was referring to the Jean Béliveau Foundation, which I had created at the end of my playing career, a vehicle that raised funds for charitable work.

"Sure, I'll provide equipment and materials. How much do you need?"

"I think with $500, I'll have enough to finish the job."

"Okay. Tell them to send me the bill. But what are you doing? How long have you been there?"

"A little more than a week. Jean, it's just beautiful here. We're building the freezer now, having a few beers, a few laughs."

I always felt that some part of Doug never grew up. Life was there to enjoy and life was short, so he made the most of it.

After we lost to Chicago in the 1961 play-offs, Frank Selke sold Doug Harvey and Albert Langlois to the Rangers in return for tough guy Lou Fontinato. Doug became New York's player-coach but lasted only a year. He had an eye for the game and was a very good judge of talent. But he couldn't stand the loneliness of coaching, the invisible barrier that separated him from his teammates, and he gave it up after a single season. Besides, his methods were unorthodox. He'd raised eyebrows in the Rangers' executive suite when he called his first team meeting in a bar. Doug left New York in 1964 and kicked around the minors for a while—as a player-coach here, a scout there—and finally ended up with the Quebec Aces, coached by his former teammate Boom Boom Geoffrion.

The Aces were heading off on a road trip, and rather than come into town to catch the bus, Doug asked to be picked up at a spot on the highway, near his home in Lac Beauport. It was an ice-cold winter's day, and when the bus arrived there was Doug, warming his hands over a fire he'd lit in an old oil drum—a fine example of self-sufficiency for the rest of the team.

When Doug went to New York, Frank Selke came in for a good deal of criticism. People said he'd banished Doug because of his work on the executive of the National Hockey League Players' Association. Selke had already traded Dollard St. Laurent to Chicago, apparently for similar reasons. Perhaps these accusations were true, but it wasn't like Frank Selke to run with the pack. I always thought that by sending Doug to New York, Selke was offering him the chance at a second career. If he'd stuck with coaching, he could have done well, but only if he had brought his personal life under control. Doug was a few months shy of his thirty-seventh birthday at the time. His playing days were coming to an end, one way or another.

OF ALL THE STARS on the 1950s Canadiens—thirteen of whom have been inducted into the Hockey Hall of Fame—the most ferocious competitor was Richard Winston Moore. Dickie and I knew each other intimately by the time I joined the Canadiens, having wreaked havoc on each other through many seasons in junior hockey. When I was with the Citadels, we hated each other with a passion and proved it night after night. Dickie wouldn't have had it any other way.

He attempted to crack the Canadiens' lineup after graduating from junior hockey in 1951 but was sent down to the QSHL Montreal Royals for seasoning, which afforded him yet another opportunity to make my life intolerable as by that time I was with the Aces.

Dickie did not last long in senior, however. When Maurice Richard was plagued by a nagging abdominal tear for most of the 1951–52 season, the Canadiens summoned Dickie to their ranks on December 15. He scored eighteen goals and fifteen assists in the remaining thirty-three regular-season games and appeared to be on his way.

Unfortunately, the injury bug bit him, just as it had the Rocket and as it would me in my NHL debut season. Dickie played only thirty-one games in the next two seasons. In his third (my first), we got to know each other even better and under much more agreeable circumstances than we had shared in junior. That year a knee injury limited him to a mere thirteen games during the regular season, although he came back to lead us in the play-offs with thirteen points in eleven games. I missed twenty-six games of my own with a variety of ailments, including a cracked ankle.

Dickie's knees were arguably worse than Bobby Orr's. Late in his career, Dickie would walk into a room and you'd know who it was without looking up by the telltale "click, click" sound of his joints.

Dickie won the scoring championship in 1957–58, playing most of the season with a broken left wrist. When he first incurred the injury, he convened a meeting to ask his linemates if they would continue to play with him; he was afraid of hindering Henri Richard's attempt at the scoring championship. Dickie was fitted with a special playing cast, and Toe Blake switched him over to the right wing on our power play to protect it. Never a big scorer in junior, Dickie ended the season with thirty-six goals and forty-eight assists, edging out "the Pocket Rocket" by four points. A year later, Dickie successfully defended his Art Ross Trophy, with forty-one goals and fifty-five assists for ninety-six points, a league record that lasted six seasons until Bobby Hull scored ninety-seven points in 1965–66.

AN EVEN DOZEN OF the 1950s Canadiens played with the club for all five Stanley Cups: Maurice and Henri Richard, Boom Boom Geoffrion, Dickie Moore, Jacques Plante, Tom Johnson, Don Marshall, Claude Provost, Bob Turner, Doug Harvey, Jean-Guy Talbot, and myself. We had a lineup filled with players who absolutely refused to accept defeat, incredible competitors all. We also had our share of flakes; Boom Boom was a blizzard all by himself.

In 1959, we went into Chicago for the play-offs. One morning Boom was reading the TV listings at the breakfast table. "Look at this," he said, excited. "*Job in Chicago.* I bet that's a gangsters-and-cops movie with lots of shooting and tommy guns." What else, in Al Capone's hometown?

Boom's bass tones became even deeper as his enthusiasm grew. "It's on at ten thirty. We'll get back to the room early so we can watch it." During the day, he mentioned our movie date several times to make sure I wouldn't forget. Boom was a peaceful man, but he loved his bloodthirsty gangster movies.

At ten thirty, we were ready, the TV tuned to the proper channel. But when the show appeared, *Job in Chicago* had become *Jobs in Chicago.* The narrative was uplifting and informative: "Job Sixty-Six, company in Oak Grove needs a plumber. Call this number and specify Job Sixty-Six." And so on, through every service industry and building trade. The only sign of gangsterism was the announcer's machine-gun delivery. Boomer went nuts, swearing in *bon Québécois* for half an hour.

In the mid-fifties, Kenny Reardon, a former Canadiens defenseman and a member of the Hall of Fame, was the team's assistant general manager. He had been known for an unorthodox skating style in his playing days. During a practice, as Kenny watched from the boards, Boom Boom did a perfect imitation of Kenny's tip-toe run, caroming off the boards on either side of the rink, cutting across behind a defenseman, braking hard in front of the net, and sending the puck way up into the whites, the Forum's remotest tier of seats.

Boomer was one half of our Class Clown tag-team act—I'll tell you about his partner in a minute—but his love of a joke very nearly killed him in 1958. We were at practice, and he seemed to brush against André Pronovost. There was no collision, but Boom was suddenly rolling all over the ice. Our reaction was predictable: we thought he was fooling around, so we let him entertain us for a while.

Finally, I skated over to him, and he gasped through clenched teeth, "Jean, I'm not joking!" I motioned for trainer Hector Dubois to come out, and he and Bill Head whisked him off to hospital.

Boom had a ruptured spleen and underwent emergency surgery minutes after his arrival. The doctors said such an attack could have happened while he was walking down the street.

Boom enjoyed good health as a player, but he's had his problems. In 1993, both he and his wife Marlene, the daughter of Howie Morenz, underwent surgery in their adopted home city of Atlanta, Georgia. Marlene had an eight-hour triple bypass operation, and Boom was treated for prostate cancer. I'm happy to say that both of them have since recovered fully.

In addition to his comedic talents, Boom fancied himself a singer and, truthfully, he did have enough of a voice to be asked to appear on both English and French television. On the road, we'd occasionally go for a few beers at a club that featured live entertainment. We'd barely have time to get settled before Boom would climb onstage and commandeer the microphone. Nowadays it's called karaoke; back then, we had another phrase for it: big ham.

Perhaps Boomer's most famous performance was on *Juliette,* the popular variety program on CBC Television. He changed the words in the song "C'est Magnifique" to suit and celebrate himself. When he wasn't doing Maurice Chevalier numbers, Boom would fall back on Dean Martin tunes. As a vocal impersonator, he was well ahead of his time.

Of course, Boom had his serious side: he always played to win. In 1961, he was shooting for the Rocket's fifty-goal single-season scoring record and netted the magic goal against Toronto's Cesare Maniago on March 16, in a 5–2 win over the Leafs at Montreal. It was Boom's sixty-second game of the year, the team's sixty-eighth.

Throughout my career, I heard complaints that I passed the puck too much, but I shrugged them off because I'd always enjoyed making plays. I think I got assists on thirty-seven or thirty-eight of Boom's goals that season, which cut down on the complaints. He finished first in league scoring with ninety-five points, five more than I. When they presented him with the Art Ross Trophy at the Forum that year, nobody booed.

Boomer and I had several set plays. Back then, most defensemen tended to be stocky and slow. A good stickhandler was usually given the blue line, and I was able to use my long reach to advantage. If I went to the right, I would try to hold onto the puck until the defenseman committed himself. If he came at me, I'd flip it to Boom, and he'd blast it. If the defender backed in, we'd take the puck right into the crease.

When you're on top of the world, which the Canadiens were in those years, a certain arrogance will surface on occasion. Boom could sneer with the best, as I saw one Sunday night at Madison Square Garden. We had beaten the Rangers 6–0, and New York coach Phil Watson was so angry that he waited until the stands cleared, then took his team right back onto the ice for an eleven o'clock workout.

Boomer and I were among the last players to leave the visitors' dressing room. As we walked along the aisle beside the rink, we were greeted by the unusual spectacle of weary Rangers sweating out stops-and-starts under the watchful eye of Fiery Phil.

Boom put his nose right up against the glass and yelled at a group of players that included Andy Bathgate, Wally Hergesheimer, Dean Prentice, and Lorne "Gump" Worsley. "Skate like hell, you bums!" he cried. "Keep it going! Keep it going! Try to get it right!" The Rangers stared back at him with glassy-eyed resignation. This was their second beating in an hour.

Character that he was, Boom had nothing on Marcel Bonin, my former Aces teammate, who found his way to Montreal from Boston in 1957. As mentioned, Marcel was fond of hunting and of borrowing other people's clothes when the occasion demanded. He could also walk on his hands as well as he could on his feet. Sometimes, while we were going about our pregame preparations, we'd look up to see a stark-naked man, wandering around the dressing room upside down. That could relax you before an important contest.

So could Marcel's habitual pregame questions. "Who are we playing tonight?" he'd ask. "Who are their toughest players? Marcel is feeling strong!" All of this would be accompanied by much flexing of very thick biceps. To drive home the point, Marcel would occasionally snap off a piece of a drinking glass, pop it into his mouth and grind it to powder inside one cheek, just like a chaw of tobacco.

Once, we were in the locker room, dressing for a big game with about five weeks remaining in the season, when Marcel made a strange announcement. "Starting tonight, Marcel is going into a slump," he said.

"What?"

"A slump."

"What are you talking about?" Goals were hard enough to come by in the NHL, and I'd never heard of a player who purposely wouldn't score.

"Fifteen goals, that's my usual production. I'm already there. If I score twenty, they'll ask me to score twenty-five next year, and I can't. So for the next seven or eight games, I'll be the playmaker. You score. Marcel is going into a slump."

In fact, in his five years with us, Marcel Bonin never did score more than seventeen goals a season, although when he was on the line with Boom and me in 1959–60 and 1960–1961, he put together fifty-one points in each of those seasons. Perhaps he could have done better, but he decided it was enough after he'd hit the half-century mark.

Marcel was a very helpful guy to have on your side when the going got rough. One night, we were involved in a brawl in Boston. Boomer was grappling with Jack Bionda, a big defenseman, and Marcel was off in the corner with somebody else. When the fight broke up, everyone skated back to their benches or to the penalty box, all except Bionda, who sat exhausted at center ice, shaken by his scuffle with Boom.

Marcel spotted Bionda just sitting there, out of gas, bothering no one. As if acting on an afterthought, Marcel casually paused in front of him, leaned over, and *whang*, knocked him out cold with one swat, then continued to our bench. Needless to say, the clans gathered and once more fights broke out all over the rink.

On another occasion, we were playing in Chicago Stadium on a very warm night. Elmer Lach had taught me not only to have my stick in motion as the puck was dropped, but to be the last man in on the face-off. I'd set up for it as usual, but when I could see that the linesman was ready to drop the puck, I'd pull back, glance around to see where everybody was, and then move in again. That night, I looked over and spotted Marcel, talking cheerfully to someone in the stands. I stepped back again and skated over to him. "Marcel, what's going on?"

He nodded at the fan. "This guy just dropped a glass of beer down the back of my neck. You know how hot it is. I was telling him that next time, he should warn me and I'll turn around so he can put it here." He gestured toward his throat. The fans and the players cracked up. What could I do or say? In those days, we could afford to act like that. We were winning all the time.

After he retired from hockey, it seemed only natural that Marcel gravitated to police work, joining the force in Joliette, about thirty miles northeast of Montreal. He was off duty on the afternoon of a robbery at a local hardware store. A silent alarm alerted the police, who trapped the thieves inside. But the crooks were armed and shots were exchanged. When the police chief arrived, he gave the order: send for Marcel.

Since Marcel was hunting that day, it took a while to reach him. An hour or so after the drama began, Marcel showed up, armed to the teeth. By this time, the press photographers had arrived as well.

Marcel told me the rest of the story. "I'm moving along, hugging the wall and trying to get to an opening where I could say something to the guys inside, when I hear this *'psst'* behind me. It's one of the photographers from Montreal, a guy I knew really well at the Forum.

"He issues instructions as if he's taking a picture of me in a hockey uniform. 'Marcel, move the shotgun away from your body a little bit; I'll have a better angle.'

"I turned around. 'Are you nuts? Where do you think you are? These guys are shooting bullets, not pucks!'"

I could understand the photographer's confusion. This was probably the first time in his life that Marcel was asking him, or anybody else, to be serious. The robbers surrendered peacefully in the end, which was just as well. Marcel was a sharpshooter; he could hit a target behind his back, shooting over his shoulder, by aiming via its reflection in a diamond ring held in front of him.

THESE, THEN, WERE SOME of the major contributors to our success in the 1950s. I'll return to Henri Richard, Claude Provost, and Jacques Plante later, and I acknowledge that I've omitted several other important names, among them Tom Johnson, Bob Turner, and Dollard St. Laurent, three remarkably consistent performers.

Tom, for example, played 857 games in thirteen seasons. When he first joined the team, he was paired with Butch Bouchard and they became close friends. Later, he played a lot with Jean-Guy Talbot. Like Johnson, Bob Turner was a westerner and a fine skater; he joined the team in 1955–56 and therefore shared in our Stanley Cup victories during his first five years in the NHL. The sad news of Bob's passing came in the spring of 2005.

But every member of the Canadiens organization made a contribution of his own. It was a decade to remember and to be proud of, always.

At the same time, the fifties were not years entirely free of pain and distress. My beloved mother was diagnosed with cancer and passed away at age forty-nine in 1957, the year my daughter was born. My father remarried, and Mida, my stepmother, helped him with the task of raising my younger brothers and sisters.

I should mention here another episode that presaged the problems I would face in the 1960s. Élise and I had been prepared for the glare of the celebrity spotlight by our time in Quebec City. We had learned to cope with media demands, although these intensified when we moved to Montreal. Every week, or so it seemed, a newspaper or magazine was knocking on the door, seeking fresh insight into the lives of the Béliveaus. We were posed in pictures of domestic bliss—cooking, eating, reading, enjoying music. Our fans expected this sort of coverage, and we were usually happy to oblige.

But there was another side to the coin. In 1955, a rumor spread that we were experiencing marital difficulties. The story originated in Quebec City, where Élise was frequently seen without me. In fact, her mother had fallen ill that year, and Élise was visiting more frequently.

The rumor was embellished to include a rival, the professional wrestler Jean Rougeau. There was only one flaw in this piece of gossip: Élise had never met the man in her life. Journalists were dispatched to investigate, but when it was denied by all concerned, the "scandal" eventually died down.

At the time, however, it was upsetting and gave mean-spirited persons cruel inspiration. One night, Élise answered the telephone and found herself speaking to a woman who'd been in the habit of calling with lurid descriptions of my alleged infidelities.

"You think you're so smart, Madame Béliveau," she said, "but you should see where your husband is at this moment."

This woman knew that, given my schedule, the chances were that I'd be away from home when she made her calls. That night, however, Élise could see precisely where I was: sitting right next to her. She so informed the caller, and we heard no more from her. But the whispers about my or Élise's imaginary carryings-on persisted for quite a while.

We got through this period thanks to the support we received from our families and our mutual love and respect. We were never threatened by the gossipmongers, because there was no basis for their speculations. The trouble is that a wounding story can strike in many directions. Several years later, I had occasion to meet Jean Rougeau, who said he felt very badly about what had happened. He, too, had a wife and family, and the slander had had a similar effect on his household.

Winning the 1959–60 Stanley Cup brought the fifties to a satisfying close. My second decade of play would be a ten-year roller-coaster ride of fresh triumphs and unaccustomed troubles, while ushering in a whole new chapter in the unfolding saga of the *bleu-blanc-rouge.*

6

THE NEGLECTED SIXTIES

Sam Pollock has called the 1960s the "forgotten decade" in the history of the Montreal Canadiens. In the endless debate over which team was "the greatest"—the 1950s Canadiens or the 1970s edition—even the most meticulous Hab historians tend to overlook the men who won four Stanley Cups in five years, or five in seven years if, like me, you consider the 1970–71 Canadiens as essentially the 1960s lineup.

Only two other NHL teams—Toronto between the 1944–45 and 1950–51 seasons, and Edmonton between 1983–84 and 1989–90—have ever won five Cups in seven years. And yet, for reasons that escape me, the 1960s Canadiens receive little recognition and even less respect.

At the time, nobody doubted our abilities. Along with the Maple Leafs (in the first half of the decade) and the Chicago Black Hawks (by its halfway point), we were recognized as the force to be reckoned with. By the end of the decade, people were using the word "dynasty." Then along came Guy Lafleur, Steve Shutt, Bob Gainey, Ken Dryden, and other standouts of the 1970s, and we found ourselves relegated to a high, dusty shelf at the back of the hockey library.

On the personal side, I can honestly say that my second decade with the Montreal Canadiens was more eventful and more stressful than the first. It came as an unhappy surprise after our previous successes. The shocks were both physical and emotional: potentially career-ending injuries, scoring slumps, the wholesale trades of all-star teammates, league expansion, being booed by my home fans, and almost never-ending speculation about my widely touted imminent retirement.

I wasn't young anymore. Indeed, the state of my health would be a continuing concern in the years between the 1960–61 season, when our five-straight Stanley Cup reign ended, and 1970–71, the final season of my playing career. Even today, the occasional older fan will remind me of a story that circulated at that time; I was described as a Cadillac chassis with a Volkswagen engine, hampered by a heart that wasn't big enough or strong enough for my body size and my demanding sport. The story was essentially true, but while the Cadillac metaphor remained a constant, the heart's smaller vehicle tended to change model every now and then.

The story originated in 1953. When I signed my first contract with the Canadiens, team management thought it prudent to secure insurance on me, considering the $100,000-plus contract we had agreed to; the team would be protected if my playing days came to an abrupt end through accident or misadventure. Naturally, I underwent a stringent physical, during which the doctors noted a "cardiac anomaly"—one or two degrees down from an "abnormality." Nonetheless, Frank Selke was shocked to be told that the insurance company would not issue the policy. The examining physician had written in the file: "He has an Austin's motor in a Cadillac's chassis." The Austin was a tiny British car, the most underpowered vehicle the doctor could think of on the spur of the moment.

No one suggested that this condition was at all life-threatening, but there were problems. My "pump" could not move enough blood through my system when I was physically stressed. Symptoms of this anomaly included fatigue, nausea, temporary loss of sight, a shortness of breath that sometimes felt like suffocation, and chest pains so sharp that I felt my heart was ready to burst. Plainly, I should have looked for other work. Instead, I went out and helped the Canadiens win five consecutive Stanley Cups.

After the 1961–62 season, however, things started to catch up with me. By now in my early thirties and chronically fatigued, I decided to visit the Leahy Clinic in Boston, where I underwent a full regimen of stress tests. I ran on a treadmill and blew up balloons, and when I'd finished, they wheeled out the electrocardiogram machine. This scientific approach to physical fitness is common in any health club today, but back then it was brand-new and faintly mysterious, at least to me. My first two minutes on the treadmill were tough and I rapidly ran out of breath. Then my system slowly adjusted, and by the end of six minutes, when the doctors called a halt, my engine was humming and I felt I could have continued for several minutes more.

Still, the doctors were amazed that I could function as a professional athlete; according to them, I sorely lacked the necessary physical gifts. At the same time, they concluded that I wasn't at risk if I kept on playing. There might be a degree of discomfort, but nothing to worry about. My body had adapted to the condition many years before, setting a pace that I could live with. That pace, as the treadmill test showed, meant that I was a slow starter, but became stronger as I went along. And while I haven't checked my statistics over the years, I wouldn't be surprised to find that I scored more often in the second and third periods than in the first.

Despite this physical disadvantage, I managed to play eighteen years in professional sport. Some athletes aren't so fortunate. You can imagine my reaction when I heard about the tragic deaths of basketball players Hank Gathers and Reggie Lewis, both of whom lost their lives on the court because of similar deficiencies. It amazes me that someone with a finely tuned athlete's body can have something so utterly wrong with his or her system, an ever-present danger about which nothing can be done and that can strike without warning. I considered myself very lucky to be able to manage my condition, and I worked hard at keeping negative factors at bay.

The physical anomalies I couldn't control were the injuries I suffered in action, some worse than others. During the 1960s, I began to feel jinxed as far as these injuries were concerned, especially since an alarming number were suffered when we played Chicago.

The worst occurred during the third game of the 1961–62 play-offs. I was in the corner, scuffling for the puck with my former teammate, Dollard St. Laurent, when suddenly the lights went out. While Dollard and I were scrambling, the other Chicago defenseman, big Jack Evans, left his post in front of the net and charged me into the boards, catching me in the head with his stick, then driving my head into the glass. Even though I dressed for the remaining games, I was finished for the play-offs. With Henri Richard out with a broken arm, we were down two centers, and the Hawks won the series in six.

I suffered what was diagnosed as a mild concussion in the Evans incident, but no concussion, mild or otherwise, lingered as long as this one did. All that summer and during September's training camp, I continued to feel its effects. Convinced that my skull had been fractured, I underwent several more examinations, but everything appeared to be fine. It didn't feel fine, though. My game was off well into the following season.

Two other injuries that seriously affected my play were likewise sustained in games against the Black Hawks. On December 17, 1966, we tied them 4–4 at the Forum. Yvan Cournoyer, Bobby Rousseau, and I were pressing deep in the Chicago zone. I came over the blue line with the puck and moved toward Glenn Hall in the Chicago net as defensemen Doug Jarrett and Ed Van Impe waited to check me. Just as Jarrett was moving toward me, I suddenly felt an excruciating stab of pain in my eye. Stan Mikita had checked me from behind, and his stick had moved up my arm and into the eye.

This was my introduction to the "banana blade," the almost absurdly curved stick favored by both Mikita and Bobby Hull. While the blade may have terrorized goalies, it was capable of inflicting grievous harm on other players and was later outlawed. If Mikita's blade had been straight, it might have clipped my eyebrow or caught my cheekbone. Instead, its sharp curve allowed it to circumvent the orbital bone that encircles and protects the eye socket and nick me directly on the eyeball. A year earlier, Detroit defenseman Doug Barkley had a promising career snuffed out due to the loss of an eye, as had Claude Ruel in junior. These thoughts were not far from my mind as I writhed on the Forum ice. The pain eased and my eye eventually mended, but it cost me seventeen games.

The press seized upon this incident as further proof that I'd become accident-prone. According to media wisdom, I grew "brittle" in the early 1960s. I was "often injured" and "never quite able to turn in a full season." This simply wasn't true. My injuries tended to attract more attention than other players', but the numbers speak for themselves. In 1960–61, I missed a single game due to injury. The next season wasn't so hot: I sat out twenty-seven games. In 1962–63 and 1963–64, I missed a grand total of three games. I was absent for twelve games in 1964–65, but only three in 1965–66. The eye injury kept me out of seventeen games in 1966–67, and I lost eleven games in 1967–68 through thumb and chest injuries. In 1968–69, I missed one game; in 1969–70, seven. In my final year, playing as a fragile basket case, I somehow managed to make an appearance in all seventy regular-season games.

In other words, in four of my eleven seasons from 1960–61 to 1970–71, I sat out ten games or more. In six of eleven, I missed three games or fewer. My absenteeism rate was, in fact, about average at slightly less than 10 percent.

None of which seemed to correct the misperception. By 1962–63, my relationship with the press had taken a puzzling turn. Not only were the "Will He Retire?" stories recycled every time I turned around, I was continually being analyzed by pundits who didn't like what they saw or who made up what they wanted to. My mental stability was called into question: was I strong enough to handle all this adversity? Two basic themes emerged in answer. One was: Jean Béliveau is profoundly wounded by the accusations that he no longer contributes or cannot play up to the standards he set in the fifties. The other: Jean Béliveau has always been a "gentle giant" and, like most gentle people, has never possessed a strong psyche or well-developed fighting instincts.

These instant analyses appeared in newspapers that were tucked under countless arms and carried into the Forum. On some nights in 1962–63, I heard the heretofore unfamiliar sound of boos and catcalls being directed at me, which in turn set off another round of "Béliveau the Wounded Giant" stories that filled yards of newsprint.

Perhaps these are best illustrated by a selection of headlines or excerpts that appeared in print over time. Most date from 1962, when we were struggling to find ourselves as a team; the last few come from 1966, around the time of my eye injury.

Even during practice, Béliveau is hitting the posts

A hot rumor circulating that Béliveau is suffering from a serious illness

Could Béliveau abandon the Canadiens in the middle of winter?

If I score 30 goals during the season, I think the fans should be pleased with my performance

Béliveau responds to the boos: 'We are not bums!'

Some stories were sympathetic, if not a little wistful.

> *Will Béliveau ever receive the homage he merits?*
>
> *Jean Béliveau: the best was never enough*

Others tried to decide my future.

> *Béliveau has become a completely different man!*
>
> *Jean Béliveau is not dying: Father Aquin confirms it*
>
> *Jean Béliveau is mortally worried: should he retire?*
>
> *At 35 years of age, is it time for Jean Béliveau to retire?*

I could go on, but these paint the picture—a miserable slump that never seemed to end. It felt at times like my Quebec City days, but with fortune reversed. Then, the media couldn't wait for me to come to Montreal. Now, it seemed, they couldn't wait to show me the door.

Fans can be as fickle as the press. I remember one night when defenseman Terry Harper took the puck from behind our net. He hadn't been playing well of late, so he was booed as soon as he took possession. Then he crossed the opposition blue line, got behind the net and, just as he was hammered by two defenders, passed the puck to a free John Ferguson, who kicked it over to Yvan Cournoyer and it was in the net. The crowd wasn't booing anymore.

Truthfully, I wasn't heckled for eighteen years solid, not seriously. There were isolated incidents, but the jeering usually originated with a small proportion of the crowd. One guy was after me all the time. He must have weighed three hundred pounds, and on one occasion I lost patience and said to him, "How can you boo me? You can't even bend down to tie your shoes." Yet fan reaction is always blown out of proportion. The press hears four or five guys sound off and it's a headline.

The headlines are to be expected, of course. There's always been tough competition among the Montreal media and consequently some sensational, if not outrageous, coverage. It's even more intense today and has contributed to the loss of two Canadiens coaches in the current era, Jacques Lemaire and Pat Burns, both of whom went on to win Stanley Cups with New Jersey. Journalists have a job to do, whether to sell newspapers and magazines or to ensure an audience for radio and television. The louder and more lurid the story, the more attention they will attract. That's obvious, but in Montreal, it's sometimes taken to extremes. When I saw a relatively minor sports story boldly featured on the front page, I frequently asked myself whether there weren't more important things happening in the world.

There were two consolations when these headlines appeared. First, I wasn't being singled out exclusively. Boom Boom Geoffrion had troubles, particularly during the season that followed the one in which he'd scored fifty goals. In 1961–62 he slumped, and his goals dipped to only twenty-three. Inevitably, everybody said he was finished.

Second, and thankfully, a number of journalists took the time to think about what was happening to Boomer and me. Paul Émile Prince, writing in *La Presse*, raised a couple of interesting points. "The marked players, like Béliveau and others, labor constantly under pressure... The fans who recognize their success want to see them do better still... they are not forgiven a slump, a bad night, a bad period. There are many things that can affect performance during a game or a series of games, with the main one being an injury. These are the things that the public often doesn't know about, or forgets, but that have to be overcome. Therefore, the role of star is not as easy as is believed."

BESIDES INJURIES AND MEDIA speculation, one other factor disturbed me and my game during the early 1960s. It should have been a happy and positive development, but it soon took on a negative spin. This was my selection as team captain, a position that fell vacant when Frank Selke sent Doug Harvey to the New York Rangers in the summer of 1961.

The honor came as a huge surprise to me because my name wasn't even on the ballot. Strictly speaking, there wasn't a ballot at all. Every player simply wrote the name of the teammate he wanted as captain on a scrap of paper. The winner was announced when all the slips were counted. As far as I was concerned, there were only three guys in serious contention: Tom Johnson, Dickie Moore, and Bernie Geoffrion.

I was not at my best the day the vote was held. That fall, we'd trained in Victoria, British Columbia, and enjoyed unusually luxurious accommodations at the Empress Hotel. Our plan was to barnstorm back across the country, playing exhibition games against Western Hockey League clubs to keep our edge. The first of these games took place in Trail, B.C., against the Smoke Eaters, a highly rated team that had won that year's world amateur championship. I was terribly sick the day of the game, running a high fever and sweating a lot.

Toe Blake came to me around five o'clock. "Jean, the people here expect and want to see you. Just make an appearance."

I could hardly stand to dress for the game and my legs were wobbly in the warm-up skate. On the second shift, I tried to go around one of the Trail defensemen, but I was so weak and my legs so rubbery I couldn't get any speed. He leaned into me, we both fell, and I tore half the ligaments in my knee. The team continued on its cross-country tour, while I returned to Montreal for treatment. I would play only forty-three games with the Canadiens in the 1961–62 season, a high price to pay for a token appearance in an exhibition match.

On October 11, the Friday before our season opener, Toe called me to the Forum for the vote on the captaincy. My leg was in a full cast and one of my friends, a car dealer in Longueuil, had lent me a four-door sedan so that I could sit sideways in the back seat while Élise drove me downtown.

I voted for Dickie Moore that Friday. I loved Boom Boom like a brother, but I felt that he didn't convey enough seriousness to be captain. As his roomie for eleven years, I knew that he had a serious side and that he was as committed a competitor as any of his teammates. If the others had come to know him as well as I did, had seen and heard his concern for the team's well-being, perhaps he would have won the vote.

Dickie's knees were a concern to some. Every time he put on his equipment we held our collective breath, willing those shaky pins to carry this consummate pro through one more game. Few players believed that Dickie would be around for the long run, which colored their voting. Similar concerns affected Tommy Johnson's candidacy. He was thirty-three and, as it turned out, a year or so away from being traded to Boston. I also didn't think Tommy had the temperament for it. He was very quiet and wouldn't have enjoyed a Montreal captain's many public duties.

But who can say why the players voted the way they did that day? When the slips of paper were tallied, my name led the list. I was stunned by the result. Unfortunately, so was Boom, who took it badly. He never said anything to me directly, but it was no secret that he was deeply disappointed.

A few weeks into the season, I went to Toe Blake and volunteered to give up the "C" I was wearing on my jersey. Toe was aware of Boom's displeasure and knew that I would be honored to wear the "A" (for "alternate") instead, if it contributed to team unity. As a coach, he wanted all of his superstars happy and productive, so he took me upstairs to meet Frank Selke.

The boss, however, would have none of it and spoke sharply to us. "There is no question of doing that. The players voted for Jean, and to name Geoffrion I would have to throw out their vote. I will never do that. Mr. Geoffrion will have to learn to accept his teammates' ballot."

As mentioned, there was never an open disagreement between Boom and me. How could there be? With one look, sometimes one word, he'd have me laughing like a fool. Then he'd join in, and everything would be right with the world. But the other teams tuned in to his displeasure and tried to exploit it. Boston coach Milt Schmidt went so far as to make a public offer for Boom: "He'll be captain of the Bruins if Mr. Selke will trade him," he said. For the second time, the rather formal Frank Selke said, "There is no question of doing that."

There was, of course, a solid statistical reason why Schmidt wanted to lure Geoffrion away from Béliveau: we were one-two in the points-per-game average. I led with 1.16, but Boom was right behind me at 1.02, followed by Andy Bathgate at .993, Gordie Howe at .977, and Bobby Hull at .924. Splitting up the dynamic duo would be a terrific boon to the other five NHL teams.

In 1960–61, Bernie had scored fifty goals, and we had finished one-two in the league scoring, with Dickie Moore and Henri Richard joining us in the top ten. The following season, both of us fell far back. In fact, Montreal's top four forwards missed a total of sixty-four games in 1961–62—twenty-seven games for me, sixteen for Henri Richard, thirteen for Dickie, and eight for Boom. It was a measure of the Canadiens' extraordinary strength that we were still the highest-scoring team in the league, and finished first that year, thirteen points ahead of Toronto, even though the big guns had been in a tailspin. Ralph Backstrom and Claude Provost took up some of the slack, but the year marked the first time since the 1942–43 season that a Montreal forward had failed to make either the first or second all-star team. Jacques Plante and Jean-Guy Talbot were first-team choices, along with Doug Harvey, who by that time was in a New York Rangers uniform.

None of which did us the least bit of good at play-off time. We got pushed around in the 1961–62 finals, and much the same thing happened in 1962–63, when the Maple Leafs put the icing on the play-off cake by defeating us 5–0 in the fifth game of our semifinal.

Frank Selke had already decided that drastic measures were called for. We'd picked up New York tough guy Lou Fontinato when Harvey moved to the Rangers in the summer of 1961, but lost him on March 9, 1963, in a scary accident at the Forum. Lou tried to throw a check on rookie Ranger forward Vic Hadfield behind our net but missed and was off balance when Hadfield turned to body him head-first into the boards. Lou lay motionless for the longest time and was finally removed on a stretcher, his head and neck immobilized. He had a crushed cervical vertebra and was paralyzed for months. He eventually made a complete recovery, but he never played in the NHL again.

Lou was replaced by rookie defenseman Jacques Laperrière for the rest of the season. Earlier that year, another newcomer, Terry Harper, had joined the team when Tom Johnson was hurt. These additions were part and parcel of Frank Selke's ongoing makeover, as he continued to ease out the team of the 1950s and put in place the team of the 1960s.

Indeed, the changes that began in 1961 all but made our blue line unrecognizable from that of the 1950s. Harvey and Bob Turner exited in 1961, followed by Fontinato and Johnson in 1963. J.-C. Tremblay was still in place, having joined us in the 1959–60 season. But when the 1963–64 season began, Jean-Guy Talbot was the only defensive holdover from our five-straight Stanley Cup run. In the meantime we'd also witnessed the departure of Dickie Moore, whose rickety knees had finally defeated the strongest heart in the game.

By the time the 1963–64 season rolled around, Selke had assembled a vastly different and far tougher Canadiens team than had previously existed—the most physically powerful in the entire league, as I'll describe in a moment. Still, I would never have anticipated Selke's most daring move, one that some observers felt was akin to curing the disease by killing off the patient. To hasten the club's rejuvenation, he decided to trade Jacques Plante and talented centers Don Marshall and Phil Goyette to the New York Rangers for Lorne "Gump" Worsley and solid wingers Dave Balon and Léon Rochefort.

Jacques Plante had been the Canadiens' goalie throughout my first ten seasons, backed up by the able and steady Charlie Hodge. From 1955–56 through 1961–62, he was a first- or second-team all-star every year but one and won six of seven Vezina Trophies as the league's top netminder. I rate him and Terry Sawchuk as the best goalies I've ever seen, with Ken Dryden, Glenn Hall, Bernie Parent, and Patrick Roy on the next rung down.

Roy finally convinced me with his excellent play and four Stanley Cups, although I still have a hard time with him and many other present-day goalies because I am not a great fan of the butterfly style, having always favored stand-up, angles goalies. I will admit, however, that few goals today are scored by shots to the upper part of the net and that perhaps 70 percent of all shots will be stopped by the butterfly technique, especially since referees have a tendency to allow interference and open assaults on goalies in their creases.

Many things we teach young goalies today are the result of Jacques Plante's innovative spirit. Everyone knows that he was the first goalie to wear a mask regularly in NHL action. Jacques had used a mask in practice, but Toe Blake refused to let him wear it in games until Plante was hit in the nose by an Andy Bathgate slap shot in New York in 1959. Andy, a classy player, had one of the hardest and most accurate shots in the league, and he put everything into this one. Streaming blood, Jacques was taken to the Madison Square Garden's clinic, where a doctor stitched him up and managed to position the nose back into place. However, when Jacques returned to the dressing room, he told Toe, "I'm ready to go back out there, but I'm wearing the mask."

Toe and Jacques had a stormy relationship in the many years they were together. Each had a strong personality and was unafraid to speak his mind. That night, something in Jacques' voice must have conveyed an unequivocal message. He played with the mask that night and, within a year, it became a permanent fixture. Before long, every goalie wore facial protection. I still shudder at the memory of Jacques' heavily stitched nose. I couldn't believe he was able to return to the game in that condition, with the mask or without. The sutures formed a big, ugly C—for courage.

Nobody approached the position of goaltender with as much precision and science as Jacques Plante. His wide-ranging mobility revolutionized the game: he was the first goalie to go behind his net routinely to intercept a pass around the boards. He would rush out to challenge forwards who chased long passes into his zone or skate into the corner to retrieve iced pucks. Other goaltenders attempted these forays, but as a rule they were clumsy skaters and often had difficulty getting back into their nets.

Jacques' speed and agility enabled him to develop a deadly poke-check. He could hold back deep in his net and then strike like a serpent at a breaking forward—hence his nickname, "Jake the Snake." Add to that a very quick glove hand and fast feet, and Plante was pretty much the ideal netminder of the 1950s and '60s.

Here is just one example of Jacques' uncanny precision. During the first period of a game in Chicago, he complained vociferously that the crossbar on his net was too low, lower than on any other net in the league, he claimed. Naturally, we thought he might simply be crouching differently.

"No," he insisted, "when I take my position, I do it the same way in every rink. I haven't changed, this net has, and it's probably out by a sixteenth, maybe even an eighth, of an inch." The matter was left at that, although Jacques continued to belabor it after the game. The next time we played in Chicago, we asked our trainers to measure the net. It was exactly one-sixteenth of an inch out of alignment.

Like many goalies, Jacques was a solitary sort and could be abrasive at times. That doesn't mean that he wasn't a team man; he was. But he had his own way about him. He received a lot of media attention for his habit of knitting—in the dressing room and on trains when we traveled around the league. His needles clicked away, knitting and purling, turning out socks, toques, underwear, and camisoles. Perhaps the concentration of manual busywork had a calming effect on his mind, especially before an important game. Personally, I think he did it to economize. For some reason, it seems a lot of goalies are tight when it comes to money. Ken Dryden used to leave his car out past Greene Avenue in Westmount and walk blocks back to the Forum just to save a few dollars on parking.

Needless to say, some of the jokers on the team were tempted to tease Jacques about his pastime, but I tried to head them off. I knew full well that his temper was not to be trifled with. "Leave him alone; it's not our business. If he's happy to handle the tension that way, he'll probably be better off after his hockey career than most of us." This turned out to be true.

After his trade to New York, it was a shock to look back at our net and not see Jacques Plante standing there. The move proved to be a jolt to him as well. After a year and a half of "rubber therapy" with a fifth-place team, he quit hockey and returned to Quebec City, where he took a job as a sales representative with a brewery.

Jacques was too young to retire, and soon the temptation to put the pads back on became overwhelming. In 1965, he, Noël Picard, and several members of the Quebec Aces joined the Junior Canadiens as reinforcements to defeat the touring Soviet national team 2–1 at the Forum. Jacques was so spectacular that the full house gave him a standing ovation that Forum regulars said rivaled those for Rocket Richard in his heyday.

The St. Louis Blues came for him in 1968. At first he was reticent, but they dangled a $35,000 contract in front of him and off he went to share the net-minding duties with Glenn Hall for two seasons. The two veterans also shared the Vezina Trophy in 1969. Later, Jacques moved to Toronto for three seasons, then joined Boston in March 1973 for the Cup play-offs. He still had a few more games in him, though, and he surfaced with the Edmonton Oilers of the World Hockey Association (WHA) in 1975. That was his final season. He had played three hundred games in the NHL and WHA after his first retirement. In my mind, he will always be "Mr. Goalie."

As I intimated earlier, the Canadiens became the toughest team in the league in 1963–64. Terry Harper and Jacques Laperrière added size to our defense, aided by the even heavier-duty Ted Harris. Later, Noël Picard did his part in our 1965 Cup win. In the meantime, Dave Balon, Léon Rochefort, Bryan Watson, Claude Larose, and Jim Roberts added a good, solid, two-way work ethic up front.

But the club's new industrial-strength character was best personified by the most formidable player of the decade and possibly in Canadiens' history, John Bowie Ferguson. Fergie was the best fighter I know of in the NHL, but he wasn't a brute enforcer. He could beat you with his fists, certainly—his hands were huge—but equally well with his play in the corners and his scoring ability. For us, Fergie's greatest contribution was his spirit. He was the consummate team man and probably intimidated as many of us in the dressing room as he did opponents on the ice. You wouldn't dare give less than your best if you wore the same shirt as John Ferguson.

He is often remembered by commentators for his "countless" penalties, but Fergie never topped 185 minutes in penalties in any of his eight seasons. Over the years, he totalled 1,214. The *NHL Official Guide & Record Book* doesn't even list players who clocked fewer than 1,500 career minutes in their top sixty penalty leaders, a roster that includes former Canadiens Chris Nilan, Bryan Watson, Carol Vadnais, Doug

Risebrough, and Chris Chelios. I'm not in the upper echelon, either; I managed only 1,029. The point is that Fergie wasn't, and didn't have to be, a nonstop brawler. His hard-earned reputation preceded him, and he could keep the opposition in line without spending all night in the penalty box.

Fergie didn't appear quite so threatening when we first met at training camp in September 1963. The guy with the big nose wasn't the greatest skater to come out of the American Hockey League, where he had played with the Cleveland Barons. He knew his limitations and was ill at ease. He came up to me one morning, worry written all over his face. "If you only knew how much I want to stay with this team..."

"I've been watching you, Fergie. Don't worry, just keep on doing what you're doing."

Fergie had been, in essence, a free agent, very rare in those days, and Toronto, New York, Boston, and Montreal all had sought his services. The Canadiens won out and considered themselves lucky, but Fergie didn't seem to understand that we were impressed by his work ethic and felt that he deserved his place with us. If he labored as a skater, his faster teammates would learn to help him compensate.

Toe put Fergie with Boomer and me right from the start, perhaps remembering how well Bert Olmstead had done with us years earlier. My regular winger, Gilles Tremblay, moved over with Henri Richard for a while, while Fergie broke in with us. He learned quickly: twelve seconds into our season opener with the Bruins, he had the unlucky Ted Green in his clutches. That first night, Fergie received two majors for fighting and scored two goals in a 4–4 tie. It didn't take long for the word to spread up and down the league. Fergie's intimidation factor influenced our fortunes for many seasons thereafter, and no doubt gave Boston pause as they evolved into the Big Bad Bruins.

That evolution was complete by 1968 when the Bruins, full of cockiness and swagger, prepared to meet us in the play-offs. They had

Phil Esposito, Johnny Bucyk, Johnny McKenzie, Wayne Cashman, Ken Hodge, Bobby Orr, Derek Sanderson, and Ted Green, a formidable array of high elbows. We had Fergie.

Over the years Fergie and Green had become regular dance partners, and early in the first period the sparks flew again between them. Ferguson grabbed Green, got his sweater over his head, and pummeled him for several minutes. The Bruins exited in four straight games.

Back in 1964, the "new" Canadiens made a strong showing throughout the regular season and once again finished first. Then we fell to the Leafs in a seven-game semifinal. I suffered a knee injury after game 4 and tried to return for the seventh contest, but we were out. The series is remembered for the brawls that erupted in games 1 and 4, especially Eddie Shack's famous "coco-bunk" head butt that sent Henri Richard off for stitches. You had only to look at Fergie's eyes after the game to know that the scene would not be repeated too often in the future. You also knew that Shack would be on his best behavior whenever he saw the *bleu-blanc-rouge*.

In retrospect, we didn't have much of a chance that year, in part because of Leafs coach Punch Imlach's canny late-season acquisition of Andy Bathgate and Don McKenney from the New York Rangers in exchange for Dick Duff, Bob Nevin, and three minor-leaguers, one of whom was Rod Seiling, then playing for the Canadian national team. This gave the Leafs the edge they needed against us, and they went on to win the Cup.

With the end of the 1963–64 season came Boom Boom Geoffrion's decision to retire. At the age of thirty-three, he chose to go to Quebec City to coach the Aces. Boom's departure meant that only six regulars remained from teams that had won any or all of our five consecutive Cups: Henri Richard, Claude Provost, Billy Hicke, Jean-Guy Talbot, Ralph Backstrom, and myself. Three of us were starting centers, so the team was still in good shape up the middle, despite the transition we were going through. I've already mentioned the physical players who made a difference on the team, but we had a group of talented goal scorers as well. Bobby Rousseau, Gilles Tremblay, André Boudrias, and Yvan Cournoyer all made their appearances in 1964, and Serge Savard, Jacques Lemaire, Carol Vadnais, Jude Drouin, and Christian Bordeleau were soon to join us.

Henri, Claude, and Ralph, by virtue of their seniority, were absolutely vital to the 1960s Canadiens. They were there every night, year in and year out, leading us to Cup after Cup, and yet remaining low-key about our extraordinary successes.

Provost was the typical front-line soldier, a likable guy, usually quiet but capable of laughter, too. NHL play in the sixties was dominated by Bobby Hull, except when the Hawks came up against the Canadiens, and the reason we prevailed against them can be summed up in two words: Claude Provost. His job was to shadow "the Golden Jet," and he carried out the assignment in honest fashion—no hooking, tripping, or slashing behind the play, just good, clean hockey. He used speed and close checking to frustrate the great Chicago left-winger, but also found time to contribute to our offense. In 1964–65 he was the first-team all-star right-winger, ahead of Gordie Howe. Hull was the first to acknowledge that Claude was the best defensive winger of his day. While others would use questionable means against him, Hull maintained that "they can't check me like Claude Provost."

Ralph Backstrom would have been a big star on any other team in the NHL, especially during his first seven or eight seasons. He had won the Calder Trophy as rookie of the year in 1959. As it turned out, he became our third-string center, playing behind Henri and myself, and therefore did not see a lot of time on the power play. He had to take on a more defensive role, even though he had been a high-scoring junior player.

If John Ferguson brought respect to the 1960s Canadiens, Henri Richard provided the character. I had enormous admiration for

Henri from his earliest days and not only for what he did on the ice. When you're the younger brother of a hockey legend, it will take time for people to recognize you for what you are. Maurice had been retired for several years before fans began to notice that Henri was a standout in his own right. All through his long career, the first question anybody ever asked him was, "How's Maurice?" Every time, he was remarkably patient: "Maurice is fine."

Henri was a highly productive hockey player (1,046 points in 1,256 games) and very physical. He was also a great team player and a superb captain after I retired. It is not by chance that Henri Richard holds the all-time record of eleven Stanley Cup wins.

IN MY FIRST YEAR with the Quebec Aces, my left-winger was Ludger Tremblay, the oldest of eleven children in a family from Montmorency Falls, just outside Quebec City. He had returned from a career in the AHL with the Cleveland Barons hoping to be closer to his roots; playing with the Aces, and working for Anglo-Canadian Pulp and Paper allowed him to accomplish it. A decade later, a taller version of Ludger Tremblay appeared on my left wing—his kid brother Gilles, fifteen years or so his junior.

Gilles' career with us would last only nine short seasons, abbreviated by an asthmatic condition that robbed the league of one of its most exciting players. Like Ludger, Gilles was blessed with unusual upper-body strength and fantastic speed. He had great natural talent and was second only to Bobby Hull at his position. Gilles could forecheck and back check with the best defensive players in the league, but when the situation required it, he was most dangerous offensively. Toe was once quoted as saying he would not trade Gilles straight up for Frank Mahovlich.

Gilles and I worked a break-in play to perfection. Whenever the slightest opening arose, I'd throw the puck up the left side and let him take it in full stride. Once he got a step ahead of a defender, Gilles would leave all but the fastest players in his wake. And while Claude Provost often played Bobby Hull to a standstill, Gilles Tremblay could do the same with Gordie Howe. Unfortunately, Gilles was snake-bitten; he lost half of one season with a broken leg and a large chunk of another with a viral infection.

I got more than my share of assists in those days with Gilles on my left wing and Yvan Cournoyer, perhaps the only player in the league who could outskate him, playing right. I sometimes felt like the Montreal Alouettes' Sam Etcheverry, laying out long bombs to Hal Patterson and other fleet receivers. Canadian Football League defensive backs had to lay off those players; similarly, NHL defenders had to treat our forwards with respect. If they came up too close, Yvan and Gilles would give them a move and blow by them. If they tried to press me, I could use my size and reach to flip a pass to the speedsters on either side. Even explosive teams such as Chicago and Boston had to be wary of our counter-attack.

Terry Harper and Jacques Laperrière quickly established themselves on our defense. Both were tall and lanky; if they stood shoulder to shoulder, you'd swear that their long arms could reach out tentacle-like and cover the boards on either side of the ice. Jacques had a booming slap shot, which enabled him to set a scoring record for defensemen in the Ontario Hockey Association Junior A league that stood until Bobby Orr came along. By contrast, Terry's shot couldn't break a pane of glass, as his fourteen goals in ten seasons with us would prove. But the gangly Regina native was a gamer who never stopped working to improve himself, and he emerged as one of the NHL's premier defensemen.

A lot of Montreal fans were displeased by Terry's awkward style, arguing that he could never be a "Flying Frenchman" or bring honor to the *bleu-blanc-rouge*. Terry has five Stanley Cup rings to prove them wrong, but his decade with us was spent with jeers and accusations ringing in his ears. This unfair treatment upset his teammates, and we would occasionally express our frustration to the press.

The fans never saw the long hours he and others such as John Ferguson put in during and after practice to improve their play. I mentioned earlier that Fergie's skating was a liability at first, but midway through his time with us, he was getting the jump on veteran defenders. In much the same way, Terry practiced until he became the strongest backward skater in the league.

His teammates weren't Terry's only admirers. Bobby Hull, for one, complained that he "could never get around or by that Harper in Montreal." And in his first televised interview on *Hockey Night in Canada,* Bobby Orr told Ward Cornell that he liked to pattern his play on that of two NHL blue liners: Tim Horton and Terry Harper.

Terry failed to improve in one respect only, namely pugilism, and he earned a reputation as perhaps the worst fighter in the league. He'd never retreat when the going got rough, and he challenged only the tough guys, which accounted for his 1–40 record in fights, his sole victory coming on points over Toronto's Bob Pulford. We admired Terry's grit. He was a real needler on the ice, and his thin-lipped sneer often drove opponents to distraction and into the penalty box.

Terry played 1,066 games in nineteen seasons in the league and earned every penny he was paid. But the most remarkable chapter of his story had been written long before he arrived in the NHL. As a twelve-year-old boy in Saskatchewan, he suffered severe burns on his legs. For several months, his doctors were convinced he would never walk again. We saw the evidence of his fortitude in the dressing room; the livid scars were a frightening sight. They also helped to explain Terry Harper's tremendous force of character.

Jacques Laperrière was a reticent man who anchored our blue line for a decade. He won the Norris Trophy as the league's top defenseman in 1966, just prior to the arrival of Orr. Ted Harris was a quiet, powerfully built Manitoban who was a top heavyweight in the league. His battles with Orland Kurtenbach of the Rangers and Leafs were legendary.

Lest I give the impression that I'm simply going down the roster and saying nice things about all my teammates, let me reiterate the point of this chapter: the Montreal Canadiens of 1964–65 to 1970–71 are probably the least-respected dynasty in NHL history, despite those five Cups in seven seasons. These guys deserve recognition and acclaim.

You've certainly heard about the Edmonton Oilers team of Wayne Gretzky, Jari Kurri, Mark Messier, Kevin Lowe, Glenn Anderson, and Grant Fuhr that accomplished the same feat in the 1980s. Edmonton was bursting with superstars back then. We had our share, but we were at heart a collection of team players whose dedication to hard work equaled or surpassed that of the Canadiens' 1950s edition. Claude Provost, Gilles Tremblay, John Ferguson, Ted Harris, and Terry Harper were card-carrying members of what Don Cherry calls the Lunchpail Hall of Fame. Cliché though it may be, they always showed up to play, and they always gave their best. We won, and kept on winning, because Frank Selke and later Sam Pollock knew how to assemble and retain extraordinary players, men who would eventually be inducted into the NHL Hall of Fame.

And so, while the decade had begun on a somber note, our prospects were definitely sunnier by 1964, a momentous year for the team during which Frank Selke was retired as general manager—over his objections—and replaced by his protégé, Sam Pollock.

One of Sam's first moves was to swap Billy Hicke to the Rangers for veteran winger Dick Duff, a trade that paid off for the remainder of the season and into the play-offs. A smallish forward, Dick was deadly around the net, with a heads-up style that nicely complemented his centerman. He could score or return a pass on a give-and-go that would lead to many wide-open nets. He joined me and Cournoyer, while Fergie moved over to the checking line with Ralph Backstrom.

Duff had a move that would drive defenders to distraction. He would come in quickly and low, kick the puck into his skates and through a defenseman's feet, and pick it up again behind the opponent. In effect, he was passing to himself, and it worked more often than not. He'd make that move while driving toward the net or crossing the ice out at the blue line, opening up miles of room for Yvan and myself.

Detroit bumped us out of first place by four points at the end of the 1964–65 season, led by centers Norm Ullman and Alex Delvecchio. However, we'd been held back by injuries, as had the Hawks, whom we considered to be our major opposition. In fact, Stan Mikita, Bobby Hull, Pierre Pilote, and Glenn Hall took the Hawks past the Red Wings in a tense seven-game semifinal, while we downed fourth-place Toronto in six games.

Who would win the final was anybody's guess. Home-ice advantage proved to be the difference. We took our first three home games and so did the Hawks, forcing a seventh game at the Forum on May 1. Both teams had seen stars come and go: Chicago defensemen Pierre Pilote and Ken Wharram missed the first two games, which we won 3–2 and 2–0, but they returned for 3–1 and 5–1 wins in Chicago. Gump Worsley was replaced by Charlie Hodge for the fourth game, and although we lost it, Charlie turned around and blanked the Hawks 6–0 at the Forum in game 5, as we scored four power-play goals and a short-handed one by J.-C. Tremblay.

We returned to Chicago eager to end matters. Ralph Backstrom gave us the lead early in the second period, but goals by Wharram and Doug Mohns early in the third meant we would go down to a sudden-death seventh contest.

Game 6 had been a rough affair, with referee Frank Udvari sending Terry Harper and Stan Mikita off together with seventeen minutes each on a minor, a major, and a misconduct. Sam Pollock made a lot of noise after the game to the effect that the crowd had influenced the official's penalty calls.

We were determined to take game 7 out of the referee's hands and to deal with Hawks goalie Glenn Hall in the process. After all, we had shut out the Hawks in the last two games at the Forum. Toe Blake, always looking for an edge, surprised many observers by returning Worsley to the net.

Serious hockey fans realize that home-ice advantage in a seventh game isn't always a guarantee of victory. When one bounce of the puck can make all the difference, the venue doesn't matter that much. Chicago had proved that in the semifinal against Detroit; both teams had traded home victories down to the seventh and final game, which the Hawks won 4–2 in Detroit. As it turned out, that would be one of only two games won by a visiting team in the 1965 play-offs: our sixth-game triumph in Toronto was the other.

When we took to the ice for the final game against Chicago, the Forum fans were Cup-starved and showed their eagerness to end our four-year drought, with a huge ovation that pumped us from the first drop of the puck. Fourteen seconds into the game, Dick Duff fed me a beautiful pass and we led 1–0. By the end of the first period, we were up 4–0 on additional goals by Duff, Richard, and Cournoyer. That score—our third-straight home shutout—held up. Shortly after 10 PM that night, I hoisted my first Stanley Cup as captain of the Canadiens.

A year later, after beating Toronto, we went into the final against the Detroit Red Wings and lost the first two games at home, an unprecedented humiliation, at least in my memory. Those games were televised by an American network and special lighting for color broadcast had been installed for the April 24 opener. We must have been dazzled by the lights, because we slunk out of town and into Detroit, our tails between our legs, after 3–2 and 5–3 setbacks.

We normally stayed in downtown Detroit at the Sheraton-Cadillac, but this time emergency measures were in order. Toe was determined to isolate us from the usual distractions, so he booked us into the peace and tranquillity of the suburbs, in Dearborn. Unfortunately, he failed to notice that our hotel was the headquarters for a convention of barbershop quartets. As a result, harmony-heavy renditions of "Sweet Adeline" and "By the Light of the Silvery Moon" could be heard at all hours of the day and night. I remember Toe running up and down the halls in his pajamas, trying to silence the rehearsing conventioneers. "My guys have a big game tomorrow night. Knock it off!" he yelled, only to be drowned out by the next chorus.

I can't recall whether Sam Pollock joined Toe in the anti-noise effort, but Sam was there, all right. A Detroit or Chicago play-off series represented a nightmare for him because these were the two most remote NHL outposts. Sam wouldn't fly, and the trains took too long when games were played every second day. His chauffeur, Brian Travers, put in thousands of miles in a hectic three-week period. Sam sat in the back, propped up on pillows, with all his files spread before him. We finally convinced him to take the plane home with us after we won the Cup in St. Louis in 1968; Brian drove all the way back from Missouri by himself.

When we arrived in Dearborn, Sam was in a mood for positive reinforcement. He handed me $500, with instructions to "find a good restaurant and take the boys out tonight. If you need more, pay it and I'll reimburse you." Sam was very conscious of the fact that we needed relief from some of the pressure. And it worked. We won the next four games, three of them in Detroit.

The following spring, we were supposed to win again and deliver a present to Montreal mayor Jean Drapeau during Expo 67 and

Canada's centennial year celebrations. Unfortunately, somebody forgot to tell Terry Sawchuk, Johnny Bower, and the rest of the Over-the-Hill Gang in Toronto. They sent us down in six games, taking the Stanley Cup on May 2.

The 1966–67 season was the last hurrah for the so-called Original Six teams. Our training camp that summer was unbelievable—110 players from our affiliates all over the hockey globe gathered in Montreal to be evaluated, with a view to the coming league expansion. Afterward, they scattered to Cleveland, Houston, Quebec City, and points north, south, east, and west.

When the NHL expansion draft took place the following spring, we were allowed to keep only one goalie and eleven skaters. But Sam's foresight paid off. While we provided the six new teams with a large number of quality prospects, we lost no core players ourselves. This allowed us to make it back to two more Cup finals, both against the St. Louis Blues.

As described earlier, our four-game semifinal sweep of the Bruins in 1967–68 was inspired by Fergie's battles with Ted Green. He won, and so did we, going on to meet and beat the Blues. A year later, Boston posed a more difficult challenge, having finished the season in second place with 100 points to our 103 and taking us to six games in the East Division final.

Fergie had shocked the hockey world in 1968–69 with a twenty-nine-goal season, playing alongside Cournoyer and me. Injuries had ravaged the team, and both Rogie Vachon and Gump were having such problems in the nets that rookie Tony Esposito ended up starting eleven games. We struggled until February, then turned it on in the homestretch to finish first.

However, the Bruins would not be deterred. We won the first two semifinal games at home in overtime, by identical 3–2 scores, and warily returned to Boston to face a supremely confident team.

Boston was doing all the talking that year. "We won't lose another game in this series," Harry Sinden told the Boston papers. Two of his Young Turks, Derek Sanderson and Bobby Orr, agreed with him. Buoyed by that spirit, the Bruins chewed us up and spat us out 5–0 and 3–2 to even the series. We took game 5 by another 3–2 score, but it was by the skin of our teeth again. Having gone up 3–0 in the second period, we hung on desperately as the Bruins bombarded Vachon with twenty-six shots.

We returned to Boston for game 6 on Friday night, with both teams expecting to face a seventh-game showdown in Montreal on Sunday. Phil Esposito set up Ron Murphy at 2:29 of the first and Boston Garden went crazy. That goal was scored at about 8:15 PM, and very few fans among the capacity crowd expected that they'd still be riveted to their seats in the early hours of Saturday morning.

Early in the third, I won a face-off to Gerry Cheevers's left and drew it back to Serge Savard at the right point. Both lines came together in a milling scrum, and Cheevers never saw the Savard shot that slid along the ice and into the far corner to tie the game.

We went into overtime and survived a scare in the first twenty-minute period when Fergie took a penalty and the Bruins almost scored. Our coach, Claude Ruel, was nervously chewing gum behind our bench midway through the fifth period when a strategic switch he'd made earlier in the game paid off. During the regular season and much of the play-offs, I had been up against Derek Sanderson, a talented but cocky center who was very good on the draw. Fergie, Cournoyer, and I had our successes against him, but by game 6, Harry Sinden was double-shifting Phil Esposito's line. Claude had reasoned that unless I played against Esposito head-to-head, our top scoring line would be sitting on the bench for lengthy periods of time.

He moved Claude Provost to the right wing, and I went out with him and Fergie. We lined up against Esposito, Ken Hodge, and Murphy, just past the eleven-minute mark of the fifth period and the ninety-first minute of the game (believe me, we were counting). I won the draw and we chased the puck into the Bruins' zone. Fergie was in the corner, forcing the defenseman to hurry his clearing pass. Don Awrey, the other defenseman, tried to tame a skittering puck near the blue line, but it bounced free. I saw Provost heading for it and knew that he'd get there first, so I turned and moved toward the net, on the opposite side of Cheevers.

In a flash, the puck was on my stick, then off again, into the top corner of the net. We had won the series, and I had the only overtime play-off goal of my career. Having bested the Bruins, we went on to beat the West Division Blues handily in four straight games.

We failed to make the play-offs the following year, and Boston's fine young team was able to win the Cup at last. I had considered retiring after the 1969–70 season, but Sam Pollock asked me to stay for one more. It turned out well for all concerned; a year later we were back, armed with fresh new weapons.

Our play-off success in 1970–71 hinged on the acquisition of Frank Mahovlich from the Detroit Red Wings, as well as the arrival of several talented players from within the Montreal organization: Peter Mahovlich, Guy Lapointe, Pierre Bouchard, and especially Ken Dryden. Frank stepped into our style of play without missing a beat. His presence also improved the performance of his talented younger brother, Peter, but I'd be lying if I said we went into the play-offs brimming with confidence that April. Our third-place finish in the East Division meant that we would be up against the first-place Bruins in the opening play-off round, and once again not many observers liked our chances.

As in the play-offs of 1969, it came down to a tremendous goaltending performance and one key game. Phil Esposito, Johnny Bucyk, Jim Pappin, and Dennis Hull can all attest to Kenny Dryden's powers that year. The six-foot, four-inch McGill University law student had come to us from the Montreal Voyageurs with about six games remaining in the regular season and he proved his worth at once. The critical game in the quarterfinal was the second, in the steamy confines of Boston Garden. We'd played a strong game to lead off the series but the Bruins were better, beating us 3–1. For some reason, Harry Sinden decided to switch goalies in the second game, substituting Eddie Johnston for Gerry Cheevers. Still, it didn't seem that this change would affect the outcome, as the Bruins roared to a seemingly insurmountable 5–1 lead midway through the second period.

Then, with about four minutes remaining in the period, Henri Richard stripped the puck from an embarrassed Bobby Orr and beat Johnston to give us a glimmer of hope at 5–2. Early in the third, I banged in a Fergie rebound. Two shifts later, I got another tally on passes from Fergie and Cournoyer, to make it 5–4. Then Jacques Lemaire stole the puck from a Bruin to tie the game with half a period to go.

Now we were the ones feeling young and cocky, and the Bruins were feeling their age. At 15:23 of the third, I thanked Fergie for his two assists by slipping him the puck from behind the Boston net. He beat Johnston and we went ahead. Big Frank iced it with an insurance goal three minutes later, and the series returned to Montreal tied 1–1.

The Bruins never recaptured their momentum after that, and we went on to win the series in seven. After outlasting a determined Minnesota team in a six-game semifinal, we beat Chicago in seven to win the Cup—my tenth as a Canadien and my fifth as captain.

That 3–2 win on May 18, 1971, in Chicago, sounded the last post for our team of the 1960s. It was time for a new generation to take over, and we all knew it. I clearly remember the plane trip home from O'Hare airport. I sat with Fergie, sharing a few beers, contemplating the future. The toughest player I'd ever known had tears in his eyes.

"I can't do it anymore," he said, resignedly. "Reggie Houle carried me all through these play-offs." Réjean, another Sam Pollock discovery, could skate like the wind. "I think I'm going to retire with you."

His heart was heavy, but John Ferguson could leave with his head high, as could Claude Provost, Ralph Backstrom, Bobby Rousseau, Gilles and J.-C. Tremblay, Terry Harper, Jimmy Roberts, Claude Larose, Jacques Laperrière, Gump Worsley, and Rogie Vachon. They were the heroes of the Canadiens' forgotten decade.

TALKING WITH FERGIE during that flight, my mind drifted back to another conversation that had taken place nine long years before. In 1962, when I felt that my personal fortunes were at their lowest ebb, I went to see Senator Hartland Molson, then the Canadiens' owner. I wasn't experiencing a burnout, as they call it nowadays, but I might have been headed in that direction. There was a great deal of pressure to perform on the ice, and I was working very hard outside the game, as well. Perhaps too hard; it was difficult for me to gain perspective on the situation. I was internalizing everything, unable to share my stress with anyone else.

"Senator," I confessed, "I'm starting to doubt that I'm ever going to play as well as I have in the past."

Hartland de Montarville Molson had always been a rock, there for me in so many different ways. Even today, it's heartwarming to think that I had this distinguished businessman and sportsman by my side for almost half a century, from the time I arrived in Montreal until his death in 2002. In my playing days with the Canadiens, he was the first to telephone if I was sick or injured. He was a friend, a mentor, a second father to me.

Back in 1962, he looked at my face and knew that I was in need of comfort and advice. "Jean," he said, "over the course of a long career, there will be many ups and downs, especially for someone of your temperament. You take everything so seriously. When you're not performing to your standards, it's understandable that you would be discouraged.

"But any doubts you are having now will pass with time. You have the talent and the strength of character to come back. The public might not realize it, but you have even higher standards than they do."

I was cheered by his words and I took them to heart. After two years of struggle, my teammates and I went on to win five Cups. In 1964, I was awarded the Hart Trophy for the league's most valuable player and followed that, in 1965, with the Conn Smythe Trophy for most valuable player in the play-offs. I did come back, but the pressure never eased for an instant.

From today's vantage point, I can say without fear of contradiction that the burden of high expectations made me a better player. I was forced to perform, night after night. I was, for better or worse, a star, and stars, especially those identified as goal scorers, must live with the world's constant scrutiny of their offensive statistics. (I used to think that the fans and the media were more familiar with my statistics than I was.) The same holds true for goalies. Their performance, like a goal scorer's, is measured in the simplest terms: goals scored, saves made. It's easy to track—not as complicated as the plus-minus statistics for a defensive player.

This is where one's character comes into play. How will a player react to and deal with the pressure, internal and external? I've always been too much of a perfectionist, wanting everything to be first-class all the way. A season of seventy wins and no losses would have been fine with me. I had to do my very best every game.

Pressure is part of any professional athlete's life; it comes with the territory. The assumptions of others will force you to improve, to perform at a higher level. And in Montreal, winning is not only expected, it's demanded.

The Canadiens of the 1960s knew this all too well, and they did their part.

7

THE PLAYERS

MY CAREER IN PROFESSIONAL sport spanned the evolution of hockey from the "old game" and the "old league" through the transition period to the modern game we know today. Later, I'll explain how I feel the game has changed and who I think is responsible. Now, however, I wish to revisit some of the outstanding players I played with and against on the ice.

My game was very different from today's, and I'll try to explain why in the pages that follow. Let's begin with a comparison of the mathematics. I played in the six-team league for fourteen of my eighteen seasons, in a twelve-team league for three seasons, and in a fourteen-team league the season I retired from active competition. The chart on the following page shows the difference forty years can make.

	1964	2004
Games (regular season)	70	82
Playoff series needed to win Stanley Cup	2	4
Travel by	Train	Airplane
Time zones	2	4
Teams in NHL	6	30
Nationality of players	All Canadian*	Multinational
Bench (players carried on NHL roster per team)	Max. 20	Min. 24
Coaches per team	1	3
Average player size	5′10″, 180 lbs	6′1″, 205 lbs

* Tommy Williams of the Boston Bruins was the NHL's lone American, or non-Canadian, in 1964.

Please remember that the addition of twelve games a season—a 20 percent increase from the days of the six-team league—means another calendar month of action. Back in my day, the season started well along into October, and the final game in the play-offs was scheduled for April.

In 1959–60, we won a fifth-straight Stanley Cup by sweeping the play-offs in eight consecutive games, playing a total of seventy-eight games that season. The Cup-clinching match took place on April 14. In 1965, we jumped all over the Black Hawks in game 7 of the Stanley Cup final, scoring three goals in the first period, including one just fourteen seconds into the game. The date was May 1, and it was the first time a Stanley Cup final had been played later than April 30. A year later, we won the Cup against Detroit on May 5, and in 1967, we lost it to Toronto on May 2.

The league flirted with final dates in the last week of May throughout the 1970s and 1980s and crossed a new threshold on June 1, 1992, when the Pittsburgh Penguins swept the Hawks in four straight. In 1994, the four-round play-offs didn't even begin until April 16. Since then, the Stanley Cup play-offs have never been completed before the end of June, and today's Stanley Cup winner will play at least one hundred games from start to finish.

The season and the play-offs stretched to the limits—thirty-six weeks on a twenty-eight-week regular season and eight weeks of play-offs—and the players went from sprinters, who were conditioned to rise to competition standards at specific points in the schedule, to marathoners who strove to maintain high performance over a much longer period of time. As a consequence, training became another science altogether.

In 1966, we were still six years away from the first Soviet Union-Canada hockey summit, although international hockey techniques and training systems were starting to draw attention. Canada's "senior teams" had suffered several embarrassing defeats abroad, and in that year the amateur national team program, spearheaded by Father David Bauer, was born.

Players from European countries and the former USSR, many of whom would eventually graduate to the NHL, played much the same game we did, but they prepared for it in ways that seemed totally alien to us. Eventually it was acknowledged that we trained wrong and we ate wrong, and the man who told us so was a Canadian who was celebrated overseas while being almost ignored in Canada. He was Lloyd Percival, the exercise guru, who would later help renowned Soviet coach Anatoli Tarasov devise new and better training programs.

Percival, a founder of the Fitness Institute and the Coaching Association of Canada, launched his strongest criticism of North American methods in 1965–66, a year before the first NHL expansion took place. The league's training practices were archaic and absurd, he charged. The basic drill hadn't evolved in forty years. Players who arrived at the training camps in late September were subjected to intensive regimens without adequate preparation. That, he said, was why so many of them were running on empty by mid-season, prone to slumps and injuries.

Certainly in the days of the six-team league we had plenty of time to slip out of shape during five idle spring and summer months. By contrast, in 1993 the Montreal Canadiens won the Stanley Cup on June 9 and reported to camp just three months and four days later. Those extra eight weeks make a tremendous difference in a player's conditioning and healing processes. If he doesn't have time to fall out of shape, he's better off, but fatigue will eventually wear him down.

In his first book on hockey, published in 1951, Percival said that any self-respecting NHL club should monitor the health of its athletes more carefully by submitting them to regular tests, always with a view to the physical and mental limitations of each individual, and that every team should include in its professional entourage a physiologist, a psychologist, and a dietitian.

"Race horses are more humanely treated and trained by horsemen than hockey players are by their team management," he wrote. "In recent years, training techniques have evolved in all major sports around the world. Only the NHL has done nothing to allow its athletes to benefit from the results of [that] research."

Toe Blake took exception to this prescription, claiming that forty-year-old training methods had shown positive results throughout that period. Moreover, players weren't thrown into the cauldron too quickly; rather, they took care to show up for training camp at 95 or 100 percent of their game shape, having spent the summer playing golf, tennis, or softball. Toe maintained that he never forced his players to perform grueling stops and starts—a Percival criticism—until two weeks into the camp, and that those players with ankle, knee, or groin injuries were excused.

"You will never convince me to have my players running to stay in shape, no more than I could convince Mr. Percival to have his runners skate. The same muscles are not used by athletes in the different sports." Toe was right on this point. Some of the early experiments in new-style training left jogging hockey players with painful shin splints.

During the debate, someone thought to interview Butch Bouchard, one of the league's senior statesmen. He defended hockey's traditional training methods as reasonably effective but went on to suggest something that was, for the time, quite radical: "Hockey should probably be like football, with one coach for the defense, one for the offense and maybe one more for the goalies." In other words, not only would extra coaching staff help in diagramming plays and implementing strategies, they would keep a closer watch on their charges and spot minor injuries as they occurred.

Hervé Lalonde, a Quebecker who was then coaching in Switzerland, Jacques Saint-Jean, the physical education director of a Montreal-area school, and Dr. Guy Charest, professor in biokinetics at the University of Montreal, agreed with most of Percival's contentions and were promoting his ideas to anyone in Quebec sports circles who would listen.

Saint-Jean had observed the Soviet, Czechoslovakian, and Swedish hockey programs firsthand and reported that, while the Europeans recognized the talents of our players, they were disappointed by our training systems. "In Europe, hockey players play more scientifically. They analyze their play. In Canada, when a team loses, the coach says: 'The puck didn't roll for us tonight,' or 'Our players were a bit off on their shots.' Often, he doesn't even know why his team lost."

This is the only argument I can ever remember Toe Blake losing, even though his point ("we use what works for us") was essentially valid. If you're weak on face-offs, you won't improve by jogging at the Y. Still, it took the Soviet-Canadan Summit Series of 1972 to demonstrate that we didn't know how to run a training camp, especially one for all-stars coming together in a short-term tournament scenario.

Our habit of playing ourselves into shape, plus our less regimented on-ice strategies, allowed us to overcome the Soviets' machine-like precision—but just barely.

Percival had startled many in the NHL establishment with his prediction that the Summit Series would not be the high-scoring romp expected by most Canadian fans. Since then, however, we've gone on to implement nearly all of his suggestions, including the hiring of physiologists, psychologists, and dietitians. Every team dressing room features a state-of-the-art gym and players are monitored at regular intervals throughout the season. Any player in the NHL today can discuss the advantages and disadvantages of pliometrics; advanced exercise regimes have become part of the everyday workload. Multicolored exercise balls, stationary bikes, weight machines, and treadmills are as much part of modern hockey paraphernalia as are composite sticks.

The Canadiens used to hold a team meeting at eleven o'clock on game-day mornings, but we didn't go on the ice. Toe wanted us up and alert, which meant not keeping late-night hours. That was his primary reason for calling us together. These days, players convene at the rink at ten or eleven for a light skate to get limbered up, although I've seen some teams conduct what appears to be a regular practice—something of little if any value, in my view.

What does have value is the new approach to diet. Today, nobody sits down to a pregame steak in the early afternoon before an 8 PM start. Instead, it's all complex carbohydrates (pasta, pasta, and more pasta) and carefully monitored food intake throughout the day and the season. When I first came up in the 1950s, I would eat around three o'clock, and when we were on the road, this meal was usually a steak dinner. When I got a little older, I ate at two thirty. When I edged into my thirties, the meal moved back to two o'clock. My body was telling me something, though I couldn't discern the message. Instinctively, however, I was adapting my eating habits.

By 1976, the Canada Cup team had added jogging to its pre-tournament training regimen, along with calisthenics and off-ice training, nutrition counseling, and close monitoring of every player's oxygen intake and stamina—exactly what Dr. Percival had ordered a decade earlier. Within two years, every NHL team was adopting the "European" approach, although dry-land training never really caught on, except for the weight machines, treadmills, and exercise bicycles.

In the early 1960s it was all much simpler. We would return from the off-season, be outfitted with white or red Canadiens sweaters, then prepare for the coming season with some intraclub scrimmaging, generally in the form of minitournaments of four teams. Twenty years later, I'd wander into the dressing room after a regular-season game and watch players who'd just come off the ice after a hard-fought game climb onto the exercise bikes for a half-hour session before they went to the showers or the whirlpool. "Warm-down periods" were unknown in our day.

Over the years I noticed a major difference in the treatment of injuries, as well. For example, if we suffered a knee injury in the 1950s and 1960s, immobilization and rest were the orders of the day, mainly because large and heavy casts prevented us from doing anything else. In the 1980s, it was a case of light on the rest, heavy on the rehab. A player who emerged from surgery would be up and around as soon as possible, working within a week or ten days alongside trainer Gaëtan Lefebvre on a recovery regimen that included leg curls and extensions on the exercise machines, lots of bicycling in the training room, and special massage.

The modern player rarely wears a cast but is fitted instead with a succession of knee braces that allow progressively greater movement without sacrificing support during his recovery period. Thanks to magnetic resonance imaging machines to better "see" injuries and hyperbaric chambers to improve blood flow to the site of the injury, recovery times have been cut in half or better.

Today's player tends to take this sophisticated medical treatment for granted. And knowing that the finest medical care and the most advanced rehabilitation programs are available, he may be more reckless on the ice. The players of the 1950s and 1960s feared injuries. We knew there were a hundred players ready to take our places in a six-team league. We knew an injury almost invariably meant a long layoff, often with an extended hospital stay. We knew too that our equipment was, by today's standards, flimsy and primitive—a bit of felt, some leather, and plastic shoulder cups—intended only to guard against damage caused by the occasional errant puck or stick. As a result, we tended to show more respect for an opponent, even if he was the dirtiest SOB in the league.

As you know, we didn't wear helmets or face shields back then, so our sticks were carried at ice level most of the time. We rarely charged opposition players into the boards from behind. Today's player sports as much body armor as a football lineman, and opponents armed with aluminum or composite (Kevlar-and-graphite) sticks aren't averse to delivering vicious two-handers across the forearm or the leg, figuring that the target's equipment will protect him—or, if it doesn't, that he won't see that player or his team again for several months, during which tempers will have cooled.

This style of hockey suggests that players no longer respect their opponents. The new game is all about interference, using whatever is at hand to impede opposition players, be it tripping, hooking, slashing, or hitting from behind.

Why is scoring down? One reason is that team stars aren't being protected. League rules against the instigation of fights make it easy for fourth-line players to attack the opposition's leading scorers with impunity, while preventing other fourth-line players from defending their own stars.

Another reason is the overemphasis on defensive strategies. Teams today have as many as three coaches to drill players on defensive systems. Name any team sport and its coaches will tell you that defense can be taught quickly and easily. "You can't teach someone to have great hands or an eye for the net, because these skills are intangibles and highly specialized," said one coach. Consequently, "the best way to influence scores, and therefore game results, is on the defensive side of the puck."

And that's what every team has focused on. In my day, a Claude Provost might shadow a Bobby Hull and the defensive pairing of Terry Harper and Jacques Laperrière might join them on the ice. Today, the defense will have all five players working a system that aims to keep the puck away from Joe Sakic or Peter Forsberg. And these defensive schemes will be practiced long and hard.

I'VE DESCRIBED THE accomplishments of my Canadiens teammates at some length, but I must acknowledge as well those players on the opposition benches who shaped our sport in the 1950s and 1960s.

It goes without saying that Gordie Howe was the pre-eminent player of my generation. Witness his twenty-one nominations to first or second all-star teams at a time when Maurice Richard, Boom Boom Geoffrion, and Andy Bathgate were his competition on right wing. Because of our size and temperament, especially off the ice, Gordie and I were compared during our playing days almost as often as he and Maurice.

Gordie was every bit as tough as reported, but his brawn was secondary to his hockey smarts. Many observers couldn't get past his famous elbows and so underestimated his on-ice intelligence.

Gordie was a master of positioning, whether in possession of the puck or not. Even in the final years of his long career, he was often the savviest player out there.

I have seen many players who stood taller than Gordie's six feet, one inch, and who outweighed his 205 pounds, but I don't believe I've seen anyone stronger, with the possible exceptions of Bobby Hull and Tim Horton. Gordie didn't have the big, square shoulders of a Kevin Hatcher or a Larry Robinson; his shoulders were thick and rounded, and they sloped over a huge chest that was all knotted muscle. He could come up behind you, gently slip his stick under your armpit and effortlessly lift you right off the ice. Trying to strong-arm Gordie off the puck in a corner was akin to wrestling with a telephone pole.

How did Gordie manage to play pro hockey into his fifties? The answer lies in his incredible strength, high on-ice IQ, and a low-key personality with a streak of meanness when the situation demanded it—the definition, in short, of a formidable player. Even in the 1950s, Lloyd Percival predicted a long career for Gordie.

Bobby Hull, on the other hand, was muscle mixed with fantastic speed, the hardest shot the sport has ever produced, and pure power on the ice. Asked to compare the Golden Jet with his son Brett, I'd say that Bobby was a couple of inches shorter, half again as strong, and twice as fast on his feet. He had an even better shot and release. Having started his career as a center, he was also an expert playmaker, apt to put an accurate pass on a linemate's stick just as an opposition winger and two defensemen converged on him. Bobby scored 610 goals and added 560 assists in sixteen NHL seasons, most of them earned before he moved to the WHA at the peak of his talent. I'm convinced that he would have challenged Gordie's 801 goals long before Wayne Gretzky had he remained in the NHL.

Bobby was the first player to have multiple fifty-goal seasons—five in all—in an era when only two other players, Rocket Richard and Boom Boom Geoffrion, had been able to accomplish the feat once. And only once in those five seasons did it take him more than seventy games to do it.

Bobby's arrival with the Black Hawks somewhat overshadowed the debut of another extraordinary hockey player, but not entirely. That man was Frank Mahovlich, who played with Toronto and Detroit before joining the Canadiens as my linemate in 1971. Frank had a love-hate relationship with Toronto. While he was a major contributor to four Stanley Cup victories in his twelve seasons there, his classic skating style was often disparaged by the fans and by Leafs coach Punch Imlach. At six feet, two inches, and a solid 200 pounds, "the Big M" was supposed to throw his weight around, flattening opposition forwards against the boards. That wasn't his way, yet no one was willing to credit him for his true skills. The scuttlebutt had it that he was lazy; hurtful criticism that no doubt contributed to a minor burnout before he was traded to Detroit.

Once, during a delay before a face-off in a game at Toronto, I told Frank that his style would fit in perfectly with the Canadiens. Frank never forgot that remark, and he brought it up in January 1971, when he joined our team on the road in Minnesota. We'd sent Mickey Redmond, Guy Charron, and Bill Collins to the Wings in exchange.

"Jean, you remember that night in Toronto, when you said I would fit in well with the Canadiens?" he asked.

"I said 'fit in perfectly,' Frank, and we'll start proving that tonight."

A month later, he set up my 500th NHL goal. My prediction proved true over the years, with Frank contributing to two Stanley Cup wins in three seasons.

But there's something more to the story. One of Frank's teammates on the Leafs must have reported my original comment to Punch Imlach. When I was going through Mahovlich-like problems of my own with Montreal's fans a few years later, Punch was only too happy to return the compliment: "Béliveau should be playing for us in Toronto, where he would be much better off," he told the press.

One September, after his team lost an exhibition game to a minor-league team, Punch was fuming at the poor performances of what he described as his "so-called superstars." It was always difficult to kick-start NHL players when the competition was AHL, WHA, or lower. The AHL and WHA players, on the other hand, were ready to run through the boards to prove their worth and sometimes scored upset victories.

After this particular defeat, Punch was heard to loudly proclaim, "If only I could get the player I really want. Jean Béliveau played for me when I coached the Quebec Aces, and I probably know him better than anyone else... I've always hoped he would finish out his career in a Leafs uniform."

Punch knew better than to question Toe Blake's handling of me, but he didn't hesitate to take the Canadiens' fans to task. "Montreal fans have never understood Jean Béliveau's style. He's a classic player; you don't have to be a big expert to know that. Imagine Béliveau being booed at the Forum. He doesn't deserve such treatment."

This was quintessential Punch. In one swoop, he had dodged the league's tampering rules by couching his comments as a concern for my feelings, antagonized his archrival, Toe Blake, and subtly let me know he hadn't appreciated my sweet-talking his star winger—a "classic player" he'd failed to defend when Frank was having problems with his own hometown crowds.

It comes as no surprise that I write about Howe, Hull, and Mahovlich; all three were automatic Hall of Fame inductees when their careers ended. But there are other Hall of Famers who, though they may have slipped the memories of today's fans, deserve homage.

Four of my era's outstanding centers were Stan Mikita, Norm Ullman, Dave Keon, and Alex Delvecchio. I knew their talents intimately; in the six-team league, we played each other fourteen times a year in the course of a seventy-game season. Opposing lines were often matched for an entire season or several seasons in a row.

It's a mistake to assume that the players of the 1950s and 1960s were somehow disadvantaged because they couldn't sit around analyzing videotape. We didn't need video. There were probably no more than seventy-five other fellows in the entire league, and we saw them every other week. When we played Boston in the late 1960s, I knew they'd put Derek Sanderson on me, along with Johnny McKenzie and Don Marcotte. In Chicago in the early 1960s, I faced the Mikita line, while Henri Richard confronted the Bill "Red" Hay, Bobby Hull, and Murray Balfour line. In Toronto, I was up against Dave Keon's line, with Red Kelly spelling him sometimes, and in Detroit, Norm Ullman would be out there.

Was the prospect of playing against a limited number of familiar faces boring for the players or the fans? Certainly not for me; I enjoyed it. When a visiting team played us in Montreal on a Saturday night, and we went at it again in their arena on the Sunday, it seemed like an extended six-period game. This happened almost every weekend. Yes, there was a finite number of players, but they were the finest players in the world. How could that possibly be boring, on the ice or in the stands?

Nowadays, teams might not meet each other in an entire calendar year. An example is this schedule of Montreal-Detroit games over three seasons in the early 1990s:

October 10, 1991	Montreal at Detroit
February 1, 1992	Detroit at Montreal
March 8, 1992	Detroit at Montreal
November 4, 1992	Montreal at Detroit
November 7, 1992	Detroit at Montreal
December 18, 1993	Detroit at Montreal
April 13, 1994	Montreal at Detroit

In calendar year 1993, the Canadiens didn't play a single regular-season game in Detroit. Their only at-home game against Detroit came just two weeks before the end of the year. To fans in both cities who would have liked to see Steve Yzerman, Sergei Fedorov, and Dino Ciccarelli take to the ice against Patrick Roy, Kirk Muller, and Vincent Damphousse, it must have felt as if these two clubs were in separate leagues, like the then Montreal Expos and the Detroit Tigers.

Would the NHL realize that it was killing longstanding and revenue-generating Original Six rivalries with such schedules and make a change to remedy the situation in the new millennium? Apparently not, as these equally rare Montreal-Detroit play dates illustrate:

November 1, 2000	Detroit at Montreal
February 11, 2002	Detroit at Montreal
October 17, 2002	Montreal at Detroit
October 20, 2003	Detroit at Montreal

Note there was no game at all between the two in 2001—a real rivalry builder. In several seasons of the Original Six era, these two teams played twenty-one games, fourteen in the regular season and another seven in play-offs. In 2003–04, if Saku Koivu, Andrei Markov, Sheldon Souray, or Jose Theodore wanted to see the Red Wings stars in action more often, they had to watch them on television. That's a major problem for today's NHL.

There is a related point concerning players' matchups. The opposition centers I most often confronted—Ullman, Keon, Delvecchio, and Mikita—are all in the Hall of Fame along with me. In the original edition of this book I noted that as of the 1993–94 season, Mikita stood as the fifth-highest scorer in NHL history, with 1,467 points; Delvecchio was tenth with 1,281; Ullman was thirteenth with 1,229, and Keon was fortieth with 986. Quite a few of those goals, I can assure you, were scored against the Montreal Canadiens. Since then, their names have dropped in the standings as the next generation of players moved through the NHL and into retirement after lengthy careers, but that takes nothing away from their accomplishments. They were the most prominent stars of their day.

In this era, however, you won't find Joe Sakic facing off against Steve Yzerman or Peter Forsberg battling Sergei Fedorov in the same game. Instead, defensive speacialists like Kris Draper, Darren McCarty, and Kirk Maltby play against Sakic and Forsberg, while Dan Hinote, Darby Hendrickson, and Steve Konowalchuk share the ice with Fedorov and Yzerman.

Today, offensive and defensive responsibilities are clear-cut and largely separate. In my day Mikita, Delvecchio, Ullman, and Keon were expected to shut down me and my line—and score the occasional goal themselves. We attempted to do the same. Matchups of this kind are simply not seen today.

Stan Mikita was the first European-born player to achieve NHL stardom. Born in Czechoslovakia, he immigrated to Canada as a child and came into the league with the Black Hawks in 1958–59. A year later he was teamed up with former Canadien Ab McDonald and Kenny Wharram on the Scooter Line.

Stan started as a chippy player who didn't hesitate to use his stick on an opponent, and he had the penalty minutes to prove it. In 1966–67, however, he changed his tune and won the Art Ross, Hart, and Lady Byng Trophies in that single season. He had excellent vision and was very smooth on the ice. He and teammate Bobby Hull were jointly responsible for introducing the "banana blade," which Bobby used to unload howitzers at cringing goalies. But Stan presented a greater threat, because he could not only blow the puck past a goalie, he knew how to pick a corner neatly, unleash a backhand shot with laser precision, or make an equally beautiful backhand pass to Wharram or McDonald.

Ab McDonald was a good, workmanlike left-winger, while Wharram was a fast right-winger with excellent hands. If an opponent was distracted for even a second, Mikita, a right-hand shot, would hit Kenny on the tape in full stride, and he'd be on top of the goalie in a blink. A couple of years later, Doug Mohns replaced McDonald, and a second-generation Scooter Line took to the ice.

Toronto's Dave Keon was a smallish center, an effortless skater who seemed capable of perpetual motion. Punch Imlach sent him out against me for several years; in 1963 and 1964, he starred in the games that eliminated us in the play-offs. My skating style demanded lots of room, and I always looked for openings for myself and my wingman to make the puck work for us. Keon was the perfect center to counter me because his mobility eliminated that open space. Even when we'd worked our way down the ice for a chance on net, he was quick enough to recover and mess with us all over again.

Dave was hard to beat, a center who could play off the wing himself, but to do that, he needed linemates who could swing him wide passes off the left wing. Another winger/center like Mike Walton or Bob Pulford could switch positions with Keon on the fly, causing problems for our wingers when we tried to match up against them.

Later on, Toronto put Norm Ullman's line against me, and Norm and I would usually take the opening face-off. Norm didn't have Dave Keon's speed or breakaway potential, but he was an excellent player nonetheless. He was steady and smart, magical when it came to working with his wingers and difficult to check because he was always on the move, skating in circles, then abruptly changing direction. He was very skilled at moving the puck from behind the net or out of the corners and at maintaining possession while he looked to make the play. Experienced wingers like Floyd Smith and Paul Henderson, who played with Norm in Detroit and Toronto, had the speed to find the openings and enjoyed simple tip-ins after Norm got the puck to one of them behind the defense.

Ullman could leave me gasping for air, so Toe Blake liked to put Henri Richard against him. Henri was his match in endurance, skating with him effortlessly, bumping him off the puck in the corners or on open ice, sticking to him mercilessly and hampering his playmaking ability.

I think you see the pattern. Punch lmlach would put his future Hall of Famer on me. Then Toe Blake would shuffle lines and put another of our future Hall of Famers on him. Imagine players like Bob Pulford, Ron Ellis, Red Kelly, and George Armstrong in the mix, add Boom Boom Geoffrion, Dickie Moore, Yvan Cournoyer, and the Richards—Hall of Famers all—and you'll begin to appreciate the level of competition that prevailed. I haven't even mentioned the Toronto defensemen—Tim Horton, Allan Stanley, and Marcel Pronovost—or our Tom Johnson, Doug Harvey, Jacques Laperrière, and Serge Savard, likewise all Hall of Famers. And then, we'd have to stare down a whole raft of Hall of Fame goaltenders like Terry Sawchuk and Johnny Bower, together in Toronto in the mid-sixties, Glenn Hall in Chicago, Gerry Cheevers in Boston, and Gump Worsley and Eddie Giacomin in New York.

Johnny Bower was the hardest goalie to outmaneuver in the entire league. He would simply refuse to go for a deke and so was difficult to score against on a breakaway. He positioned himself in such a way that he drew you toward him, almost as if you were being drawn into a funnel. I remember sending John Ferguson in on him several times. Fergie didn't have the greatest moves in close, so quite often he'd just keep on going and run right over Bower. Allan Stanley, Carl Brewer, Kent Douglas, and Tim Horton would come steaming to their goaltender's rescue, but Johnny would get up, shake himself off, and mumble,

"It's part of the game, guys." They were happy to hear that, because nobody was anxious to "correct" John Ferguson's behavior.

Terry Sawchuk was different. He was an angles goalie who wanted you to shoot. But if you preferred to put a move on him, he was happy to oblige. Both he and Bower were pushing forty in 1967 when we lined up against the Leafs in the league final, and both delivered outstanding performances. Sawchuk was especially amazing during a 3–0 shutout in the second game, April 22, in Montreal, after we had taken the series lead with a 6–2 win in the opener. Later in the series, I walked in on him in Toronto, and how he caught that puck I'll never know.

When I started out, most opposition centers were much smaller than I was, and that remained the case until the second half of my career. George Armstrong and Alex Delvecchio were good-sized men, as was Eddie Litzenberger, but the rest were built like Ullman, Mikita, Keon, and Henri Richard—maybe five feet, nine inches tall and between 170 and 180 pounds. Then, in the mid-1960s, along came Phil Esposito, Garry Unger, Walt Tkaczuk, Gordon "Red" Berenson, Ivan Boldirev, Peter Mahovlich, and Darryl Sittler, all of whom raised the height and weight figures to record levels.

IS THERE ANYTHING I don't like about the modern game? My main criticism is the nonstop stickwork—the slashing, the hooking, the cross-checking, the tripping—and the inadequate response of the officials. When I was playing, referees Bill Friday, John Ashley, Frank Udvari, and others didn't adjust their calls to suit the time clock. If you tripped someone in the first minute of play, or late in the third period, or halfway through overtime in a play-off game, it didn't matter: you were going off for two minutes, end of discussion. Today, the officials allow the players to get away with far too much, and it detracts from the game. Using the stick to check is the lazy player's crutch: when an opponent makes a play on you, all you have to do is turn around and hook him. Chances are you won't be penalized.

The only way to check a player properly is to keep skating. If players were coached to remain in motion, the game would return to good, clean body-checking, hip-checking and shoulder-checking. Once again it would be a thrill to watch the talent perform to their full potential. But don't misunderstand me: I don't advocate letting the stars run free. We certainly weren't free to do what we wanted in the 1950s and 1960s. Maurice and I always had someone on us, but we found ways around it. When I had a checker all over me in the opponent's end, I'd latch on to some other guy, one of their defensemen. If the checker had orders to follow me at any cost, so much the better. I'd be tying up two players instead of one, which left somebody else on our team in the clear.

What impresses me most about today's game is the amazing supply of talent that's come on stream. The number of teams in the NHL has quadrupled in a single generation and still the league has found enough young players to make the teams competitive and to draw people to the arenas. The anti-expansion doomsayers have been proved wrong; the NHL hasn't spread itself too thin. Instead, interest in hockey is growing and its importance rising correspondingly, because the sport remains what it's always been—the most exciting game played on two feet. Some might argue that I'm looking at the sport through rose-tinted glasses, but I see a game that is as exciting as it ever was, even while changing with every generation.

WHEN I BEGAN TO make notes on some of the athletes who had impressed me during my era, as well as those who have played in the NHL since, my thoughts drifted to figures outside the hockey arena. I had the opportunity to meet many other sports figures during my career.

In the early 1950s, professional wrestling in Montreal and Quebec was almost as popular as hockey, and "Whipper" Billy Watson, Wladek "Killer" Kowalski, Jean Rougeau, Larry Moquin, and Yvon Robert would perform to capacity crowds. There was some crossover between the contact sports of boxing and wrestling, and frequently big-name boxing stars would be brought in as draws to warm up the audiences. I met both Jack Dempsey and Joe Louis when they made guest appearances to promote the Monday wrestling programs at the Tour de Québec.

Later, after I'd moved to Montreal, I got to know Whitey Ford, Billy Martin, Mickey Mantle, and other New York Yankees stars who were invited to the same sports banquets as me and my teammates. Of course, harking back to the John Nault days in Victoriaville, I favored the Boston Red Sox and was a great admirer of the incomparable Ted Williams.

For some reason, the Canadiens always had an affinity for Boston's teams. Whenever we could, we would check out Celtics basketball games on Sunday afternoons at the Garden, before our contests against the Bruins. If we arrived in Boston during the baseball season, off we'd go to Fenway Park to take in a game.

Once, Ted Williams invited me into the clubhouse, and we spoke privately for twenty minutes or so. When I came out, the local reporters clustered round, wanting to know what we'd discussed. Apparently I'd been more favored than I knew; Ted never gave them more than a couple of sentences. In fact, he and I started off talking about baseball and hockey, then moved on to the great passion of "the Splendid Splinter," fishing. Williams often traveled into the wilds of Quebec on fly-fishing expeditions.

Several years after I retired as a player, Élise and I were driving through Maine to Cape Cod, Massachusetts, when I read in the paper that the Yankees were in Beantown for their traditional September showdown with the Red Sox. The three-game set would start the following night. I turned to Élise and proposed a change in plan: "Let's go to Boston tomorrow."

The following evening, I took her for a walk around the perimeter of Fenway Park, just to give her a taste of the atmosphere at a big-league stadium. I had no intention of going in. We'd assumed that there were no tickets available for such a classic contest and were simply killing time before a meal. As we passed by a ticket window, a man behind the wicket called me over. "Jean! What are you doing here?" He knew me by sight because he also worked at the Boston Garden. "Going to the game?"

"No, just showing my wife the sights."

"Wanna go?"

"Sure!"

He returned in a moment with two tickets that placed us beside George Steinbrenner, the Yankees' owner. It was a special pleasure to sit there, unrecognized, and watch the Yankees stars put on their show, with George in the stands and Reggie Jackson and friends down on the field. Our seats were right behind the Yankees on-deck circle, and we saw Jackson take his big warm-up swings, the Boston fans heaping abuse on him all the while. Halfway through the game, he hammered a homer over the fence in right center field, about 420 feet away. He wore a satisfied smile on his face as he stared down his tormentors in the stands on the way to his team's dugout.

In 1971, when I retired, the Expos had a night for me at Jarry Park, and I had my picture taken with Willie Mays, then in the late stages of his career as a member of the San Francisco Giants.

My most treasured baseball memory, however, dates from earlier that year, in January, and took place away from a ballpark. On the night in Montreal I scored the hat trick that gave me my 500th goal,

Élise and I had planned to go out to dinner with my business manager, Gerry Patterson, and his wife. The postgame interviews went on and on, and it was late when our foursome finally gathered. I felt bad, thinking there wouldn't be anything suitable open at that hour, but Gerry reassured me.

"Don't worry," he said. "We're going somewhere very special, very exclusive—it's a new place in Westmount Square."

We crossed Atwater and walked half a block west to an apartment building, then rode the elevator to one of the higher floors. On one of the apartment doors a hand-printed sign read: Only 500-Goal Scorers Allowed.

Inside, we were greeted by Rusty Staub, a Montreal Expo player who possesses a talent for fine cuisine. That evening we feasted into the early morning hours on oysters Rockefeller and Dover sole. Rusty had been at the Forum that night and left to prepare the meal the moment I'd scored my big goal. He was a fine ballplayer and a talented amateur cook who turned professional when he opened an East Side Manhattan restaurant, named Rusty's, after retiring from baseball. Following the tragedy of September 11, 2001, when two jetliners were flown into the World Trade Center, he was an indefatigable volunteer worker, raising millions in relief for his fellow New Yorkers. He's a great guy, and I've jokingly taken the credit for helping to launch his second career.

Throughout the years, I have met the greats from many different sports: baseball's Tom Seaver and Pete Rose; pro basketball stars Bill Russell, Bob Cousy, John Havlicek, and Wilt Chamberlain; and Hall of Fame jockeys Willie Shoemaker and Eddie Arcaro. I occasionally followed the vibrant local boxing scene in Montreal and made the acquaintance of Robert Cleroux, Yvon Durelle, Archie Moore, and George Chuvalo, as well as two tough competitors in the lightweight class, Armand Savoie and Dave Castilloux, who recently passed away.

My most exciting foray into another sport occurred in the late 1960s, when I was filming a commercial for American Motors at the Mont Tremblant racetrack. Al Unser Sr. was featured in the commercial as well. When we broke for lunch, Al invited me to play his game for a couple of laps—using a regular North American compact car.

"Come on, Big Jean, Ah'll take you for a little spin," he drawled. Here was the racetrack, here were the cars (admittedly, not the cars that Al was accustomed to), and here he was with some free time and a new friend to scare the wits out of.

Unser took me around that track at about 150 miles an hour. Or so it seemed; I refused to open my eyes to look at the speedometer.

"That's it, Al," I said. "You've just confirmed that car racing will never be a serious second-career option for me." That was it for lunch, too. I was afraid to go anywhere near food: my stomach was still circling the track.

Al Unser went on to win four Indy 500s, including back-to-back victories in 1970 and 1971. As with that day on the track at Mont Tremblant, I was retiring just as Al was getting up to speed.

Ironically, that's how I felt about hockey, too.

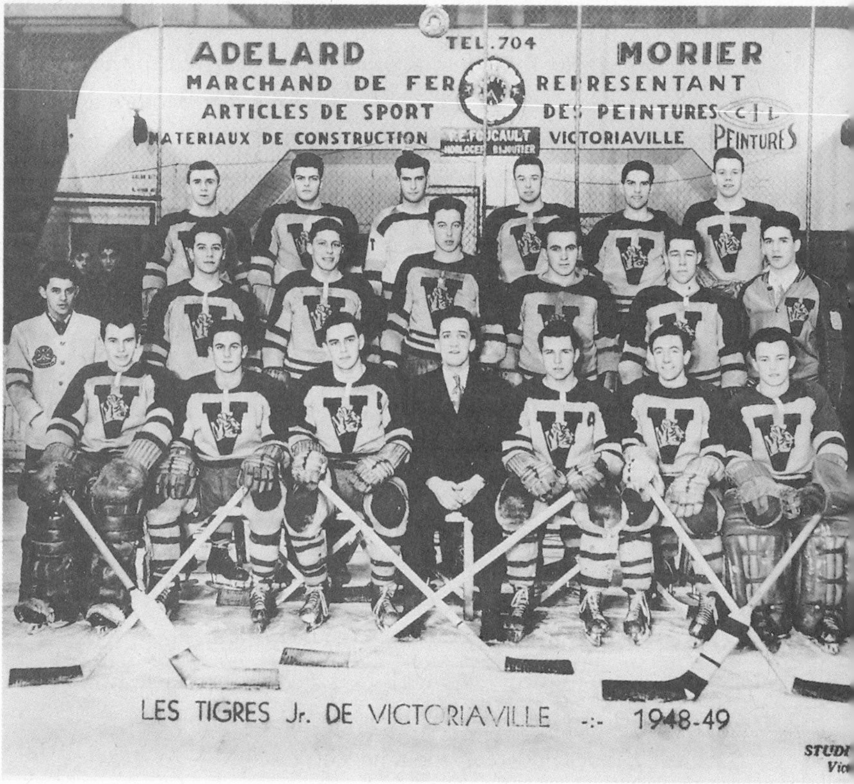
ADELARD
TEL.704
MORIER
MARCHAND DE FER
REPRESENTANT
ARTICLES DE SPORT
DES PEINTURES
MATERIAUX DE CONSTRUCTION
VICTORIAVILLE
PEINTURES
LES TIGRES Jr. DE VICTORIAVILLE -:- 1948-49

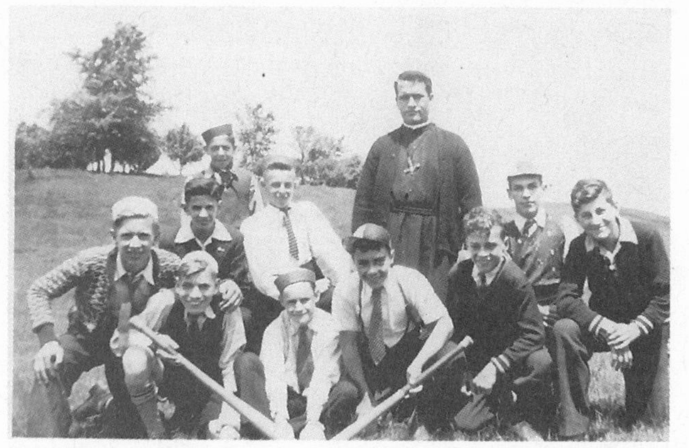

top left— Jean (middle row, third from left) played his first year of Quebec junior hockey in his hometown of Victoriaville.

bottom left — Jean (to the right of the Brother, in white shirt) with some of his Académie Saint-Louis de Gonzague classmates.

below — Jean (middle of back row) was a big cog in Victoriaville baseball in the summertime.

Citadelle
QUEBEC

top left — Jean (far right, front row) was an alternate captain with the 1950–51 version of the junior Quebec Citadels.

bottom left — Jean as a lanky sixteen-year-old with the Intermediate B Victoriaville Panthers in 1947–48.

above — The star of the Quebec Aces senior-league team was a popular man with the ladies in the two seasons encompassing 1951 through 1953.

above — Quebec's number 1 junior star cradles the puck.

facing page — *top left:* The infant Jean Béliveau in 1932; *top right:* Jean at four years old; *middle left:* Jean Béliveau: A boy and his tricycle; *middle right:* Jean, already showing some height at twelve years old; *bottom right:* Jean, a serious student at age fifteen.

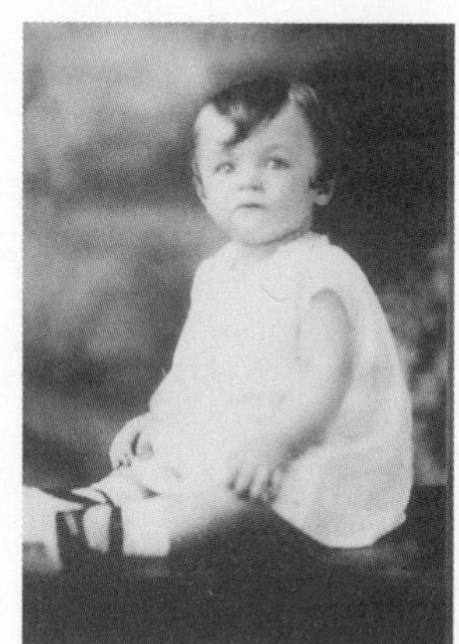
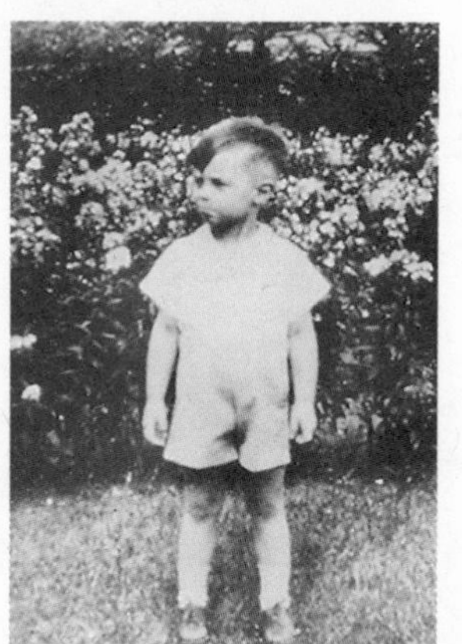

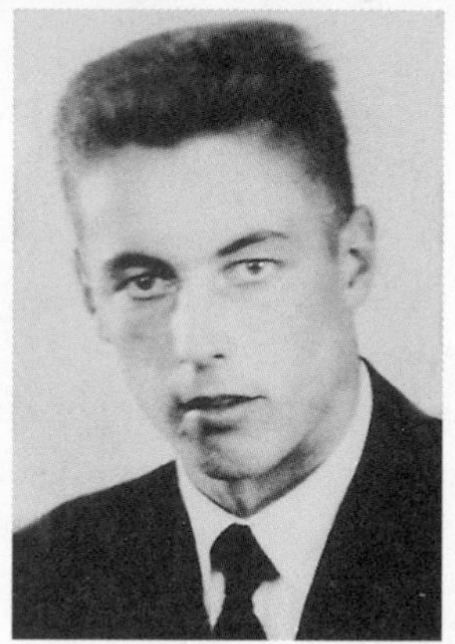

8

THE COACHES

IN JULY 1969, I was hired to do a series of television commercials for Purepak containers and was pleased to learn that one of the commercials would be filmed in Los Angeles. A patch of temporary ice was installed at the Great Western Forum and filming went on for about a day and a half.

We had just wrapped up when a Purepak executive asked if I would be interested in attending a session of the preseason training camp of the National Football League's Los Angeles Rams. I would indeed.

We drove south to California State University, Fullerton, that afternoon. There I was given my first close-up look at a professional footballer's preseason training regimen. It was an education. What was most striking was the sight of 300-pound linemen sweating out a scrimmage in 102-degree-Fahrenheit temperatures, then putting in another hour or two under the hot sun as the defense, offense, and special teams split off to continue work on their particular drills.

I was marveling at the players' stamina and athleticism when I was spotted by head coach George Allen. We'd met only once before, at a sports banquet, but he greeted me with surprising warmth and invited me to dinner with the team that evening.

The daily agenda at the Rams training camp was fairly typical of all NFL teams. The players reported at seven in the morning for taping and calisthenics, followed by breakfast, playbook study, and a "midmorning" workout at nine thirty. After lunch and a short rest period came more playbook study, followed by a return to the practice field at three o'clock for a scrimmage and other drills. At six, the team gathered for a meal. Then the various squads retreated to their corners of the meeting hall for a final round of playbook study, breaking off at nine when, exhausted, they trooped to bed for lights-out at ten.

In the 1960s, hockey players went through their own version of Hell Week in September, but we were spared the hot midsummer sun, the hours of playbook study, and the endless repetition of what seemed to me to be rather basic drills.

I sat at George Allen's table along with his coaching staff, and we spent an amicable hour discussing professional sports in general, with me asking questions about football and answering others about hockey. Toward the end of the meal, George surprised me again with a request that I say a few words to his players at their team meeting. "Just talk about the success you and the Canadiens have had over the years."

Fortunately, there was something to talk about. Two months earlier, we had won our second Stanley Cup in a row, our fourth in five years and my ninth overall. But I doubted that these experiences would be of interest or use to a roomful of tackles and guards. "I don't mind talking to your players," I told him, "but what can I possibly say? I don't think many of them know who I am and I doubt they know hockey."

"You'd be surprised," he responded. "A lot of the players live here in the off-season and go to the Kings' games. Don't worry, they'll have heard of you. Tell them how you and the Canadiens approach each season. We have an older team, a veteran team, and I'm trying to get them to think 'championship.' You're a champion; I'd really appreciate it if you could communicate that attitude to them."

When he introduced me to his players, George stressed two factors: my age—thirty-seven at the time—and my long career in a demanding sport. "He's a guy who plays a tough game in a tough league, as tough as the one you play in. He's been with his team for sixteen seasons, going on seventeen. Does anybody here hope to do the same? Can anybody name a football team that's won four Super Bowls in five years? Jean Béliveau proves that age is no detriment if you stay in shape."

George Allen gained another fan that day, both for his gracious comments and for the way he demonstrated that he was always thinking about his team and his sport. He would take advantage of any opportunity to motivate his players, to give them an edge during a demanding season. In other words, George Allen was a coach.

For sixteen seasons, between 1952 and 1968, three men held primary responsibility for directing my daily hockey fortunes. All three joined me in the Hall of Fame. Punch Imlach is the only one who was inducted solely for his coaching prowess and who appears in the Builders category. Dick Irvin and Toe Blake entered the Hall as all-star players in their own right, but I think each would agree that his accomplishments behind the bench overshadowed the successes of his playing days.

There was a lot less emphasis on coaching "style," or schools of coaching, back in the 1950s and 1960s. Terms like "strategist," "tactician," or "bench general" weren't commonly used then. As coaches, very little differentiated Imlach, Irvin, and Blake. All three were veteran hockey men who had played the game; all had been well schooled in the basics. They were successful because they understood the demands and responsibilities of leadership. A coach cannot mount an effective game plan if he's unable to convince his team to play it for him. To do so, he must earn the players' respect.

I've already introduced Roland Hébert, my first coach in affiliated hockey during that initial season with the Victoriaville Tigers of 1948. Roland understood the basic tenet of coaching at the junior level: the most promising players need lots of ice time. He made sure I got it, often putting me out there for forty minutes a game.

When I moved to Quebec City, Pete Martin of the Citadels provided more of the same, and the pattern of my progress toward the NHL was firmly established. Every year I improved as I was matched up with better teammates and faced off against stronger opposition. The Quebec media often complained about Pete Martin's leadership, and the team engaged former NHL player Kilby Macdonald as a "special adviser" during my time there, but I can honestly say that I had no complaints about Pete's handling of me. I will admit, however, that George "Punch" Imlach introduced me to a game that was played and coached at an entirely different and considerably higher level.

Punch played for Frank Selke's Toronto Marlboros in the late 1930s, but moved to Cornwall, Ontario, in 1941 after he and Selke had a blowup over salary. That dispute colored their dealings ever after. After playing a season in Cornwall, Punch enlisted in the Canadian Army and served three years in a "hockey company" that happened to include such figures as Jack Riley, Tommy Ivan, Jimmy Conacher, and Buzz Bastien. Punch obtained the rank of lieutenant, was demobilized at the end of the Second World War, and promptly attended the Detroit Red Wings' training camp. But he had lost ground through the war years and fell short in his attempt to play in the NHL.

To his credit, Punch was a realist: he was in his late twenties in an era when few players continued past their early thirties. He needed the promise of a secure future and found it when coach Lex Cook offered him a job playing with the Quebec Aces. Punch accepted, but held out for an off-ice job as well, in the accounting department of Anglo-Canadian Pulp and Paper. Two years later, he became a playing coach when Cook went off to Dallas.

In 1956 the Aces won the Edinburgh Cup, the Canadian minor-professional hockey championship, by which time they'd literally become Imlach's team; when attendance dwindled in the mid-1950s, Punch and two other investors purchased the Aces from Anglo-Canadian, hoping to move them into the American Hockey League. Punch had a 25-percent interest in the team, but not enough money to persuade the AHL to expand to Quebec City. The Quebec Senior Hockey League was too small a pond for Punch, and he was its best-kept secret. In 1957 he was hired as general manager of the Springfield Indians, a team owned by the legendary Eddie Shore but operated by the Boston Bruins.

When he arrived in Springfield, Punch was dismayed to learn that he was expected to coach the Indians as well as manage them. A season-long feud developed between Shore, who contested every move Punch made and was on the telephone to Boston demanding his dismissal at regular intervals, and Punch, who took the Indians to the American Hockey League final, a feat no one had expected. Nonetheless, Shore wasted no time ending the affiliation with Boston in the off-season, and Imlach was offered a position akin to today's director of player development, managing the Bruins' minor-league teams.

Then, Toronto's Stafford Smythe came calling. When the 1958–59 NHL season began, Punch was Toronto's assistant general manager. The Leafs got off to a dreadful start under Billy Reay's coaching that year and were in last place with a 5–20 record in late November. It was obvious that the Leafs were not playing for Reay. When Punch convinced the hierarchy to promote him to general manager, he fired Reay and took over the coaching duties himself.

Punch canceled his first team practice and instead summoned the players one by one to a meeting room, where he secured a promise from each that he would follow Imlach's lead. Punch put his stamp on the Leafs from the start, signing Johnny Bower and trading for defenseman Allan Stanley and forwards Larry Regan and Gerry Ehman, character players all. On the final night of the season, the Leafs overcame the Red Wings 6–4 at the Olympia to make the playoffs. They went on to eliminate the Bruins in a seven-game semifinal before we beat them in five for the Cup.

Punch was new to the NHL, but he'd spent more than a decade in the minors and knew exactly what he wanted. His plan for Toronto involved a slightly older, well-balanced team, with eager young forwards up front for speed, supported by experienced guys on defense and a pair of veteran goaltenders—exactly the kind of team that had flourished in the QSHL during the postwar years. For most of his first tenure with Toronto, from 1958 to the 1968–69 season, the Toronto Maple Leafs looked and played remarkably like the Aces.

Punch insisted on mutual trust, and he gained the confidence of his players by treating them as individuals. When I started with the Aces, Punch told me he didn't want to make any major changes in my game, but he had me work on small things that would improve my performance.

"After a couple of steps, you take big strides and you can really move," he told me. "But you have to improve your quick starts." Following every practice, he'd place me on the red button of the faceoff circle, with one of the forwards out on the circle itself. The forward would chase me all over the ice, then we'd switch places and I would chase him for a while. This went on for weeks, until Punch was satisfied that I was faster off the mark.

Much has been said and written about Punch Imlach, especially about his move to Buffalo in 1970 and his subsequent brief return to the Leafs for the 1979–81 seasons. Some of these comments may have left the impression of a man well past his prime, out of touch with the modern game; that's not the Punch Imlach I knew. When the Leafs were going through the roller-coaster ride of the Harold Ballard years, I took these anti-Punch remarks with several grains of salt. Punch had a philosophy: "About 10 percent of players can motivate themselves. The other 90 percent you drive hard, and some of them might even thank you later on when they realize what you've done for them. A coach's most important job is to motivate his players."

At the time Punch was struggling with Ballard's Leafs, both Dick Irvin and Toe Blake would have been out of coaching for more than a decade; had they been active in the 1970s, they might have shared Punch's fate. A profound change had taken place in the player-coach relationship, with players frequently second-guessing or questioning the coach's most basic decisions. None of these three had been raised to tolerate this sort of insubordination. In the "old days," a coach could occasionally dictate like an army sergeant—"We do things my way, period"—because there was always a line of hopeful talents in the minors ready to take our places.

Players of my generation were likewise bothered when we saw what was happening. We realized that the youngsters of the 1970s had grown up with a different culture. The Canadiens' management group tried its best to instill team values in young men who had come of age in a climate of rampant individualism and decreased personal responsibility. Suddenly, it had become a bother for players to wear a jacket and tie on game day and to dress well on the road.

Having been raised in the postwar era, our generation responded to lines of authority fashioned after the military model. By the late 1970s, however, this approach had little mainstream appeal. Young players seemed unable to relate to it and senior management seemed unable, or unwilling, to compromise. In the past two decades, I have heard veteran hockey people complain about a generation of "only children," young men whose parents' lives revolved around their sons' development and success. Every coaching move had to be explained and justified over and over, whether it be the lowest echelons of minor hockey or the ranks of the pros. Coaching by negotiation is quite different from the methods of my day.

WHILE PUNCH IMLACH, Dick Irvin, and Toe Blake all were disciplinarians, they approached problem solving and communications issues in different ways.

Dick Irvin, for example, had an acid tongue, capable of stinging his victim by long distance. During the four years I was courted by the Canadiens, Frank Selke took a laissez-faire attitude, confident that I would show up when I was ready. But Dick was not averse to sending pointed messages across the miles.

I was in my first season with the Aces when a story came down the wire from Montreal: "Boom Boom Geoffrion Greatest Rookie to Enter NHL, Says Dick."

"That kid is a better player right now than Rocket was in his first season," he was quoted as saying. At the same time he took care to add that, when I joined the Canadiens, he would put me at center between Boomer and Dickie Moore.

Irvin was hardest on those players he perceived as shirking or showing signs of physical weakness. This sometimes led him to confuse an injury with malingering or to jump to the premature conclusion that a particular player wasn't suited to the wear and tear of the NHL. And there were injuries aplenty. Maurice Richard, Gordie Howe, and I almost saw our careers end before they started because of rookie-season injuries. Rocket had seemed particularly vulnerable ever since suffering a severely broken ankle in his first season of senior hockey. A year later, he broke his wrist, and he followed that up with another ankle break in his first season with the Canadiens.

"Richard may be too brittle to play in the National Hockey League," opined Irvin. This was not what Maurice wanted to hear. Dick was oil to Rocket's flame, and the two of them became a dangerous combination—one of the reasons why, in the aftermath of the Richard Riot, Frank Selke informed Irvin that he wouldn't be coaching the Canadiens anymore.

My first season was curtailed by injury, and the least sympathetic person in the organization was Dick Irvin. I cracked my ankle in a road game but didn't know it was fractured. Nor did Dick, who considered my distress a minor incident. I'll never forget the slow walk along the platform from the train and through Windsor Station the morning we got back to Montreal. By the time I made it outside, the entire team had dispersed; that's how long it had taken me to hobble the two hundred yards or so to the street. The next day, X-rays revealed the crack, and I was in a cast, feeling both bad and relatively lucky. Gordie Howe had suffered a fractured skull and severe concussion in his freshman year; I always wondered if Dick would have thought Howe was exaggerating.

Irvin and Frank Selke were friends, and when Frank relieved Irvin of his coaching duties, he offered him a position in the team's front office. Dick refused it and instead moved behind the bench in Chicago. A little more than a year later, he died of bone cancer. Nobody had known that he was ill when he was still with Montreal, but he must have been suffering the painful effects of that debilitating disease for most of the two years he was my coach. In short, he was tenacious, and he expected us to be the same.

Toe Blake, who would be my coach for the next thirteen years, was regarded by many as Irvin's best student and true heir. He led the team to eight Stanley Cups and it's astonishing now to recall that Kenny Reardon, the Canadiens' assistant general manager, had to lay his job on the line to ensure that Toe would be hired in the first place. It helped that Kenny was the son-in-law of Senator Donat Raymond, then the team's owner.

With Dick's departure, Raymond and others favored Billy Reay as the new coach. Frank Selke wanted one of his former Toronto players, Joe Primeau. Selke had just let go a coach who he felt could not channel the Rocket's will to win, and he may have believed that Toe was simply too much like Dick.

The newspapers were promoting veteran Quebec hockey coach Roger Leger as the ideal candidate. The French-language media in particular were lobbying for a greater French-Canadian presence on the team, both in management and on the ice. Irvin was often assailed for his indifference to that need and for what some saw as a bias in favor of big, scrappy players from western Canada. Selke was sensitive to these charges and had done his best to improve the on-ice French-English ratio by pouring time and money into the Quebec minor leagues. And the French players had come—Plante, Geoffrion, St. Laurent, Talbot, Henri Richard, Provost, Goyette, Pronovost, Bonin, and Béliveau.

But for the position of coach, Ken Reardon, himself a westerner who'd made good with the team, knew there was no better candidate than Toe Blake. Toe had seen his own playing days end during the 1947–48 season when he broke his leg. Sent to our affiliate in Houston and coaching on crutches, Toe led his team to the league championship. The following September, the Canadiens assigned him to Buffalo, but he had a run-in with the owner there and left to coach the Valleyfield Braves in the QSHL. He was successful and might have been an automatic choice for the Canadiens but for the fact that he'd antagonized Frank Selke during his years with the Braves.

Eventually Reardon prevailed, and Toe rejoined a team he'd left six years before. Only two of his former teammates—Rocket and Butch Bouchard—remained on the roster. Although still captain,

Butch would play only sporadically that year and on several occasions went to Toe and suggested retirement. Toe wanted him to stay because, like Imlach, he wanted a full quota of veterans on his team. On the last night of our Stanley Cup final against Detroit on April 10, 1956, a 3–1 win that gave us the championship in five games, Butch was there in uniform to receive the Cup.

As for Toe, the man Frank Selke had been reluctant to hire went on to win five straight Stanley Cups. Toe's greatest quality was his ability to motivate a collection of superstars to work together as a unit, perhaps the key to victory in any team sport.

In the spring of 1993, the Canadiens surprised a lot of people by winning their twenty-fourth Cup. Quebec and Pittsburgh, two teams with superior talent, were eliminated in the play-offs. Both had great players but neither squad was playing as a team—not the Nordiques, because they were unaccustomed to success, nor the Penguins, because they had stopped listening to their coach. You can't win the championship if your superstars put themselves ahead of the team's well-being.

Toe drilled that lesson into us time and time again. I learned it and later, as captain, was expected to pass it on. Nothing is won by a single player's effort alone, least of all the Stanley Cup, which is now decided over four rounds of play. You need the commitment of every player—soldiers and superstars—and Toe treated them all as equals, from the venerable Rocket to the freshest rookie. More important, he had us totally convinced that his egalitarian approach was the only one that would work.

Toe believed that hockey was a simple game and that the most successful teams were those that focused on the basics. Our pregame preparations reflected his philosophy. Game plans went on the blackboard, but we seldom needed them. "Hockey is very easy," Toe used to say, raising his arms to demonstrate. "It is played in two V's—one moving away from our net, and the other moving toward theirs."

As a center, I was expected to do my job in both ends, to key the transition game when we got the puck by joining with our defensemen, and to put myself in position to start or support the next play. Toe believed that constant movement of players and puck was critical: give the puck to a teammate and then hustle to find open ice so that he can give it back to you. We were expected to play with our heads up, fully functioning, anticipating the opportunities, getting into the flow. Today, wingers camp out "high" along the boards near their own blue lines, waiting for a breakout pass from a defenseman down "low" in front of the net or along the back boards. As I mentioned earlier, we didn't do this very often. Inactivity on the ice drove Doug Harvey nuts, and he simply refused to pass to us unless we were on the fly.

Nowadays, of course, this style of play is known as the "Russian" or "European" game. When the hockey pundits of the 1970s and 1980s dumped on the North American game and lauded the Europeans as innovators, I had to laugh. The Montreal Canadiens played that style in the 1950s, with puck control in all three zones. Toe insisted on it. He wouldn't tolerate lazy play or poor execution of the basics: "How can you catch a pass? You've been skating with your stick up around your waist. If you want the pass, keep your stick on the ice."

We followed Toe's game plan faithfully and no one dreamed of questioning his leadership. That's not to say we didn't have our quirks and idiosyncrasies, but Punch, Dick, and Toe knew them and made allowances—though not many.

An example was Doug Harvey's penchant for controlling the play. Sometimes he'd hold on to the puck for long minutes, daring the world to snatch it away. One night in Detroit he was happily stick handling a bit too close to our net, while Toe fumed behind the bench. "The way Harvey's playing around, he'll get a penalty in the next thirty seconds." Sure enough, Doug kept up his wizardry until someone poked the puck away, and he had to hook the guy in an effort to retain or regain possession. Doug went off for two minutes, and Toe's blood pressure went up into the rafters.

Toe wouldn't stand for anything less than a 100 percent effort that night or any other night. His hat pushed back on his head, he would pace back and forth behind the bench and talk to the clock, but we knew his comments were directed at us; the only people in the rink who heard them were those of us on the bench and possibly the fans in the first two rows of seats, which is just as well. But Toe never scolded us in public, never went face-to-face with his players the way, say, Quebec coach Pierre Pagé did with Mats Sundin and Martin Rucinsky the night the Canadiens eliminated the Nordiques in the 1993 play-offs.

Toe trusted his players, and we trusted him. He always treated us like men, not children. He'd go to the wall for players he believed in, even if the fans or the media were less than supportive; I think particularly of Jimmy Roberts, Claude Provost, André Pronovost, and Terry Harper. Montreal fans have always embraced the spectacular players and scorned the "plumbers," but plumbing is nothing to be ashamed of. It takes skilled tradesmen to win Stanley Cups, a lesson some fans and media commentators seem slow to learn.

A classic illustration of this in the 1990s concerned forward Mike Keane. When Pat Burns was coach, I read many articles questioning Keane's continued presence on the team and Burns's "unreasonable" devotion to him. Then Jacques Demers took over as coach and made a lot of trades, but he was determined to keep Keane.

Keane, like Jimmy Roberts, had more heart than talent, but he made a huge contribution to the team. Every time a coach sent him or someone like him onto the ice, you'd see an honest worker doing his best. Toe recognized the type; he was an astute judge of talent who'd never ask more of a player than he could give. But if someone was mired in a slump, Toe would be the first to help him pull out of it and as soon as possible.

Our roster didn't change much during Toe's first five years. There wasn't any need. We were winning everything in sight. In the early 1960s, however, change seemed to sweep through the club. After the Maple Leafs had manhandled us in both the 1963 and 1964 play-offs, Frank Selke and Toe moved quickly to build a bigger and much stronger team, adding players like Terry Harper, Jacques Laperrière, Ted Harris, Claude Larose, and John Ferguson. We weren't "the Flying Frenchmen" anymore. We were deluxe plumbers, according to many, but we won four Cups in the next five years, and Toe was there for three of them.

Coaching was a lonely profession in the 1960s. There were no assistants for company behind the bench during games, and the only people coaches could socialize with on the road were the training staff and the journalists, who weren't nearly as numerous as they are today. The workload Toe carried was especially evident when we traveled. We played home-and-home series back then, which meant that, in the case of a Chicago series, we'd play at the Forum Saturday night, hop on the midnight train, then ride all night and the next day to Chicago, usually arriving about an hour before Sunday's game time at a suburban station. There we'd climb on a bus and rush downtown with a police escort. Because our schedules were so tight, the team's assistant equipment manager, Eddie Palchak, would go ahead of us on Saturday morning, taking a second set of equipment with him so that it would be there waiting when we arrived. The only things we'd carry with us were our skates.

In those days, Toe was both coach and road secretary. He carried our train tickets and meal money and other incidentals in his briefcase. One night it was snowing heavily when we finally arrived in Chicago at 6:35 PM. The game was scheduled to start at seven thirty.

Our police escort was waiting, but there was no bus. Toe realized he had forgotten to reserve the bus.

I suggested we ask the cop to radio for taxis or see if there were other cops available with their cars to take us to the stadium. With a storm on, it was hopeless to try for enough cabs. Thankfully, an enterprising constable thought of the paddy wagon. I rode in the police car with three other players, while everyone else—including Sam Pollock, who had come along with us—piled into the paddy wagon. Away we went, with the lights flashing and the sirens wailing.

When we pulled up with a flourish in front of Chicago Stadium, there was a crowd milling around outside. The doors to the squad car and the paddy wagon opened, and a gaggle of athletic young men in suits and overcoats tumbled out, toting skates and looking haggard. The illustrious Montreal Canadiens organization lost a bit of its glamor that evening, but I hope those cops received the complimentary seats they deserved.

While Toe was not as acerbic or abrasive as Dick Irvin, he had a temper and was the fiercest behind-the-bench competitor I'd ever seen, which probably led to his leaving the game when he did.

Our five-straight Cup string ended in Chicago in 1961. We had finished seventeen points ahead of the third-place Hawks during the regular season, the one in which Boomer scored his fifty goals, but Boomer was sidelined with a serious knee injury when we faced off March 26 for game 3 with the series tied at one each. The late Danny Gallivan described that game as the best he ever broadcast. The crowd was in shirtsleeves because the night was unseasonably warm, and the arena got hotter as the evening wore on. The teams were tied 1–1 after the regulation three periods, and we had two goals called back in overtime by referee Dalton McArthur, who had been feuding with Toe throughout the game.

A little more than halfway into the third overtime, Dickie Moore was sent off for tripping and the Hawks' Murray Balfour, who'd started out with the Montreal organization in the late 1950s, scored his second goal of the game on the ensuing power play. Toe, his face redder than the goal light, made a beeline for McArthur and took a punch at him, for which Clarence Campbell fined Toe $2,000, a fortune in those days. We bounced back to take the fourth game in Chicago 5–2, but Glenn Hall shut us out 3–0 in both the fifth and sixth games. The league final proceeded without us. With Chicago battling Detroit for the Cup, we were on the outside looking in for the first time in years. We wouldn't win a Stanley Cup or even appear in the finals for the next three years, but we were competitive each season and made it back to the Cup in 1965.

In the meantime, there were signs that Toe was struggling with the pressures of his job. When he'd started out behind the bench, television was not much of a factor in sports. By the mid-1960s, however, we were televised at least twice a week. This prompted more print coverage, which led to higher expectations and an ever more critical and demanding attitude on the part of the fans.

As an aside, the glare of public scrutiny has become even hotter in recent years. In May 1994, immediately after the Canadiens had been eliminated by Boston in the seventh game of the divisional quarterfinal, Guy Carbonneau, Patrick Roy, and Vincent Damphousse decided to unwind on the golf course. The morning was cool and wet. They weren't playing, just taking a stroll to decompress, when they were confronted—some might say ambushed—by an enterprising newspaper photographer. Guy was not in the mood to tolerate this intrusion and gave the journalist what we call in French *le doigt d'honneur*—"the finger of honor"—a gesture that was duly reproduced on the front page of the *Journal de Montréal* the next day. The furor died down within a couple of days; nonetheless, Guy Carbonneau was gone when the next season came around.

The occasional bashing from the media and the booing from the fans really got to Toe, especially when we brought up the highly touted and very exciting Yvan Cournoyer in 1963–64. Toe relegated "the Roadrunner" exclusively to power-play duty, and the fans were quick to show their displeasure. One night, we had to grab him during the first intermission before he could make his way into the stands to silence a nonstop boo-bird.

On another occasion, Toe ran afoul of a somewhat exalted member of the audience. For years, the first two seats in the second row behind the right-hand end of our bench had belonged to Canadian National Railways (CNR). One seat was usually occupied by a distinguished-looking gentleman in a three-piece suit who muttered to himself throughout the game. I never heard precisely what he had to say, but Toe could obviously pick up fragments as he walked behind the bench.

On one particular night, after the siren had signaled the end of the first period, I was walking toward the dressing room when Toe pulled me into the coach's cubicle.

"Who's this guy on the right-hand side of the bench who's always mumbling?" he asked me.

"Second row, brown hat, blue suit, and round glasses?"

"That's him."

"Donald Gordon. President of CNR."

I understated the case. Donald Gordon was not simply the president and chairman of CNR, he was a Canadian business icon. During the Second World War he had served as chairman of the Wartime Prices and Trade Board, and he had held several executive positions with the Bank of Canada before joining CNR in 1950. It was his task to modernize the government-owned railway, a process that included the integration of more French Canadians into senior management. Queried about his rate of progress in this regard, Gordon had once flippantly responded that he was "doing his best with what he had to work with," a remark that launched a media storm in Quebec.

He was burned in effigy on Dorchester Boulevard in front of CNR headquarters. Political scientists later identified this incident as one of the first public stirrings of *indépendantiste* sentiment among students of the time.

"Are you sure of that?" asked Toe.

"Yes, I'm sure; I've met him at the Beaver Club, at the Queen Elizabeth Hotel. Why do you want to know?"

"Well, just before we came in here, I told him to go to hell."

Toe looked worried, perhaps imagining the next day's conversation between team owner Senator Hartland Molson and Donald Gordon, two captains of Canadian industry. I did my best to set his mind at ease. "Relax, Toe, you probably made his day. He'll be on the phone with his friends all over the country, bragging that the famous Toe Blake told him where to get off."

Toe reached the end of his emotional rope in April 1968. We usually sequestered the team in the Laurentians during the play-offs, and we were camped that year at La Sapinière in Val David, about an hour's drive from Montreal. We came downtown for games or a late-morning practice, after which the bus would take us back up north. Toe liked to sit in the last row on the left side; my usual seat was right in front of his. Just before the bus pulled into the hotel parking lot after one of our practice sessions, he tapped me on the shoulder. "Come and see me in ten minutes," he said.

When I entered his room, I found him pacing like a caged bear.

"Jean, I don't know what's wrong with me. Something is going to snap here." He clutched his head with both hands, and repeated, "Something's going to snap."

I realized that apart from his wife Betty, I was probably the only person he could talk to about his anxiety. Thirteen years of performance pressure threatened to overwhelm him. We sat and talked for a couple of hours, until he felt calmed.

For years, Toe Blake had been the man most responsible for our Stanley Cup successes. Outsiders had speculated that the most influential person on the team was named, variously, Plante, Harvey, Richard, Geoffrion, Moore, or Béliveau. The players, however, knew better: Toe was the true cornerstone of the Canadiens' dynasty. On Saturday, May 11, we defeated the St. Louis Blues to win the Stanley Cup final in four straight games, taking each game by a one-goal margin. It was our last contest in the "old" Forum; demolition crews were scheduled to show up Monday morning to begin extensive renovations that would raise the roof, remove the pillars that obstructed sightlines, and deliver a "new" Forum to Montreal hockey fans at a gala reopening six months later.

Late that Saturday night, long after the party had ended in the stands, the veteran sports photographer Denis Brodeur waited in the Forum. He suspected that something was up, and his intuition did not go unrewarded. Just before midnight Toe emerged from his office, uncharacteristically hatless, overcoat on his left arm and a large suitcase in his right hand. Denis waited until Toe, walking slowly, with his head down, reached the exit in the northwest corner of the Forum, and then he clicked the shutter. The next day, this photograph appeared in newspapers all across North America with the announcement that Toe Blake had resigned as coach of the Montreal Canadiens. The team had had only two coaches in twenty-eight years.

A month later, Sam Pollock appointed Claude Ruel as Toe's successor. "Piton," as Ruel was known, was the consummate company man, well liked by everyone and a superior judge of hockey talent. He had coached at other levels of the Montreal organization, but was best known as an instructor of young players rather than a take-charge coach.

Claude was inevitably lost in the huge shadow cast by Toe Blake, although his early results were undeniably impressive. With Claude at the helm, we finished first in the East Division that year and went on to win the Stanley Cup for the fourth time in five years after a second straight sweep over St. Louis in the final.

Claude's major problem was communication. We were a veteran team and we understood that he knew the game, but sometimes he'd go to the blackboard and simply fail to make his intentions clear. It took a while for us to realize that Claude was equally frustrated by his poor delivery and lack of presence, and that he wanted to do something about these shortcomings.

In the middle of a January night in 1969, I was awakened by the phone ringing by my bedside. It was Jacques Beauchamp of *Le Journal*, asking if I would be at the Forum later that morning. He knew very well I would be. We had a mid-morning practice no matter how late a game or a road trip had kept us up the night before. I'd fallen into the habit of arriving even earlier to have a coffee in the cafeteria at around eight thirty. I reminded Jacques of this and asked why he was calling at two thirty in the morning.

"Because Claude Ruel will hand in his resignation to Sam Pollock this morning, that's why."

Piton usually arrived at the Forum just fifteen minutes or so before practice. When I saw him coming through the door shortly before nine o'clock, I knew that Beauchamp was right. I was upbeat and smiling when I greeted him. "Boy, Claude, you're early this morning. What's up?"

For a second he appeared to be debating what to tell me. Claude Ruel has big, brown eyes, and when he is down, he can look sadder than a basset hound.

"I can't take it anymore, Jean. I want to go back to scouting. That's where I'm happy," he confessed.

When he had signed on, Claude was prepared for increased attention from the media, but he probably hadn't realized that his appointment was more than just a coaching job—at least as far as Quebec francophones were concerned.

"You're the first French Canadian to coach this team in I don't know how long," I told him. "You can't quit. A lot of people are depending on you. Stay with me on this. I'll talk to the other senior guys on the team and we'll support you."

To tell the truth, I don't think Claude was persuaded, but he reluctantly agreed to try it my way. Right after practice I called together Henri, Jacques Laperrière, J.-C. and Gilles Tremblay, and Claude Provost and made them aware of the situation.

"We've got to pull for this guy. We've got to keep him here at least until spring. He's the first French Canadian behind the bench in our lifetime. We can't let him go in the middle of the season." It didn't take much to make the case; everybody loved Piton.

But Claude detested the social and media responsibilities attached to his job. In Los Angeles, when the *Times* asked for an interview with the coach of the Montreal Canadiens, Claude went into a panic and asked me to accompany him to the interview. I tried to dissuade him.

"Claude, you're the coach. They want to talk to you. Maybe they don't want a player there; they might want to ask you questions about certain players." He wouldn't accept these objections, and I ended up going along.

We saw another sign of Claude's growing anguish one night in Minnesota. There were about three or four minutes to go in a close game when I returned to the bench after completing a shift. Claude was nowhere to be seen.

Yvan Cournoyer called me over.

"Where's Claude?" I asked.

"Claude said you're to finish the game for him." Which I did, making line changes both from the bench and on the ice.

The following season, 1969–1970, we failed to make the playoffs—something that hadn't happened since 1947–48, the year Toe

Blake broke his leg. Claude took the defeat personally, even though we had finished the season in fourth place, tied with the New York Rangers in the East Division at ninety-two points, just seven behind the Bruins and the Hawks, who tied for first. (New York got the nod for play-off action because its goals for/goals against statistics were better than ours. St. Louis won the West Division that year with six fewer points than we had. The West's fourth-place Oakland Seals had thirty-four fewer points than us, but nonetheless made the play-offs.)

Claude tried again to resign, but Sam Pollock absolved him of all responsibility and convinced him to stay. He also hired Al MacNeil as assistant coach to take some of the pressure off for the 1970–71 season.

Sam had another sales pitch to make at the end of that season, this one to yours truly. I didn't feel that my contribution had been up to par—only nineteen goals and thirty assists in sixty-three games—and I'd decided to retire.

Sam asked me to stay another year. "The team is changing," he said. "We're in a transition period. Please play one more year. Don't worry about the points; I'm not. It's hard to go through a full season without a slump. I'll feel more at ease if you're in the room. We have a lot of youngsters, and I want you there to make it easier for them." I didn't know that he'd already spoken with Claude Ruel, and that Sam also wanted a veteran captain in place in case Claude couldn't last the upcoming season.

I relented. "Okay, but I'll leave after next season. I'll be forty next year. That's definitely the end." We shook hands on it.

As it turned out, 1970–71 was a season to remember for many reasons—my 500th goal, the trade for Frank Mahovlich, the late season call-up of Ken Dryden, our Stanley Cup win, and Claude Ruel's mid-season resignation. When Piton went to Pollock for the last time, Sam did the merciful thing and returned him to a lower-profile position elsewhere in the organization.

Al MacNeil took over as head coach and did a great job before he ran into the same media buzz saw that had nicked Claude. Al led us to third place in our division with ninety-seven points, but that was far behind the Bruins' 121. Still, we managed to upset Esposito, Orr, and company in a seven-game quarterfinal and then held off a tough Minnesota team in six to come up against Chicago in the final. We were aided by young players like Phil Roberto, Marc Tardif, Chuck Lefley, Pete Mahovlich, and Réjean Houle, but the going was rough and would get rougher still.

I remember John Ferguson exploding in frustration after a game against the hard-fighting Minnesota North Stars. Fergie remained in a surly temper for the rest of the play-offs, a mood that wasn't improved when the final's fifth game resulted in a 2–0 loss on Chicago ice, giving the Hawks a 3–2 series lead.

Al had kept Henri Richard warming the bench for almost the entire sixty minutes, and the Pocket was livid when the media gathered in the dressing room. He blew up, calling MacNeil the worst coach he'd ever played for. I was in the shower when I heard the commotion and emerged to find Henri holding forth in a loud voice, surrounded by eager journalists. I immediately dragged him into the showers and kept him there until the reporters left, but the damage had been done.

The monster's bite was soon forthcoming. Back in Montreal the next day, we picked up the French-language newspapers and discovered that our team had a "language issue." Nobody felt worse about this sort of coverage than Henri, a man with his share of the famous Richard temper, who hated to lose as much as his elder brother. But Henri could not take a benching in stride. Try as he might, he couldn't defuse the situation, although he went on to win the Stanley Cup for Al MacNeil with two goals in our 3–2 seventh game victory in Chicago, after we had trailed 2–0.

A native Maritimer, MacNeil was "promoted" to coach and general manager of the AHL Halifax Voyageurs the following season, and Scotty Bowman, who had taken the expansion St. Louis Blues to three straight Cup finals, was our new coach. Scotty remained behind the Canadiens bench for eight years, winning five Cups of his own.

In 1978 it came as a shock when Sam Pollock stepped down as general manager, appointing his assistant, Irving Grundman, as his successor and ending thirty-two years of Selke-Pollock stewardship in the front office. Irving had joined the team when the Bronfman family purchased the Canadiens in 1971. A Montreal businessman, he was also a town councillor in suburban Ville St-Laurent.

Still, as was the case when the legendary Toe Blake departed, we managed a Stanley Cup win the following season. The 1979 championship was Scotty's last for the Canadiens, however, and he joined the Buffalo Sabres as their general manager, a week before the NHL meetings and entry draft. For some reason, Irving Grundman was in no rush to name Scotty's replacement and, for the first time, no coach sat at the Canadiens' table during the annual draft that June.

I was a team vice-president by then, and in July I urged Irving to hire someone soon. He said something about taking care of it. Time went by, and in August we spoke again.

"Irving, you've got to get someone in place, to give him a chance to acclimatize to the Canadiens organization and prepare for the new season." We talked for a while, and Irving finally confessed that he was considering Bernie Geoffrion.

Boom Boom had retired from the Canadiens in 1964 after struggling for two years with a pair of bad knee injuries and drastically lowered production. Frank Selke had asked him what he wanted to do.

"I want to coach the Canadiens," he replied, with typical flair.

Papa Frank drily reminded him that the position wasn't vacant, thanks to the presence of one Hector Blake. Boom's salvation lay in the fact that Floyd Curry (who had been coaching the Quebec Aces, now a Montreal farm club) could not speak French, and it was decided that Geoffrion would replace him. Boom later said publicly that he felt he had been promised a shot at coaching the Canadiens when the opportunity arose. He went to Quebec City, coached the Aces to two consecutive first-place finishes but was fired.

Later he told me his version. "I came back to Montreal, and David Molson told me that I could have the Junior Canadiens if I wanted, but I wasn't going to take a step backwards. I told him I was going to un-retire, and that I would return to the Forum and beat his ass." Boom was busily negotiating a deal to play with Harold Ballard's Leafs, which would have been something to see. But the league intervened and the last-place Rangers claimed his playing rights. He signed with them and, in his first game back at the Forum, scored two goals against us.

Geoffrion later coached the Rangers and the expansion Atlanta Flames, but left both jobs for health reasons. Now, Irving Grundman wanted to bring him back to Montreal as head coach, right on the firing line.

At a late-summer meeting when the subject came up again, I told Irving, "I don't think Boom can do the job, for three reasons. First, I don't believe he can fill Scotty's shoes. Second, in New York and Atlanta he developed ulcers from coaching and had to quit. Third, don't forget that his son Danny is on the team. It's always difficult for a coach to have a son or brother out there; he's got enough to worry about as it is." (Danny would play only three seasons in the NHL, retiring from the Winnipeg Jets in 1982.) I gave Irving my honest opinion, but he was the general manager and the final decision was his.

On September 4, ten days before the start of training camp, the media convened in the Forum's Mise au Jeu lounge for a press conference. I was sitting with Toe Blake in the back row when Irving entered the room with Boom Boom. My former roommate wore an

Armani suit and dark glasses. His hair was permed, a popular style at the time. Toe and I looked at each other but said nothing.

Boom's first official statement was one he never should have made, publicly or otherwise.

"Pressure?" he said. "I'm used to it; it doesn't bother me." Conscious of his history in New York and Atlanta, perhaps he thought it was good strategy to pre-empt the obvious question.

About six weeks passed. One November morning before practice, he came to see me. The team was playing like the Keystone Kops; they couldn't seem to do anything right that month. And when the Canadiens are playing poorly, they hear about it everywhere they go. They can't escape a bad performance in Montreal.

"The stress is killing me," he moaned.

"Boom," I reminded him, "it's not good for a coach to quit in the middle of the year, though it depends on what you have in mind for your future. If you quit after a month and a half, you can say goodbye to coaching in this league forever. So try to make it to the end of the year. The organization and I will support you a hundred percent in whatever you do, but don't go now."

Two weeks later, he was back.

"That's it, Jean. I'm going to see Irving."

Boom resigned on December 12, 1979—day 100 of his mandate as Montreal's coach. It was probably the longest hundred days of his life.

When I was speaking with Boom, I couldn't help remembering the very similar conversation I'd had with Claude Ruel in early 1969. He had finally resigned on December 3, 1970. Nine years and nine days later, Irving Grundman introduced the Canadiens' latest new head coach. His name? Claude Ruel.

Since then, the Canadiens have been coached by Bob Berry, Jacques Lemaire, Jean Perron, Pat Burns, Jacques Demers, Mario Tremblay, Alain Vigneault, Michel Therrien, and Claude Julien. Of that group, only Perron and Demers have said they were comfortable with the pressures of coaching in Montreal and dealing with the Montreal media every day.

When I announced my retirement in 1971, I did so very publicly during the NHL meetings in Montreal. I told everyone what my plans were—and weren't: "There are two hockey jobs I don't ever want: coach and general manager." I must have been convincing, because I never received a serious offer of either.

Mind you, I wasn't completely inexperienced in the coaching game. In the 1968 season, the team was playing in Boston. Since I had suffered a minor knee problem in New York the night before, I was sitting out this game in the press box. At intermission, one of the trainers waved to me from the bench.

I went downstairs and Larry Aubut announced, "Toe just got kicked out of the game. You're coaching." We were down 1–0 at that stage, and the Bruins added another early in the second before they took a penalty.

I'd always wondered why Toe never put Jacques Lemaire on the point. The rookie had the best slap shot on the team—hard, heavy, and accurate. Here was a chance to test my theory. I sent him out, and he promptly scored. For the rest of the game, Jacques was on the point for every power play. We won 5–3.

After the game, Toe was sitting in his usual seat at the back of the bus. When I climbed on board, the players spread it on thick: "Coach, where do you want to sit? Up front? Middle? At the back? Can we get you a drink, Coach?" They hammed it up for the longest time, making sure that Toe heard every word.

So why would I ever want to coach again? I'm batting 1.000—one game, one win—and it's always wise to quit while you're ahead.

9

THE BOBBY ORR REVOLUTION

ONE SPRING NIGHT in 1964, we gathered a collection of hockey veterans in Oshawa, Ontario, to honor two of hockey's finest skaters.

One was the fabulous Jo-Jo Graboski, a legend in senior amateur ranks who had played with the Quebec Aces well before my time. Jo-Jo was referred to as "venerable" even in the early 1950s, but Punch Imlach would occasionally ask him to act as the Aces' skating instructor because he had much to teach. He once made a prediction that impresses me still: "Skating is going to become the major factor in this game, you mark my words."

That evening in 1964, after more than a decade had passed, we swapped some Aces and Imlach yarns before the banquet started. Jo-Jo asked if I remembered his prescient analysis.

"Absolutely," I said. "The Canadiens' game has always been built on skating."

Jo-Jo nodded in satisfaction and then nodded again in the direction of another head-table guest, a rather bashful all-Canadian kid with close-cropped blond hair.

"Ah," he said, "but that's the guy who will really make my words come true."

I can't recall who else attended the banquet, but I'll never forget Jo-Jo's words or my first introduction to Robert Gordon Orr. That night, the past and future of brilliant skating met on the same dais, and I felt privileged to witness the event.

Time passes quickly in hockey, and memories are short. Therefore, let me say, for the benefit of the latest generation, that Bobby Orr was a phenomenon equal to, if not greater than, all the "next ones" and "great ones" who have come along since. The stories of his exploits in the junior ranks of the Ontario Hockey League began to circulate when he was just fourteen and competing against players four and five years his senior. Like Gretzky, he was small and light, but Orr played defense, where his slight build was exposed. He stood about five feet, eight inches, and weighed perhaps 140 pounds—much smaller than his opposition. But he starred in every game he played, and everybody, from stick boys to scouts, believed he had a one-way ticket to the NHL. He would later "fill out" as a solid six-footer.

The Boston Bruins stumbled on Orr by accident in 1960 at the Ontario Minor Hockey Association bantam play-downs in Gananoque, Ontario. He was then two inches shorter and thirty pounds lighter, but had so dominated the peewee ranks in his native city of Parry Sound that he'd been moved up into the older age category. Lynn Patrick, the Bruins' general manager, and Wren Blair, then coach and general manager of the Kingston Frontenacs of the Eastern Canada Professional League, attended the bantam play-offs to scout two local defensemen, Rick Eaton and Doug Higgins, who were up against Parry Sound in the first game of the tournament.

Nobody remembers what Eaton and Higgins accomplished that day, because the attention of the Bruins' brain trust was entirely captured by a miniature dynamo who wouldn't let anyone else come near the puck. After a "Who is he?"—"I don't know, I'll find out" exchange with his boss, Blair came back with a name.

The next question was, "Is he sponsored?" In that era, prior to the implementation of the universal draft, NHL teams "owned" territories and sponsored players in regions all over the map. Sometimes their domains overlapped. For example, when the Montreal Royals faced off against the Regina Pats in the 1949 Memorial Cup final, both teams were affiliated with the Montreal Canadiens. When the Citadels played against the Barrie Flyers two years later, we were up against five or six future Boston Bruins.

Blair scurried off to discover if this kid was already sponsored by an NHL club. To his relief, no one had yet claimed him. On that day, unknown to the Orr family and the rest of the hockey community, Boston began a low-key but determined campaign to acquire the talented youngster and to secure his signature on a Junior A card. They started off with goodwill gestures: funding was provided for the Parry Sound Minor Hockey Association, and Blair's Kingston team "dropped in" to the city for exhibition games. Later, Blair made regular visits to the Orr family home and established a relationship with Bobby's parents, Doug and Arva.

The secret couldn't, and didn't, last long. A Canadiens scout had attended the bantam championships and reported back to Frank Selke. While Bobby continued his stellar play over the next two seasons, Scotty Bowman was sent to check him out, and both Detroit and Chicago made overtures by telephone. Ironically, it was the Toronto Maple Leafs who paid the least attention to the gold mine in their own backyard.

In August 1962, Blair's persistence bore fruit. He persuaded the Orrs to allow their fourteen-year-old son to attend a junior tryout camp sponsored by the Bruins in Niagara Falls. Despite his agreement, Doug Orr worried how his son might fare against the bigger boys. Bobby, however, was the revelation of the camp, even though some of the older players had obviously targeted him for special attention. After a summer of anxiety and suspense, the Bruins finally signed him to the coveted Junior A card and assigned him to the Oshawa Generals of the Ontario Hockey League.

In his first year, he scored thirteen goals and earned a spot on the OHL's second all-star team. A year later, he scored thirty, breaking the league record held by Jacques Laperrière and making sports headlines all across Canada. Barely sixteen, he also became a story in the United States, where the Bruins had been floundering dismally. In 1959–60, they wound up in fifth place, miles out of the play-offs, and followed that with five straight last-place finishes. In 1965, Lynn Patrick was replaced as general manager by Hap Emms, and the pressure was on to sign the youthful savior as soon as possible.

The Boston organization was convinced that Orr had the talent to make the jump to the NHL, even at age sixteen. The theory was that his gifts would be better utilized, and he would develop more rapidly at a level where everyone played his caliber of game. He was clearly too good for his minor-league competition and might start to stagnate or coast if no one pushed him to greater heights. It was the same reasoning I had followed in my career: when possible, move up and play with and against better players. Once you've bested your regular competition, you will stop improving.

Bobby's parents rightly resisted placing their son in the NHL, pointing out that sixteen was much too young to take on the strongest hockey players in the world, none of whom appeared to be playing for Boston. But the Bruins finished second last in 1966, prompting their restive fans to look northward to a far-off Toronto suburb for salvation. In the meantime, Bobby wasn't coasting in Oshawa. In his final two seasons, he scored seventy-one goals and 119 assists. Although suffering a groin injury, he led the Generals to the Memorial Cup final against Edmonton, where they lost a close series in six games.

Bobby's first legacy to the NHL was a gift to every player, the result of his father's determination, like my father's, that his son would have financial security, respect, and freedom of choice. In the spring of 1966, Hap Emms seemed to do everything he could to alienate the Orrs. He ordered Bobby not to play in the Memorial Cup final against Edmonton because of his injury, even though Bobby was determined to appear and, in fact, did so. Emms also submitted an insultingly low contract offer for his future star.

In Bobby's final season with Oshawa, the media routinely referred to him as the Bruins' "million-dollar superstar-in-waiting." So when Doug and Bobby first met Emms to discuss a contract, they were flabbergasted by his offer of $8,000 in salary and a $5,000 signing bonus. Emms further antagonized them by citing the example of Gilles Marotte, another prospect from Quebec discovered by Roland Mercier: the previous year, Marotte had let the Bruins decide for him what a fair salary should be. Emms rather loftily suggested that Bobby should do likewise until he proved himself with the team.

The Orrs walked out and returned with Alan Eagleson in tow. The Toronto lawyer had begun to make a reputation for himself by representing Maple Leafs such as Carl Brewer, Mike Walton, and Bob Pulford. When Emms discovered that all future negotiations would be conducted through Eagleson, he balked, and most of the summer passed without further contact.

Eagleson, no stranger to the theory and practice of well-placed publicity, let it be known that he was negotiating with Father David Bauer's Canadian national team for Orr's services. (This was within the realm of possibility. When Punch Imlach and Carl Brewer became embroiled in a contract dispute that same fall, Brewer left the Leafs for "amateur" hockey.) The Boston papers picked up the story, and Emms was caught in a tornado of adverse comment, as Eagleson had intended.

On Labor Day weekend in 1966, Emms sailed into Parry Sound harbor, and, after an all-night negotiation session chaired by Eagleson on Emms's boat, Bobby Orr joined the Boston Bruins. He did a little better than Emms's original $13,000 offer, signing a two-year deal for approximately $70,000, bonuses and incentive clauses included. That contract resulted in many league stars winning salary increases in the next two years, myself included. The deal also firmly established Alan Eagleson as a player agent. Later that year Eagleson began to lay the foundation of what would become the NHL Players' Association.

Bobby was all of eighteen years old when he started with Boston, but I can honestly say that I have never seen another player of that age with his maturity and hockey sense. He scored his first career goal in the NHL against us, in his second-ever game. It came on a slap shot from the blue line and raised eyebrows and the roof at the Boston Gardens. The game was played on a slow Thursday in early October, but the arena erupted in a long and drawn-out standing ovation that had Toe Blake saying, "I ain't ever seen anything like it."

Toe was describing the crowd's response, but his words might just as well have applied to Bobby, who went on to win the 1967 Calder Trophy as the league's top rookie that season. Of course, he alone could not salvage the Bruins, and they once again finished in the league basement. But the following season was a different story, as Boston finished third in the East Division. Three years later, we were fighting Boston for our play-off lives. They had found Phil Esposito, Ken Hodge, Wayne Cashman, Johnny McKenzie, Dallas Smith, Gerry Cheevers, and Don Awrey to support their superstar defenseman.

Like any of us, Bobby had his ups and downs. He was the finest player of his era, but he would suffer occasional bad games, and the people he made mistakes against were superb players themselves, capable of capitalizing quickly. It simply proved he was human.

In his early days, too many opponents on the ice and critics in the stands were looking for feet of clay. He took unnecessary chances, they said. He got caught up-ice. He was weak inside his own zone. He held on to the puck too much. Yet, watching him play and playing against him, I knew right away that his was a special talent. Also, having experienced the same seesaw of big buildup and big criticism in my early years in the league, I knew what he was going through and sympathized.

Later, sports journalists would employ a familiar technique to sucker NHL players into knocking Orr, with questions like: "What are Orr's weaknesses? What do the Canadiens see in his game that you can exploit?" I always refused to bite on that particular hook. I knew from close-up observation that Bobby Orr could be his own toughest critic. Sometimes, after making a mistake on the ice he would go back to his bench and rage at himself. But I also noticed that he did something only the greatest players do: he corrected his errors and didn't repeat them. Orr knew better than most that there was no such thing as a perfect hockey player, but in my opinion he came as close as anyone who played in the NHL.

Earlier I wrote that I regard Doug Harvey as the league's best ever all-round defenseman, able to dictate the terms of any game in which he played. Defensively, Orr was second to Harvey in that respect: in fact, another Boston player, Eddie Shore, might claim the number 2 spot.

Simply put, however, Bobby Orr had the greatest impact of any player to come along in my lifetime. He earned his place in hockey history by single-handedly changing the style of play, and hence the game itself, forever. In my mind, there can be no greater legacy. What is most remarkable is that he accomplished it in fewer than ten full seasons, before being betrayed by knees that, while braced by six operations, finally collapsed under the relentless punishment of the sport. Bobby's premature retirement at the age of thirty is one of the saddest episodes in the modern NHL.

How did Bobby Orr change hockey? He redefined the defenseman's position, allowing him a new, more aggressive offensive role, and opening the door for all-out attacks off quick transitions. His rushing exploits made it difficult, if not impossible, for defensive teams to zero in on Boston's forwards. Bobby could race ahead of the play, immediately putting pressure on our defensemen while catching forwards off guard. Or he could come from behind a screen of teammates, cut left or right at speed and draw two or three defenders to him before laying off a pass to a Bruin in the clear. Prior to his arrival in the league, defensemen rarely "jumped up" into the play. Rearguards were supposed to "head-man" the puck, quickly getting it up to fast-breaking forwards, while slowly following—not leading—the play up the ice.

The greatest change in the game in the last thirty-five years is this vastly increased mobility of defensemen. Before Orr, defensemen generally were large, husky guys, heavy hitters who for the most part moved slowly and awkwardly. Naturally, if a defenseman was a lumbering skater, he wouldn't be able to join in the offensive flow. He'd be constantly backing up or standing still, incapable of coming up to challenge an attacking forward.

Slow skaters are always at a disadvantage, no matter what their position. If a player slows down at the opponent's blue line, his pass, his shot, and his moves will all be slow. But if he's skating as Orr did, all his moves are executed at the same high speed: carrying the puck, stickhandling, and releasing the shot. Orr set the pace not only of his games but of all future games, by cranking up the speed of play to previously unknown levels.

In addition to his speed, Orr was good in all departments, a master of all the game's technical skills. Harry Sinden offered perhaps the best comparison of Orr, Gordie Howe, and Bobby Hull: Howe could do everything, but he couldn't do it quickly; Hull had great speed but couldn't do everything; Orr, however, could do everything at high speed, which changed the rules forever.

Orr created problems that opposing teams had never before encountered. For example, when the face-off was in our defensive end, the right- or left-winger (depending on where the face-off took place) would go directly to the point. With Orr on the ice, wingers would have to be in motion sooner, while Boston's wingers would block them and give Bobby more time and space to wreak havoc just inside the blue line. This disrupted our strategy in a way that the fans could not appreciate at first. When the Bruins faced off in our zone, it didn't matter who they had up front—Esposito, Hodge, Cashman, Bucyk, or McKenzie. How we lined up was dictated by one factor: the position of Bobby Orr. When the puck was dropped, our attention was divided, with nervous glances in Orr's direction predominating.

Don Cherry tells a funny story about the players' attitudes to Bobby. "We were playing the Washington Caps, and Bobby was out for a face-off. The Caps' center was lining up his players around the face-off circle and motioned to a rookie defenseman to stand over to the right. At that moment the rookie looked at Bobby, but Bobby shook his head and told him to go back over to his left. The kid did it! He thought so much of Bobby that he knew Bobby wouldn't lie to him. And Bobby didn't—the puck went to the kid."

Bobby's talent led to other changes, as well. For many years, the strategic standby was man-to-man or man-on-man defense. This meant that we would pick up our assigned man as he came out of his zone and into ours. It was difficult to cover defensemen, however, because they'd normally be so far behind the play. Quite often, the plan was to get back to our blue line quickly and "stand up" the attackers there. If the other team managed to set up inside our zone, our wingers would generally cover the point men.

According to orthodox thinking, when we were forechecking attacking forwards or defensemen in their defensive zone, we might put one or two forwards in deep to press, with the third stationed out high near the blue line to cut off breakout passes. When defensemen were slow, this scheme worked well. When Orr arrived, it went right out the window. He could easily sidestep one or two forecheckers and lead a four-on-three or other odd-man rush. Toe Blake always counseled us not to let Orr get wound up in his own end, because that's where he gathered his speed. If he got going and the play ended up in our end, the wingman would have to favor him, which would sometimes provide an opening for one of the Boston forwards.

Orr was closely watched, but we couldn't watch him in the same way as, say, Claude Provost did when he was shadowing Bobby Hull. Orr was a defenseman and a beautiful playmaker at the same time. If you went in too deep after him, he had the skill to pull back a little, feed a perfect pass to a winger, and trap the forechecker. That puck would be on his teammate's blade, not in his skates or out of reach too far ahead.

Killing penalties against Boston was difficult, as well. In a regular power-play defense, the forwards place themselves between the point men and the wingers on their side, observing their usual lane boundaries. If Orr was out there, we'd naturally lean toward him more, which would open up ice from the middle to the deep end of our zone. Even if we were outnumbered "down low" in the process and the Bruins scored, we wouldn't change that strategy. It was important to favor Orr rather than a winger, no matter how good the forward was, because Orr proved capable of getting off a dangerous number of shots.

In the 1969 semifinal against Boston, we were tied after four games and returned to Montreal for game 5. En route to our Laurentian retreat at La Sapinière, I began to read the game summaries and noticed that Orr was taking a lot of shots from the point. He had scored the winning goal in game 4 after Gerry Cheevers had somehow managed to get his glove on the puck after a hard shot by Yvan Cournoyer. Bobby took the rebound, raced up the ice, and put the game away. We had to intensify our approach and free our defenders from their lanes.

"The four defensive players should be aware of his presence at all times," I told my teammates. "He's getting seven, eight, and nine shots a game." To contain Orr, our checkers had to take different angles on him, constantly attacking him from all directions and forcing him to be on his guard through a full 360-degree compass on the ice.

Bobby was all of twenty years old that season, and most of our game plan involved neutralizing him. For the next few games, that's exactly what we did, and we cut down on his offense from the point. But he was good all over the ice.

Despite these woes, we had plenty of success against the Bruins. The Orr-Esposito editions never beat us in the play-offs, although they did win the Cup in 1970 and 1972 when we weren't there to face them. I always thought that, man for man, we had the edge in skating. With players like Cournoyer, Jacques Lemaire, Frank Mahovlich, Claude Provost, Henri Richard, Ralph Backstrom, Mickey Redmond, Chuck Lefley, Bobby Rousseau, Réjean Houle, and Marc Tardif up front, and Guy Lapointe, Serge Savard, Terry Harper, and Jacques Laperrière on the back line, we could play the game at Bobby's pace. Our strategy was to play a tight, careful first period. If we could stay within one goal of the Bruins, we'd get our legs back in the second and third periods and surge ahead.

When Orr started having serious knee problems, he lost a bit of speed, which certainly affected his game. Being an offensive-minded defenseman, it was very difficult for him to see an opening and not go for it. But even when he started to slow, he was head and shoulders above the competition—which explains his eight Norris Trophy selections in a row as the NHL's top defenseman. I was also impressed by the fact that Orr seemed to be well liked by his teammates and was regarded as a team man by everyone who played with him.

Of course, it wasn't long before other defensemen sought to emulate him, players such as my younger teammates Serge Savard and Guy Lapointe, and New York's Brad Park. Within a few years, a stream of talents who'd been profoundly affected by his example flowed into the NHL, players like Larry Robinson, Ray Bourque, Doug

Wilson, Paul Coffey, Sergei Zubov, and Borje Salming. And since their heyday, an entire generation of defenders has come and gone with Orr's stamp on it—Chris Chelios, Phil Housley, Al MacInnis, Brian Leetch, Jeff Brown, Gary Suter, Steve Duchesne, Larry Murphy, Al Iafrate, Kevin Hatcher, Rob Blake, Scott Niedermayer, Nicklas Lidstrom, and Bryan Fogarty. A few, like Housley, Brown, Fogarty, and Leetch, reminded me of Bobby in terms of acceleration and offensive skills, but none possessed what I call the complete package.

The only defender I believe could match Orr for speed was Paul Coffey, even though their styles were radically different. Coffey skated with his knees bent, almost in a sitting position. Orr's posture was more upright, even at full speed.

Players like Denis Potvin and Larry Robinson were great defensemen, with a predominantly physical style. They could control the game, but they lacked Orr's speed. Indeed, Potvin resembles Ray Bourque more than Orr, especially in terms of strength, endurance, and the quick release each had with the puck.

Potvin has acknowledged his debt to Doug Harvey, as well. As recently as the spring of 2005, Denis was quoted in the Montreal *Gazette* recalling that Harvey's style was often invoked by his coach in junior with the Ottawa 67s. "Another thing I remember [being told]... when he was going up the ice, Harvey always had the puck in front of him, not to one side or the other. That meant he could make his pass or take a shot efficiently with either the backhand or the forehand."

In the same article, Potvin described the defenseman's range in terms that were eerily familiar. "One thing you have to learn is that you may not be the fastest skater in the world, but there is no out-of-bounds in hockey. There is a point where that really fast skater has to turn and come to you. That's what positioning was all about." I could see Toe Blake standing in front of a blackboard, saying much the same. He would draw an hourglass on the board. "This is what a real hockey rink is shaped like." It was Toe's way of saying that this was the area in which the game was effectively played. All the rest was "wasted ice."

Further evidence of Bobby's influence is found in the scoring statistics. In 1,113 games over nineteen seasons, Doug Harvey scored eighty-eight goals and had a total of 540 points. I had to look it up. If you'd asked me beforehand whether he had scored more or fewer than one hundred career goals, I'd have said more, by far. In fact, the most he managed in a single season was nine, and he never accumulated more than fifty points in a year. Tom Johnson, another excellent Hall of Fame defenseman, totalled only fifty-one goals in sixteen seasons.

Enter Bobby Orr. In just 657 regular-season games, he turned in 915 points, a phenomenal 1.39-points-per-game average. In six of his NHL seasons he accumulated point totals of 139, 135, 122, 120, 117, and 101. In five of them, he racked up 102, 90, 89, 87, and 80 assists, breaking all records for defensemen. He did something no other defenseman has ever done, before or since: he won the scoring championship, and he won it twice. In 1970, he received the Norris (top defenseman), Art Ross (scoring championship), Hart (most valuable player), and Conn Smythe (play-off MVP) Trophies and was named Canadian Sportsman of the Year. He was twenty-one years old.

Even the statistics of others reveal the Orr effect. During the 1993–94 season, Paul Coffey became the first defenseman to surpass my 1,219 total career points. I was fifteenth overall when that season began, and everyone else on the list was a forward, like me. In 1985–86, Paul scored forty-eight goals; two seasons before that, he'd bagged forty. His output in those two seasons alone equaled Doug Harvey's entire career scoring tally.

Ray Bourque was the next defenseman to leave me in his wake, and a bunch of players, Mario Lemieux and Mike Gartner among them, led a cavalry charge of talented "offensemen" who went by me in the 1990s.

The transformation of the 1980s and 1990s is also reflected in the rise in netminders' lifetime goals-against averages. Ken Dryden's was 2.24; Jacques Plante's, 2.38; Glenn Hall's, 2.51; Terry Sawchuk's and Johnny Bower's were 2.52, and Bernie Parent finished at 2.55.

Going into 1993–94, Ed Belfour's stood at 2.70; Patrick Roy's, 2.79; Curtis Joseph's, 3.06; Mike Richter's, 3.27; Ron Hextall's, 3.30; Andy Moog's, 3.32; Kirk McLean's 3.35; Bill Ranford's, 3.43; John Vanbiesbrouck's, 3.45; Kelly Hrudey's, 3.48, and Grant Fuhr's was 3.64.

A decade later, a defensive trend was definitely re-established. Some of these goalies had recently retired, while others were still playing, but the career numbers were lower again: Belfour was down to 2.43; Roy, 2.54; Joseph, 2.75; Richter, 2.89; Hextall, 2.98; Hrudey, 3.43, and Fuhr, 3.38.

Roughly speaking, the average difference between these last two sets of figures is somewhere between a goal and two, and the most significant influence on each is the advent of bigger, more skilled and mobile defensemen. In the 1970s and early 1980s, suddenly mobile defensemen led to swollen offensive statistics. Then, when all defensemen learned to play both ends of the new game, the defensive side reasserted itself.

And it's all because a defenseman from Parry Sound liked to skate fast and carry the puck.

WE CAN'T LEAVE A discussion of Bobby Orr without examining the world of the attacking hockey player, and how more mobility on the blue line meant more mobility all over the ice. This was especially true for centers. Now that defensemen could jump up into the attack, offenses were five-on-five, or four-on-five, involving a lot more skating and more intricate patterns of attacking play.

The new attackers traveled in all directions, rather than simply north-south; it was not unusual to see centers cycle with mobile defensemen, circling and switching places on the ice in mid-play to gain advantage against the defenders. And, as centers might be caught in a defensive position by counterattacking opponents, it would be to their advantage to be big, fast and strong, like the defensemen they were replacing if only for a few seconds.

An ironic side effect of the post-Orr mobilization of defensemen is that offenses boomed all over the league. It would take almost two decades for the neutral zone trap and other collective defensive tactics to control runaway scoring. More on this in a later chapter.

As a former center, I cannot help but be impressed by the legacies of Wayne Gretzky and Mario Lemieux, two remarkably talented but dissimilar players, and by present-day superstars like Peter Forsberg, Sergei Fedorov, Mike Modano, and Joe Sakic, to name a few.

The first thing I noted about Wayne Gretzky was that he had adapted his size and style to the modern game. If he'd played in our time, he would have been checked very closely and probably more effectively than he experienced in his day. He would have been relieved to see less stickwork in the six-team league, but we knew how to check a player like Gretzky in other ways. I doubt he would have enjoyed two-hundred-point seasons back then. Very few of our games were lopsided 10–2 blowouts; 3–2 or 3–1 scores were far more common. Still, he'd have won the scoring title more than once, especially if he'd played with a solid supporting cast.

I've frequently been asked if I could find any fault with the play of "the Great One," and the answer is always no. He could make those exquisite soft passes right on the stick. I used to tell my wingers, "When you see I'm not free, keep skating. I'll push it up ahead of you. Find the opening and we'll make a play." Gretzky could make that play as if by instinct, anticipating the intended's position with uncanny accuracy. He had great peripheral vision on the ice, and if a teammate was about to get open, he'd find him, a lot like Norm Ullman used to do.

What I liked most about Gretzky was his obvious unselfishness. It used to be said that I passed the puck too much, and no doubt Gretzky heard the same thing. But as a centerman, it was his job to make those passes.

I liked what I saw of Gretzky away from the rink, as well. He's a gentleman and lives his life responsibly, and clearly his family is enormously important to him. I have a lot of admiration for his efforts to promote the game, too. It seems that from a young age, Wayne understood he had two contributions to make as an outstanding hockey player: his memorable and record-breaking performance on ice, and his off-ice ability to sell the game across North America and in particular in the major United States markets. He was the NHL's premier pitchman throughout his playing career, especially during his days in Los Angeles, St. Louis, and New York. Mario Lemieux's courageous battles against back injuries and Hodgkin's disease prove that he's made of stern stuff as well as being a fantastic talent. Mario is probably the present-day player closest to me in style, and I'm delighted that people have compared us. I concentrated on taking advantage of my long reach to make plays all over the ice, along the boards and in the corners, starting from the right side. I've seen Mario—a right-hand shot to my left-hand shot—do the same thing on the opposite side.

Some have complained that Mario doesn't pass enough, but that's ludicrous. Just ask his wingers Kevin Stevens (fifty-five goals and fifty-six assists in 1992–93) and Rick Tocchet (forty-eight goals and sixty-one assists that same season) whether Mario passed enough for their liking, even while missing twenty-four games due to injury.

The Canadiens tried to secure Mario in 1984 when he was with the Laval Voisins of the Quebec Major Junior Hockey League. The trade of Pierre Larouche to the Hartford Whalers in December 1981 for a switch of first-round picks in 1984 was Montreal's first step toward this end. The Whalers were near the bottom of the NHL heap, and had they continued their downward spiral to the bottom of the league standings, Montreal would have owned the first overall pick in the "Lemieux draft," as it became known. But the Whalers rose in the standings, finishing fifth from the bottom, and the last-place Penguins claimed Mario's services.

Perhaps this was just as well. If Mario had become a Canadien, he would have had to suffer through a year or two of Béliveau and Richard comparisons. Moreover, the Montreal fans would have made heavy demands on his off-ice time, and he has proved to be shy of the spotlight's glare and of public events in Pittsburgh.

There are several other powerful centers today who have not been able to avoid comparison with me. The most obvious is Eric Lindros, whom Maurice Richard once called a "mean" Jean Béliveau. While I always hesitated to differ with Rocket, I don't think our styles are similar at all. Eric looks and plays like a tank and is not all that smooth when it comes to face-offs and playmaking. He plays a much more physical game than I did; sadly, he has suffered the injuries to prove it.

Before joining the Flyers, Eric had played well with the Canadian team in the 1991 Canada Cup. He laid some spectacular hits on several European players, causing injuries. "That's trouble," was my first reaction, and I think my early opinion was vindicated by what has happened since. He's now a Ranger and his career is in jeopardy after a series of spectacular concussions. His younger brother, Brett, ended his career prematurely because of concussions.

There are plenty more wonderfully skilled centers in the game today, and they are a pleasure to watch. High among them has been Ottawa native Steve Yzerman, a very fluid and intelligent player. He's a beautiful skater and a great playmaker, with quick hands, not only around the net, but also for making a play. He lays a good pass out there for his wingers and will almost always find the player who has shed his checker.

His former teammate, Sergei Fedorov, moved into the top ranks of the league over the last decade. Similar to Yzerman in many ways, he's even more of a defensive talent, which makes him a valuable commodity in today's NHL. The Yzerman-Fedorov combination was probably the best one-two center pairing since Wayne Gretzky and Mark Messier of the Oilers' glory years and the Pittsburgh duo of Mario Lemieux and Ron Francis, recalling a time when most teams had two or three stars in the middle.

When Francis played with Hartford between 1982 and 1991, he was that team's offensive star. Some observers argued that he cared most about his statistics, but when he moved to Pittsburgh he showed his true character. He took on a defensive role behind Mario Lemieux and became an important member of that team. I remember when the Penguins were trying to avoid elimination by the Islanders in the seventh game of the 1993 play-offs: Francis kept rallying his teammates, tying the game in the final moments of regulation time, before the Isles prevailed in overtime. He seemed to take that loss harder than any of his teammates.

He delivered the goods with Hartford and Pittsburgh over the long term before wrapping up his career with the Toronto Maple Leafs in the 2004 play-offs: Francis is the answer to a terrific trivia question; even veteran hockey fans are astonished to find that he retired with the number 5 ranking in the NHL scoring list with 1,798 career points, higher than Marcel Dion, Phil Esposito, and a raft of others.

Lemieux and Francis won two Stanley Cups in the early 1990s. Two players who mirrored the Yzerman-Fedorov matchup, Joe Sakic and Peter Forsberg, captured two championships for the Colorado Avalanche in the mid-1990s. It became obvious that teams had trouble defending against an opposition with two superstars at center.

A trio of American-born centers showed me how much the game has developed south of the border: Chicago's Jeremy Roenick, Buffalo's Pat LaFontaine, and Mike Modano of Minnesota/Dallas. Roenick is a fine, dedicated player who is not afraid of the traffic. If the opposition gets lazy and tries to check him with the end of the stick, or if they give him too much open ice, they'll pay for it. Roenick skates well and has a very quick release on his shot.

LaFontaine and Modano went in opposite directions in 1993–94. LaFontaine was plagued by injuries that would lead to his premature retirement, while Modano had the season of his career. Modano is big and strong, a hard worker, who had the good fortune to be coached by Bob Gainey and Ken Hitchcock. Every year he's become a better two-way player without losing his offensive game, and in 1998 he led the Dallas Stars to the Stanley Cup.

The latest generation of superb young centers includes Joe Thornton, Vincent Lecavalier, Pavel Datsyuk, Jason Spezza, Olli Jokinen, and Brad Richards. It will be a pleasure to see what they bring to the sport in the coming years.

THE LAST OF BOBBY'S legacies came long after he and the players who were in the league when he arrived had retired. As I've mentioned, Orr's hiring of Alan Eagleson was a watershed in the 1960s, and it paved the way for the representation of players' interests by professional agents. That, in turn, led to more money for all of us.

In December 1966, the Bruins were in Montreal. Bobby was having dinner with Eagleson at the Queen Elizabeth Hotel when two of his teammates appeared at the table and asked them to join them upstairs. Eagleson was surprised to find the entire Boston team gathered in Bobby's room, and he was overwhelmed when they asked him to form a players' association. Within a year, nearly every player in every NHL club had joined his National Hockey League Players' Association (NHLPA).

But Eagleson had proceeded cautiously, and he had left the Canadiens until last because he was wary of me as captain and of my position in the Canadiens' organization. Montreal's management had always taken good care of its players. We went first class all the way and were considered to be a pretty conservative bunch, content with our situation. Eagleson assumed that he'd have a tough time selling us on the idea of an association.

I remember our first meeting very clearly. My teammates listened as Eagleson talked and talked, pushing a bit too hard, perhaps because he'd misinterpreted success as complacence. As captain, I'd always felt that I had to be as objective as possible, to say and do what was right for the team whether or not I agreed as an individual.

After Eagleson had spoken for about an hour, I got up and said that I was in favor of the Canadiens joining the NHLPA. "It will be good for you young guys," I said.

Eagleson didn't know that one of the reasons for the team's success was that everyone was free to speak his mind. All in all, I still believe that the NHLPA helped the players, especially in its early years—just as, at one point, Alan Eagleson was good for hockey.

A great deal has been written about Eagleson and John Ziegler, the Detroit lawyer who was league president from 1977 to 1992, and about the roles they played in the development of the NHL and professional hockey in general throughout the 1970s and 1980s. A lot more has been written about Eagleson's eventual falling out with Bobby Orr and the later charges of racketeering and fraud brought against Eagleson in the United States and Canada. His subsequent guilty plea to Canadian charges led to an eighteen-month jail sentence, disbarment, and resignation from the Hockey Hall of Fame.

If I have a personal quarrel with Alan Eagleson, it relates to the management of the NHL players' pension fund, a story to come in a later chapter.

THE SECOND FLOOR

FOR THOSE CANADIENS who decide to hang up their skates, then agree to wear a suit for the team, promotion to the front office—also known as "the Second Floor"—is usually announced at the retirement press conference. In my case, however, the foundation for such a relationship had been laid in the days when I was playing with the Quebec Aces.

In late 1951 or early 1952, I was visited by Zotique Lespérance after one of our games. At that time Zotique wore three hats: newspaper columnist with *La Patrie*, broadcaster with CKAC radio in Montreal, and vice-president of sales and public affairs with Molson's Brewery Limited, as the company was then called. What might sound to us today like a bundle of conflicting interests was relatively commonplace back then; journalists were poorly paid and many moonlighted where they could, sometimes supplementing their income by serving as part-time public relations consultants for sports teams or commercial sponsors.

"I'm not here tonight as a sportswriter or broadcaster," Zotique said with a chuckle. "I'm here as a delegate of Molson's Brewery. We've been watching you. If you ever decide to come to Montreal, we'll have a job for you."

I was nonplussed by his offer—I didn't know a thing about the beer business—but it stuck in my mind. That summer, back in Victoriaville for the off-season, I looked up a local hotel owner who was also a close friend of my family. I told him about Zotique's invitation.

"In my position, I should not favor any one company," he told me. "I sell every product and I've dealt with all of the breweries. But if you're asking me as a friend, I'd say it's a good idea to go with Molson. It's a family-run company, and they have a reputation for being very fair with their people."

What I didn't comprehend entirely, of course, was that Molson's was interested in me for several reasons: I was the right athlete (a prominent French-Canadian hockey star) in the right place (Quebec City, but Montreal-bound) at the right time (just as television was discovering the world of sports, and as the province of Quebec was discovering television).

In 1952, Molson's marketing and sales managers had decided to concentrate on television to promote their product lines. Molson's and Imperial Oil co-sponsored Canadiens games on radio, but Imperial Oil took the lion's share of the available advertising time. If Imperial was unwilling to take a chance on TV, Molson's was prepared to jump in. If Imperial maintained its dominance there as well, Molson's would remain as secondary sponsor but would seek primary sponsorship of the Quebec Senior Hockey League's Sunday afternoon telecasts.

Frank Selke, the Canadiens' general manager, was the man with his finger on the switch. If Molson's could help him, he would be disposed to help them. Zotique Lespérance talked to Selke in the summer of 1953 and proposed a mutually beneficial deal.

"I'm off to Quebec City, where I'm going to offer Jean Béliveau a position with the brewery, starting in the fall," Zotique said. "After a training period, he will become a full-timer in our sales promotion department. Whether he does well with the *bleu-blanc-rouge* or not, he'll still be our employee. We have a reputation for keeping our people." This was no exaggeration. At that time, Molson's was one of the few major corporations in Montreal with a "cradle-to-grave" employment policy. Others included Canadian National and Canadian Pacific railways, Bell Telephone, Northern Electric, and Canadian Marconi.

Selke's ears perked up when Zotique added what proved to be an attractive carrot. "Of course, he will work for us in Montreal during his trainee period." Then followed the stick: "In exchange for bringing him here from Quebec City, we want you to sell us the television rights for the senior-league games at the Forum on Sunday afternoons."

"My friend," Selke replied, "that's a bargain, and I'm going to hold you to it."

Back in the provincial capital, Zotique made his case to me on August 9. "Jean," he said, "this means job security for you. You will start at $10,000 a year, plus benefits, a pension plan, and health and dental coverage, which is certainly far above scale for a trainee." He was right: in 1953, a $10,000 salary was almost triple the amount needed to raise a family of four in middle-class comfort. Four days later, I was in Montreal, in the offices of Hartland de Montarville Molson. We sealed the deal with a handshake and began a business relationship that lasted for decades.

Later that afternoon, Zotique hustled off to the Forum. "Frank, Jean will begin work in Montreal for Molson in October."

"Zotique, you have your senior-league TV advertising rights."

Six weeks later, I signed with the Canadiens a five-year contract that would pay me a total of $105,000 in salary and bonuses. That same month, I started work at Molson's, and for the next eighteen years I was in double harness. It wasn't small-time or occasional employment with the brewery; I was a full-time Molson's employee who happened to have special dispensation to play hockey for the Montreal Canadiens. The distinction between my two employers blurred in 1957 when Thomas and Hartland Molson cemented ties with the club by purchasing Canadian Arena Company, the corporate entity that owned the team and the Forum, from Senator Donat Raymond.

Although I was one of the NHL's best-paid players from the start of my career, my hockey salary alone in no way guaranteed that I was "fixed for life." No player of my era was in that position. Molson's, thankfully, presented the opportunity to develop a second, parallel career long before I had to consider retirement from the game. Needless to say, I jumped at the chance.

When the Canadiens were at home, we practiced in the mornings and wrapped up by noon. I would shower, don my suit, and go to my office. My first few years were spent at what I call Molson Business School. Every year I "majored" in something new, working in their marketing, production, distribution, or public relations departments. As time went by, my responsibilities increased, and by 1962 I was sports promotions director for Molson Lévis Limitée, a division based in Quebec City. Eventually, Élise and I purchased a second home in Ste-Foy, just west of the *vieille capitale,* and lived there for five months of the year. Every year, in September, I reported to the Canadiens' training camp in Montreal.

In May 1964, the company announced several executive appointments at Molson (Québec) Limitée: Charles L. Dumais became chairman of the board, Paul Falardeau was named executive vice-president and general manager, and I became vice-president.

Recently, I came upon a photograph of the three of us taken during the press conference in Montreal, seated at a table with David

Molson, a cousin of the senator and president of Canadian Arena Company. We were energetic, serious, and capable, prepared to do great things for the company. Barely three weeks after this photo was taken, Charles Dumais died, tragically young. He was sleeping on his boat, which was moored in the St. Lawrence River at Sorel, when he was overcome by fumes from the vessel's gas heater. It was a great loss to the company and to his hometown, Quebec City. Charles was well respected and would have done great things had he lived.

WHEN I PUT MY PLAYING days behind me in 1971, I was able to look back on the experiences and memories of not one but two careers. In "retirement," my plan had been to continue with the brewery, but David Molson and Canadiens' general manager Sam Pollock persuaded me otherwise.

"Hockey is changing," David said. "There will be a lot of marketing to be done for every professional sport, not just hockey. You're going to be the Canadiens' spokesman."

I appreciated his logic and I was willing to give the marketing side of hockey a try. In reality, as team captain, I'd been the Canadiens' spokesman for a decade already. Arrangements were made for the transfer of my Molson pension plan and benefits package, and in June 1971 I moved into the Canadiens' front office as vice-president of corporate affairs, across the hall from Sam.

It was easy to accept the new position. I had great respect for David and great admiration for Sam, perhaps the finest hockey man who ever existed—and I say that knowing that Frank Selke preceded him. When people asked how the Canadiens sustained their success over such a long period, my answer was immediate: Selke and Pollock. Together they oversaw the club's fortunes for thirty-three seasons, from 1946 to 1978.

I first met and played against Sam Pollock's teams in junior. His Junior Canadiens won the Memorial Cup in 1950; in the early 1960s, he moved up to the Eastern Professional Hockey League with the Hull-Ottawa Canadiens. I admired not only his supreme hockey knowledge, but also his ability to shoulder a tremendous workload. Whenever a deal beckoned, Sam would go day and night until it was resolved, leaving no detail to chance nor any opportunity for the other side to develop cold feet. He selected hockey players in his own image, those who combined talent with hard work—which, when you think about it, is a short but apt definition of a winner. Sam was a motivator long before the word became overused. Watching him run as hard as he did always got others moving.

In a long career, Sam earned everything he achieved. He started at the bottom of the Canadiens' organization as a scout and coached his way up through the junior, senior, and minor-professional ranks before becoming assistant general manager and director of player personnel. In 1964 he replaced his boss, Frank Selke.

I knew that Sam, along with David Molson, offered the best education in sports administration available at the time. The list of future NHL coaches and general managers who have passed through Pollock University is long and impressive and includes Cliff Fletcher (St. Louis, Atlanta, Calgary, Toronto), John Ferguson (New York, Winnipeg, Ottawa), "Professor" Ron Caron (St. Louis), Scotty Bowman (St. Louis, Buffalo, Pittsburgh, Detroit), Bob Gainey (Minnesota, Dallas, Montreal), and Jacques Lemaire (New Jersey, Minnesota).

Sam not only built the Canadiens, he helped build the National Hockey League. When the league was contemplating expansion in 1964–65, it asked a general managers' committee headed by Sam to study the viability of such a move. The committee recommended that the league double in size to include franchises in major American markets in California (Los Angeles and Oakland), the Midwest (Minnesota and St. Louis), and the industrial east (Pittsburgh and

Philadelphia). It was the only way the league could hope to secure a network television contract.

The committee further recommended that those new teams be stocked with quality players and begin play in their own division to ensure they would not be relegated to second-division status in the first decade of post-expansion play. That's how the league's West Division came into being and why Scotty Bowman's veteran-laden St. Louis Blues ended up against the Canadiens in the 1967–68 and 1968–69 Cup finals.

Sam also designed the draft system that would distribute the league's talent across many more teams. Each of the Original Six teams was allowed to protect eleven skaters and one goaltender, then allowed to "fill" with a player from its unprotected list for each player it lost in the draft. NHL president Clarence Campbell had argued for protecting only nine players, but the six teams were not in that generous a mood.

Whether nine or eleven, so few protected players hurt most other teams, but not Montreal. We had more farm teams and more players in reserve than any other club, as well as a far more elaborate scouting system. As mentioned earlier, Sam succeeded in turning expansion to the Canadiens' advantage while offering the richest collection of available players to the new teams. Part of his preparation for the draft was the compilation of a complete classification of all our talent, which is why our 1966 training camp featured more than 110 players. Our scouts worked overtime that year, but when the 1967 expansion draft took place, we kept more of our nucleus intact, while furnishing more players to the new franchises, than any other of the Original Six teams.

Since the late 1940s, Frank Selke had built up the Canadiens' farm system and nurtured it carefully before turning over its management to Sam Pollock as director of player personnel. Those players we "grew" but couldn't keep were sold at Sam's own "market garden" once or twice a year and the proceeds funneled right back into the system. Other teams scrambled to copy our method, but Sam was always two or three jumps ahead. While his committee was studying the broadcast potential inherent in league expansion, he quickly foresaw that many minor leagues would atrophy with the arrival of television, and he was the first general manager to start divesting his organization of multiple farm teams.

Expansion presented an opportunity for the Canadiens to make a profit after many years of patient cultivation, and to invest that profit for the medium and long term. Sam traded off a significant number of players to guarantee a one-time shot at the top two francophone juniors in the country at the time, Réjean Houle and Marc Tardif. In short, the Montreal Canadiens benefited at every turn. As a player and team captain, I can say that Trader Sam was regarded with awe in the dressing room. Moving upstairs to work alongside this man was a privilege.

That fall, I joined Sam and his public relations staff—Camil Des Roches and, two years later, Claude Mouton, whom I hired—and we began involving the team in the community to a greater degree through blood donor clinics, cultural exchanges, and charity appearances of every kind. All such programs have since become standard fare for the Canadiens and every other team, but we were innovators. My associates believed that a new age was about to dawn, and that previously discounted activities such as marketing and communications would assume far greater importance in the coming years. Sam wanted to position me as the person who could oversee their development.

A few months into my new duties, the Molson connection was severed when, to take advantage of various tax provisions, the family sold the team to a consortium headed by Edward and Peter Bronfman and John Bassett of Toronto. Bassett dropped out after a year, leaving the Bronfmans to go it alone. Seven years later, the team was sold again and found itself back in the familiar hands of Molson Breweries of Canada Limited, which paid $20 million after a bidding war with its rival, Labatt's Brewery of Canada Ltd. The Bronfmans retained Canadian Arena Company, which owned the Forum, and Molson signed a ten-year lease for its use.

While I was happy to welcome my friends and former fellow employees at Molson back to the fold, it was time to say goodbye to Sam Pollock. During the seven years of Bronfman ownership, Sam had built up a good deal of equity in the Bronfmans' enterprises, including Edper Investments and Canadian Arena Company. At fifty-two, he found himself at a crossroads. The Canadiens were solid at every level and under his stewardship had just won three straight Stanley Cups.

"I've been in hockey since high school," he explained to me, "and it's time to move on. I have an opportunity to continue with the Bronfmans and I'm going to take it." Needless to say, the business world admired Sam's managerial and administrative skills as much as the hockey world. He went on to become chairman of the board of John Labatt and Company in Toronto.

The only hitch in Sam Pollock's happiness concerned the selection of his replacement as general manager. It wasn't in his nature to leave loose strings, and he agonized over the question of succession.

Morgan McCammon of Molson, who was appointed president of the team, twice met Sam and me to discuss the matter. The most obvious candidate, by which I mean the individual whom the media had instantly identified and who had campaigned most actively and overtly for the job, was coach Scotty Bowman.

Scotty had been trained by Selke and Pollock and had worked within the Canadiens organization as a coach and scout after a high stick from Jean-Guy Talbot had fractured his skull and ended his playing days with the Junior Canadiens (then coached by Sam) in the early 1950s. When expansion arrived in 1967, he left his position as Sam's assistant with the Canadiens to become coach of the St. Louis Blues, where he did a tremendous job. He returned to Montreal after our 1971 Stanley Cup win. In the eight seasons between 1971–72 and 1978–79, he won five Stanley Cups and, along with Al Arbour of the New York Islanders and Fred Shero of Philadelphia, was ranked among the foremost coaches in the league. Whatever his personal quirks, Scotty had proved himself behind the bench. (He went on to win four more Stanley Cups, for a record nine, and chalked up more than a thousand game victories, another NHL all-time coaching mark.)

The trouble was, he'd "proved" himself in other ways behind the scenes, resulting in negative entries on his balance sheet. When Scotty took issue with a player, for any reason at all, he would run upstairs to Sam's office and demand an immediate trade. Bringing all his experience and wisdom to bear, Sam was able to calm him down; Sam knew no player was capable of turning in eighty perfect games. But Scotty had ongoing fractious relations with a number of the more colorful players, especially Peter Mahovlich. With Scotty at the helm, it seemed likely that our team would change dramatically from year to year, if not from hour to hour.

There was a problem, of course, in taking a position against him. Scotty had run an effective media campaign for the post and the short list of candidates was very short indeed—down to a single name, as far as several observers were concerned. Like any good general manager, Sam Pollock had refrained from tipping his hand, but I'm pretty sure that he'd made up his mind about Scotty's aspirations long before.

Another candidate was Sam's assistant, Irving Grundman, who had learned a great deal about hockey and hockey management during seven years under Sam's tutelage. He was a quiet, reflective man, who carefully weighed every option before rendering an opinion. Sam and I both agreed that he should get the job, and Morgan McCammon's endorsement made it unanimous.

When you vote against the candidate who is almost universally regarded as the heir apparent, you have to be ready with solid reasons. The president will want to know what's going on, as will the other members of the board. My views and those of Sam became known, but they were expressed to a very small circle. Scotty had a year remaining on his coaching contract, after all. As it turned out, he stayed in Montreal for another season before moving on to Buffalo as coach and general manager.

I was asked once if I thought Scotty's performance as Buffalo's general manager vindicated our decision. It's a difficult question to answer. On the one hand, he wasn't an unqualified success, winning 216 of 404 games and batting .500 in play-off action. I thought him a great coach but an impatient general manager. On the other hand, Irving Grundman wasn't entirely successful, either. There's no doubt Irving was well respected as a gentleman and a businessman. He never claimed to have Sam Pollock's store of hockey knowledge, and he tried very hard during his stint as the Canadiens' managing director (as the general manager's position was then titled) to learn how the game was run. On balance, I don't think Sam and I made a mistake by selecting Irving over Scotty, if only because I don't think the results would have been any better under somebody else.

Our decision undoubtedly disappointed Scotty, and he didn't hide his feelings during the 1978–79 season. Unhappy as he may have been, however, he still saw to it that the team won a fourth consecutive Stanley Cup that year.

THE TEAM OF THE 1970S, which won five Stanley Cups of its own, was clearly Sam Pollock's creation, a testament to his abilities and vision.

I described earlier how Sam's January 1971 trade for Frank Mahovlich delivered a Stanley Cup to the Canadiens in the year I retired. It also delivered one in 1973, after John Ferguson and I were gone. Frank's presence raised his brother Peter's performance a couple of notches, but his most important contribution was as another senior veteran in the dressing room alongside Henri Richard (my replacement as captain), J.-C. Tremblay, Terry Harper, and Jacques Laperrière. They settled a team that had a corps of mid-level veterans in Serge Savard, Guy Lapointe, Yvan Cournoyer, Jacques Lemaire, and Claude Larose, and a large group of rising young players such as Yvon Lambert, Steve Shutt, Guy Lafleur, Marc Tardif, Réjean Houle, Murray Wilson, Larry Robinson, and Ken Dryden.

When the World Hockey Association claimed the likes of Big Frank, Tremblay, Houle, and Tardif, and when Jacques Laperrière retired after the 1973 Cup, Lemaire, Cournoyer, Savard, Jim Roberts, and Lapointe stepped forward to help Henri Richard provide veteran leadership. Sam's system continued to produce new stars such as Bob Gainey, Doug Jarvis, Doug Risebrough, Mario Tremblay, Bill Nyrop, John Van Boxmeer, Michel Plasse, and Michel "Bunny" Larocque. At the same time, the Bruins, Hawks, and Leafs were being devastated by defections to the WHA.

If Sam experienced one setback in the 1970s, it was minor and came at the hands of Ken Dryden, the goalie who, in taking a break from his law studies at McGill University, had backstopped the team to Stanley Cups in 1971 and 1973. After accomplishing this feat, Dryden felt obliged to make what Sam felt were exorbitant salary demands. The WHA was offering journeymen goaltenders up to $100,000 a year; indeed, Ken's older brother, Dave, also a goaltender, had already made the move to the new league.

Dryden felt he was worth a lot more in this heated marketplace. Sam, however, adamantly refused to alter his practice of steadily increasing a player's salary over an extended proving period. When the two reached an impasse, Dryden quit the team to article for a Toronto law firm at $135 a week.

Sam never really discussed the Dryden situation with anyone, especially during the 1973–74 season that Ken sat out, but I could see he was concerned by it. Not only had a player turned his back on a good sum of money to prove his point—a previously unheard-of stand—but that player was Ken Dryden, an athlete whom Sam greatly admired.

Sam couldn't seem to draw a bead on Kenny, and neither could his teammates. We had known he was an Ivy League scholar enrolled in McGill's law school when he originally joined us at the tail end of the 1971 season. As such, he was a first for our dressing room. I've always encouraged my teammates to respect the personalities of every individual in the room, because it takes all kinds to make a successful squad. Ken proved his worth spectacularly and continued to do so the following season, when he won the Calder Trophy as the league's top rookie.

Still, as his captain for two months and then as a Second Floor executive, I noticed that Ken placed a little extra distance between himself and his teammates. You couldn't construe his demeanor as antisocial or egotistical; far from it. Ken just seemed to be both a participant and an observer at the same time. His return after his self-exile put the Canadiens back on the road to the Stanley Cup, and Sam was the first person to acknowledge that fact.

Nonetheless, it must have been disconcerting for Sam to negotiate with Ken at the beginning. Sam was a fiscal conservative who believed in the traditional approach, of rewards granted for services rendered and championships earned. I never had difficulty negotiating my salary with him, and we were always on the same wavelength in our contract discussions. Then again, I retired before the WHA threw the pay scale out of whack, so I didn't experience the explosion of salaries as a player.

To be sure, I was offered an opportunity to join the new league and make that fabulous money. The Quebec Nordiques were one of the WHA's founding teams, and it seemed natural that the new franchise should go after the two players whose names loomed largest in the Quebec public's imagination, Guy Lafleur and Jean Béliveau. Guy was out of the question; he had signed a three-year deal with the Canadiens and still had two years and an option year remaining.

As for me, well, there were attractions. In 1971, Jacques Plante was the Nordiques' general manager and Paul Racine, one of the club's principal backers, was a shopping-center magnate who had known me for many years. In other words, the two fellows making the offer weren't fast-money boys or strangers from another hockey planet. One was a former teammate and the other a man at whose home I had often enjoyed a postgame beer in my junior days. When we met, it was like a family reunion.

Paul was a go-getter who had spearheaded construction of the massive Laurier shopping center in Ste-Foy and others in the United States. He had investors, but he drove the deals and was a very wealthy man by the time he became the first president of the Nordiques.

Paul and Jacques came to me with a four-year deal, guaranteeing the full sum—literally millions of dollars—even if it turned out I could play for only one season.

"Whatever you put on the table, I won't go back on the ice," I told them. "Ten million, twenty million, it doesn't matter. I'm forty, going on forty-one. I can't play the quality of hockey I like any more. If I could, and if I wanted to play again, I'd play with the Canadiens."

I understood that they didn't want me solely for my playing skills. They wanted the name Béliveau on the marquee and on the front page of the season-ticket subscription forms. Both Jacques and Paul were certain that they'd make money on the deal. Yet it was Jacques, as a former player (one who would return to play yet again), who immediately appreciated what I was saying.

I know some players have returned to the professional game after a few years away, but by and large I view it as a mistake to trade on the past. Jacques Plante proved to be an exception to the rule, but he was a goalie, not a skater, and his powers did not decline. You have to ask yourself tough questions: Are you helping your teammates? Are you producing on the ice? Or are you merely helping the owners, because your name is up in lights? If you're satisfied to play that kind of hockey—scoring fifteen goals and deceiving yourself that you've had a good comeback season—it's your choice, and you'll have to live with yourself. All I can say is that after the story of the Nordiques' offer surfaced, I received a great deal of mail from Quebec City. Most of it came from people who congratulated me for resisting a cynical decision and for turning down the proposal.

The Canadiens of the 1970s were an all-star group, with Hall of Fame talents such as Cournoyer, Dryden, Lafleur, Robinson, Savard, Lapointe, Shutt, and Gainey lining up for four straight Stanley Cup parades down St. Catherine Street. In many ways, however, Jacques Lemaire may have been the most important of all. His nickname was Coco, but someone with a sense of his presence on that team would have understood why he was referred to by his teammates as "the Quiet Man." Jacques was a low-key but highly effective leader who did all his talking on the ice.

If Ken Dryden was a college-educated intellectual, then Jacques Lemaire was a hockey intellectual, a fact few realized until his playing career was over. He scored Cup-winning goals in the 1978 and 1979 play-offs and consistently brought out the best in Guy Lafleur. Still, I think his post-career contributions proved even more influential.

After Jacques retired as a player, he coached in Europe, in the U.S. college ranks, and in the Quebec Major Junior Hockey League, before returning to the Canadiens as assistant to coach Bob Berry. He replaced Berry late in the 1984–85 season at a time when the team was playing below .500 hockey for the first time in twenty-five years, and he very nearly took it to the Stanley Cup final. He resigned the coaching position to become general manager Serge Savard's right-hand man in 1985. Both Savard and Ronald Corey were impressed by his scouting abilities, which paid off handsomely for the club. He studied every player in the league, much as Sam Pollock had done before him. When the time came for trades and acquisitions, Jacques drew on his master file for instant and accurate evaluations.

Jacques was a major contributor to our 1986 and 1993 Stanley Cup wins, helping Savard identify and acquire important talents such as Bobby Smith, Gaston Gingras, Brian Skrudland, Mike Lalor, Kirk Muller, Vincent Damphousse, and Brian Bellows. There's no doubt he is one of the foremost students of the game, and although his departure was a loss to the team, I think New Jersey was perfect for him. Jacques itched to get behind the bench but knew he couldn't do it under the media microscope in Montreal. With Larry Robinson as his defensive coach, he proved his mettle with the Devils and won a Stanley Cup for the franchise. Recently he has invigorated the Minnesota Wild franchise, one of the most successful expansion teams of recent vintage.

Scott Stevens, the Devils' captain and a twelve-year veteran of the league, paid the Lemaire-Robinson duo (and indirectly the Montreal Canadiens) a compliment during the 1994 play-offs. In an interview with Réjean Tremblay of *La Presse,* he remarked: "I couldn't imagine how much I had to learn. Larry especially taught me how to play my position, but he also taught me patience. I had the tendency to commit myself too quickly, to get caught out of position. He also showed me a bunch of little tricks that were taught to him during his years with the Canadiens: how to hold your stick when a player is skating down on you; how not to fall for a move. Teaching is what distinguishes Larry and Jacques Lemaire. They themselves learned from the best. The Canadiens teach young players what to do. That is why, good year or bad, the Canadiens always have a top team."

By the time of my second retirement from the Canadiens, in 1993, Frank Selke and Sam Pollock were long gone from the Second Floor, as were Toe Blake and Scotty Bowman from the bench. But their lessons live on, passed down from generation to generation, on and off the ice, everywhere that hockey is played.

11

THE MONEY GAME

ON SEPTEMBER 14, 2004, Canada defeated Finland to win the World Cup title in six straight games. The next day, the National Hockey League locked out its players, suspending play while negotiations carried on for five more months. On February 16, 2005, the NHL announced the cancelation of the 2004–05 season.

In separate news conferences, NHL commissioner Gary Bettman and National Hockey League Players' Association executive director Bob Goodenow presented similarly pessimistic pictures of the chasm separating the players and the league owners. Both had attended dozens of meetings and negotiating sessions, and there was considerable pressure from many quarters to reach a deal. But in the end they had to admit defeat.

"Even next year's season could be compromised," the commissioner said. "Both sides are back to where they were on September 15, and they are entrenched."

Having followed the saga closely for months, it was obvious to me that neither side would flinch. How could they? During the previous three seasons, each had vowed it wouldn't give an inch in negotiations for a new collective-bargaining agreement once the old one expired in 2004. It was generally accepted that there would be either a strike or a lockout in September 2004 and that it could be a long one. When the showdown came, both sides kept their word.

The February 16 cancelation date came one year and four days after the league fired a significant shot across the bow of the NHLPA. On that day, financial consultant Arthur Levitt announced that the NHL's 2002–03 losses of US$273 million on revenues of $1.996 billion threatened the league's very future. Levitt, a former chairman of the United States Securities and Exchange Commission, had just completed a ten-month independent study of the NHL's finances. And while the players' association was quick to question his numbers and his independence, I remember reading the story in my morning newspaper and, for the first time, feeling genuine concern about the health of professional hockey.

When I started out, a players' association or union was an owner's nightmare at worst and a player's afterthought at best. It wasn't until June 1967, just prior to expansion, that the National Hockey League Players' Association was finally recognized by the NHL as the exclusive representative of all players employed by the league's teams. In 1968 Alan Eagleson, recently appointed executive director of the NHLPA, declared that the players should receive a cut of television revenues and share in the expansion-fees bonanza, valued at $2 million from each of the six new teams. The first collective-bargaining agreement between the NHL and the NHLPA was executed in May 1976, and a second followed in August 1981. By the late 1980s and early 1990s, it was fair to say that the union was on an equal footing with the league; in 1992, it surged ahead.

That is what the latest round of hostilities has been all about: the NHL trying to recover its power position over its players. The odds of that happening aren't good. I've watched the league and its players grow farther apart over many years, and I believe the seeds of today's distrust and animosity were planted decades ago.

EARLY IN THE 1970S, Bob Baun, a recently retired Maple Leafs and Red Wings player, was making the transition to post-hockey life and attempting to put his financial affairs in order. He wondered why a sixteen-season NHL career was worth only $7,600 annually in pension payouts. Even more puzzling, he couldn't understand why Gordie Howe's twenty-six years in the NHL paid him only $14,000 a year.

These modest returns mirrored the pension fund's modest beginnings. In 1947, a special charity hockey game was played in Chicago between the then Cup champions and an all-star team drawn from the other five clubs. Twenty-five percent of the proceeds went into what was called the Players Emergency Fund and the rest to local charities. The year following, a more formal pension fund was established with regular paid contributions from individual players and the league. The teams' contributions comprised the gate receipts of an all-star game plus a levy on all tickets sold for play-off games. In the early fifties I was putting in $900 a year, a considerable amount at the time. Later, my annual contribution rose to something like $1,500.

While the fund was run by the league through the NHL Pension Society, the players' association had two representatives on the society board. In 1969, Alan Eagleson rubber-stamped an agreement by which the league alone would fund the plan. The owners then claimed there was no longer any need for players to be represented on the board. Eagleson accepted this argument, and his motives for doing so have been in question ever since. In my opinion he was wrong to agree to it; a review process of some sort was necessary if we were to keep track of our money.

I had always prepared a personal financial statement at the end of every year, and the only thing I could never establish to my own satisfaction was the value of my pension. In the early 1980s, when interest rates went up to 18 and 20 percent, Canadians were allowed to roll their pensions into RRSPS, which I did. I'd always felt that the interest paid on the pension fund's investments was too low, although, as noted, I had no firm numbers to justify that opinion.

Bob Baun and a teammate, the late Carl Brewer, had similar concerns, and they spent a lot of their own time and money trying to get to the bottom of the players' pension situation. They were joined in the quest by a group of former players that included Eddie Shack, Andy Bathgate, Gordie Howe, and Bobby Hull. But their demands for information about the management of the fund were met with stonewalling by the league; the situation festered for years.

In 1990, the Toronto-based group that included Brewer and Shack hired lawyer Mark Zigler to study the pension plan. He determined that there was a surplus of roughly $25 million sitting in the fund, and he found evidence that the league owners had used some portion of this—I think the figure was $13 million—as an excuse to take what is called a contribution holiday. The owners took the position that if there was indeed a surplus, they shouldn't have to add fresh money to the pot. The ex-players argued that the surplus should have been added to the fund and later disbursed in increased payments to retirees. They were prepared to take legal action to establish their claim, and in 1991 they launched a lawsuit against NHL president John Ziegler, the NHL Pension Society, and the NHL owners.

To make a long story short, a number of irregularities in the administration of the fund came to light, and after a four-year fight through the courts, the Supreme Court upheld the players' claim to the fund's surplus to the tune of $41 million. The decision affected some 1,300 former players and has reverberated through the league ever since. It also eventually helped end the NHL-related careers of league president Ziegler and NHLPA executive director R. Alan Eagleson.

I was in the Canadiens' front office, in management, when this battle was being waged, but I had no difficulty arguing in favor of the Canadiens' alumni association supporting the players' court case against the league. This was a delicate situation in some respects: the Canadiens had treated the alumni very well over the years, granting free use of the Forum for money-raising exhibition games and skate-a-thons, for example. I had to tell the team's president that we wanted to take some of these proceeds and use them to support a suit against the team and its NHL partners. In my view, no other project affected the well-being of former players as much as this one, and the Canadiens alumni sent a contribution of $25,000 toward the players' legal expenses.

I was comfortable taking a pro-player *and* pro-league stance after I retired from playing, for the simplest of reasons: thanks to Sam Pollock, I was among the two or three best-paid players in the league. My salary of Can$100,000 in 1970–71, my final season, topped the list. And yet, as a manager with Molson in the off-seasons, I was familiar with the process by which management decisions were generally taken, and I understood that company executives didn't adopt adversarial positions just for the sake of doing so.

In some respects I was part of the "money game" even before my NHL career began, supplementing my Quebec Aces wages with work for team sponsors. My involvement with Molson predated my signing with the Canadiens and continued long after. And when I joined the NHL, I brought money with me, in that Frank Selke had to sign a rich and well-publicized contract to secure my services. Shortly after, it was common knowledge that he loosened his purse strings again to ensure that Rocket Richard was similarly compensated; the Red Wings had to do the same for Gordie Howe. Still, the league's overall salary structure at that time wasn't affected, and players labored for decades in blissful ignorance of their bench mates' salaries. Today, all league salaries are easily found on the Internet and can be accessed in moments. Everyone is fine with that, especially the agents.

How have we moved from those Original Six days, when the league operated like a conservative old boys' network, to today's situation where professional hockey is held ransom in a money game with crazy stakes? There are at least four answers to that:

Expansion: the growth of the NHL from six teams to twelve in 1967, followed by additions every other year or so until it became a thirty-team league in 2000;

Television: the arrival of color, high-tech cable and then satellite network television propelled professional sports to a pre-eminent position in the world of entertainment;

The World Hockey Association: a rival league turned the NHL's salary structure on its ear in 1972 and contributed to expansion by adding four teams to the NHL when the leagues merged in 1979;

New revenue streams: the discovery of lucrative and multiple new sources of income for the clubs in the 1980s and beyond.

Hockey historians pay little if any attention to the period between 1967 and 1975 when all of these factors helped launch an irreversible assault on the owners' supremacy.

Starting in 1967, the league looked to expansion for its financial future. The owners grew rich on expansion fees—the money new teams paid for admission to the NHL club—but very little trickled down to the players. Every time the issue was raised in negotiations, the league smugly replied that expansion was benefiting the players quite enough by providing more jobs in the sport's highest league. The players were becoming more frustrated, and the word "strike" was whispered, yet few players of that generation could imagine what such an action would entail.

In the late 1960s and early 1970s, the expansion frenzy hit every major professional sport, with the NHL, NBA, major-league baseball, and the NFL morphing into leagues that stretched from coast to coast through growth or mergers. Behind it all was television; the economics of pro sports and the rising popularity of sports television are inseparable.

The television networks learned early that there was a gold mine in bringing sports to their audiences, and some of that wealth found its way back to the leagues and teams. However, the first real boom hit when color television burst onto the marketplace in the mid-1960s. Suddenly the networks were making technical demands for better on-field and on-ice facilities to enhance their broadcast images. Soon, watching a game at home was as exciting as attending in person.

Arena ice had to be painted blue so that it would look white on camera, and special lighting was installed to heighten the color impact. When the new lighting started melting the ice, other solutions had to be found, including expensive air-conditioning systems that addressed the problem of hot lights as well as warmer outside temperatures when the season stretched into early summer.

The first expansion of the six-team NHL was prompted by the desire to secure a U.S. network television contract. CBS broadcast games for a brief period, but this arrangement ended even before I finished playing; the league has been unable to sign another major U.S. network contract since. Instead, the NHL turned to the cable and satellite networks, systems that allowed games to be broadcast in real time, thereby allowing such innovations as the Sunday NFL double-header. This led to inequities within the NHL: those clubs in larger television markets were able to benefit from higher revenues, just as Montreal and Toronto were the major beneficiaries of the CBC's *Hockey Night in Canada*.

The NHL owners were not alone in appreciating that televised hockey could be lucrative. Another group of businessmen felt they could do a better job of landing television contracts in the major North American markets, and in 1972 they formed the World Hockey Association to challenge the NHL's hegemony. The WHA's owners planned teams in New York, Chicago, Cincinnati, Los Angeles, Detroit, Miami, Houston, and San Diego, as well as in Edmonton, Vancouver, Winnipeg, Toronto, Ottawa, and Quebec City.

In the short term, the WHA represented competition to the NHL for both players and television contracts. Over the long term, it had consequences for the players that far outlasted its own existence. The flight of players to the rebel league was in effect the NHLPA's first player "strike" and the start of the power pendulum's swing to the players' side for the first time in the history of the NHL.

The players saw the WHA as an opportunity to make their point without labor action, and an impressive number of them crossed the street. The NHL was bound to have problems, thanks to its owners' stubborn attitudes; they laughed that the new league was an underfinanced nuisance that would eventually drown in its own red ink. They were right in the end, but it still cost them dearly.

The new league made its debut on October 11, 1972, when the Alberta Oilers visited the Ottawa Nationals, and the Cleveland Crusaders were home to the Quebec Nordiques. Name players like Bobby Hull, Bernie Parent, Johnny McKenzie, J.-C. Tremblay, and Gerry Cheevers had defected to the WHA, and others such as Gordie Howe and his sons Marty and Mark, Frank Mahovlich, Marc Tardif, Réjean Houle, André Lacroix, Mike Walton, and Danny Lawson would follow. The NHL's Toronto and Boston teams especially were decimated by defections, and it showed in their performances in the mid-1970s.

In seven short seasons, the WHA proved innovative in its own way: the Winnipeg Jets welcomed Swedes Anders Hedberg, Ulf Nilsson, and Lars-Erik Sjoberg into their ranks, quickening the flow through the European pipeline. The Birmingham Bulls took another tack, signing seven top eighteen-year-old junior stars who became known as the Baby Bulls: goalie Pat Riggin, forwards Michel Goulet, Keith Crowder, and Rick Vaive, and defensemen Rob Ramage, Craig Hartsburg, and Gaston Gingras. Another significant player to sign a WHA rookie contract was Cincinnati's Mike Gartner.

These moves shook the hockey world on both sides of the Atlantic. Within a few years, dozens of Europeans were earning hockey salaries in North America. And the Baby Bulls would eventually force the NHL and the junior hockey leagues to lower the draft age from twenty to eighteen, something that riled the junior-league managers for years.

But by 1977 the WHA teams were experiencing financial difficulties. That year and the next, approaches were made to the NHL board of governors with a view to a merger of the two leagues. This would have made life easier for everyone; the bidding war between the leagues had driven players' salaries out of sight—and several hockey entrepreneurs into bankruptcy—in five short years. A year before the arrival of the WHA, highly rated NHL players were being paid in the range of US$150,000. When Bobby Hull, Derek Sanderson, Bernie Parent, and others received offers of $1 million each from WHA teams, those NHL salaries doubled and tripled. Players like Parent and Cheevers enjoyed enriched contracts when they returned to the NHL, and all seven Baby Bulls were well paid during extensive NHL careers, after receiving $60,000 a year from the Bulls in their WHA rookie seasons, far more than they would have been paid in junior. The NHL players won their first "strike" hands down.

Before Sam Pollock left the Canadiens, he accurately predicted the change on hockey's horizon. Professional sport generally would become even more of a business than before, he said. Front offices would need the services of capable administrators, tax-law and investment specialists, and marketing and communications gurus. The competition was about to become fierce.

The Canadiens had their first glimpse of this new reality almost immediately and right in their backyard. In May 1977, when we won the Stanley Cup and the Quebec Nordiques defeated the Winnipeg Jets to take the WHA's Avco Cup, talk circulated of a "super series" between the two champions. It didn't develop much beyond media speculation and a mini-tempest on talk shows, but it gave those of us on the Second Floor a clear indication of the passions inherent in a Quebec City–Montreal rivalry.

When the first merger feelers were advanced in 1977 by the strongest WHA franchises, Pollock had grave concerns about any agreement that would bring the Nordiques into the league. In his view, the province of Quebec was exclusive Montreal Canadiens territory, and Sam wanted to keep it that way. By the time of his departure a year later, there was yet another reason for the Canadiens to oppose the Nordiques' entry: the two teams now belonged to rival breweries. Carling O'Keefe Breweries of Canada Incorporated had become the Nordiques' majority shareholder in 1976.

Molson's ownership of the Canadiens made the team susceptible to pressure of various kinds. When it became apparent that Montreal intended to oppose Quebec City's admittance to the NHL, anti-Canadiens sentiment grew in and around the provincial capital. Molson sales representatives and distributors there reported the serious threat of a boycott of all Molson products. For a time, it seemed that such a boycott might spread as far west as Edmonton and Winnipeg.

On June 22, 1979, that possibility evaporated when the Nordiques and three other WHA teams—the Hartford Whalers, the Edmonton Oilers, and the Winnipeg Jets—joined the NHL. The Canadiens were no longer Quebec's uncontested team, and Molson was no longer the only brewery with an NHL squad in the province. Indeed, we were under attack by an aggressive franchise determined to get out from under the long shadow cast by the building at Atwater and

St. Catherine. The Nordiques were very much an expansion team that season, but they boasted well-recognized names in their lineup, many of them French, and many more French names among their management.

A key player in the Nordiques' organization was the president of Carling O'Keefe Breweries, a tireless marketing specialist from Montreal named Ronald Corey. Another was Marcel Aubut, the team's thirty-year-old general counsel, who assumed the presidency and became the impetus behind the merger talks. These two men showed vision and daring, and the Nordiques were competitive on the ice within three short years. Unfortunately, one of their very first marketing ploys was to position themselves as French Quebec's team and to subtly paint Montreal as the team of the English-speaking establishment.

Still, the Nordiques-Canadiens rivalry between 1979 and 1995 was one of the most exciting in NHL history and one of the positive side effects of the NHL's financial revolution. One other telling point: only one of the four WHA merger teams, the Oilers, still plays in the city of its birth. The Nordiques broke a lot of hearts in 1995 when they moved to Colorado—and won the Stanley Cup on June 10, 1996, to boot. Three weeks later, on Canada Day, the Winnipeg Jets were transferred to Phoenix after a long and emotional battle by hundreds of Winnipeggers to keep their team. On April 13, 1997, the Hartford Whalers played their last game and moved to North Carolina. In the years since, the Colorado Avalanche have won another Cup, developed a great fan base and are solid NHL citizens. The jury is still out on Phoenix and Carolina. WHA, R.I.P.

The fourth factor in the overall shake-up of professional sport was the development of multiple revenue streams and advanced marketing programs. These began in the early 1970s and, as with expansion, television licensing, and the WHA, they changed the rules of the game on the ice and off. One has only to compare the clean white side boards of the Original Six era and right up until the early 1980s with today's circle of advertising billboards around every league rink to see there's money even in the stage set.

BY THE EARLY 1990S, change was the predictable constant in our sport. The league's team list changed regularly, with further expansions in 1991, 1992, 1993, 1998, and 2000 that added nine new teams, above and beyond those franchises that moved to other cities.

If the owners profited from found money in expansion and sponsorship, so did the players. Salaries rose to stratospheric heights, and the balance of power between players and owners shifted completely, as demonstrated by two unprecedented labor actions.

The first, in 1992, effectively cost John Ziegler his job as NHL president. The league was still locked in the pension fight with its retired players, and I remember warning management that the negative fallout from such a one-sided issue would hurt the NHL. My words fell on deaf ears, because another hockey story had captured the headlines—the possibility of the league's first strike.

Despite contrary evidence from several sources, John Ziegler had convinced the board of governors that there was no real danger of a strike during the 1991–92 season. (I've always wondered if he received assurances to that effect from Alan Eagleson.) He clamored loudly for a player vote by secret ballot and eventually got one. If he'd wanted to force a showdown, he should have acted in September 1991, when the players had just reported for training camp and hadn't yet been paid for the upcoming season. By April, they had their checks for the year, the pressure was off, and they were prepared to gamble.

The players voted 500–4 in favor of a strike, and Ziegler's days with the league were numbered. The ten-day walkout resulted in the signing of the first collective-bargaining agreement that was openly favorable to the players. When that deal concluded two years later, the owners came back to the table determined to play hardball. The result was a 103-day walkout that began in October 1994 and didn't end until January. The eighty-four game regular season was reduced to forty-eight games, and the play-off season began on January 26 when play resumed. Today there are some owners who are still trying to make up for the losses they suffered in that abbreviated half season.

The ten-year collective agreement the parties then signed in late 1995 was a slam dunk for the union. By its second year, the owners knew they were in trouble. A particular aggravation was the free-agency clause. Under the agreement, the eligible age for unrestricted free agents was set at thirty-one, a provision that came into effect in 1998. The league had hoped this clause would check the escalating salaries of the stars by slowing demand for their services and allowing more of the teams' salary budgets to go to the greater number of players.

The UFA clause, as it was known, produced exactly the opposite effect, limiting the supply of superstars and sending demand for them through the roof. Bidding wars broke out everywhere; the New York Rangers, for example, made a one-time offer of $15 million (all NHL salaries have been expressed in U.S. dollars since the 1990s) to Colorado's Joe Sakic. To keep him, the Avalanche had to match it and they did, retaining his services for another Stanley Cup win in 2001.

The salary issue has come to overshadow all others and with good reason. Let's compare some figures from 1994, the year of the half-season work stoppage, and 2004–05, the year the season was canceled altogether, with a few numbers from my day.

In 1970–71, my final season as a player with the Montreal Canadiens, the entire team was paid a total of $1,110,687.73 to win the Stanley Cup. That figure includes every player's regular-season salary and signing bonuses, as well as all play-off monies. In his eighteen-year NHL career, Maurice Richard made less than $500,000 in total.

In 1994, Montreal Canadiens' general manager Serge Savard signed Patrick Roy to a new contract that paid the golden goaltender $4 million a season. (I firmly believe Patrick was worth every penny in the context of the salary levels of the day; he was the best goaltender in the league in the early 1990s.)

Under its terms, Patrick was paid more to play two regular-season games than I was paid for my first five regular seasons, not including play-offs, and 3½ times more per season than the entire Canadiens team earned in 1970–71. Patrick earned more in two months than did Rocket Richard in his entire career.

At the time of the 1994 strike, the average NHL player salary was $733,000. By 2004–05, that figure was $1,830,126. How does one arrive at an *average* salary of almost $2 million? It isn't difficult when the league's stars are paid five times that amount. In the 2003–04 NHL season, Peter Forsberg of the Avalanche and Jaromir Jagr of the Capitals and Rangers led the way, each with $11 million annually. Close behind at $10 million each were Sergei Fedorov of the Mighty Ducks, Pavel Bure of the Rangers, Nicklas Lidstrom of the Red Wings, and Keith Tkachuk of the Blues.

St. Louis and Colorado seemed particularly well heeled, with the Blues' Chris Pronger ($9.5 million), Doug Weight ($8.5 million), Pavol Demitra ($6.5 million), and Al MacInnis ($6 million) all members of the NHL's top 35, and Forsberg being joined by teammates Joe Sakic ($9,880,939), Rob Blake ($9,326,519), and Teemu Selanne ($5,800,000) in the top 40. Selanne and fellow newcomer Paul Kariya took hefty pay cuts to join the Cup-contending Avalanche a year after their Mighty Ducks lost in a seven-game final to New Jersey.

When teams like St. Louis spend $40,500,000 on five players, and Colorado $36,007,458 on four, you know something or someone has to give. Indeed, in June 2005, Blues owners Bill and Nancy Walton Laurie (she of the Wal-Mart Waltons) cited significant losses over previous seasons and projected losses to come when they announced that the team and the Savvis Center were up for sale. The combined deficits for the Blues and the arena since opening in 1994 were said to have surpassed $225 million. When the Lauries purchased the team and the facility in September 1999, the asking price was $100 million. They also assumed $96 million in accumulated debt. Their plan had been to maximize use of the building by attracting an NBA franchise; it never happened.

Given that history, my question is, who in the world would want to buy such a money pit? If Nancy Walton Laurie, with a net worth of $2.9 billion ranked number 61 on the 2003 Fortune 400 list of richest Americans, can't afford to own an NHL team, who could blame her sister, Ann Walton Kroenke (number 56 on the same list, with a net worth of $3 billion), if she decided to divest herself of the Colorado Avalanche? (The Kroenkes do have the advantage of owning the NBA Denver Nuggets, who fill their venue on forty or more dates every year.)

In 2004, NHL owners generally cried poor, saying player salaries represented 75 percent of their hockey-related revenues, far above the proportions in other businesses. The league claimed that over the ten years of the latest collective agreement, NHL-wide revenues had grown 173 percent, but hockey salaries had ballooned 261 percent. It added up to an aggregate league loss of $1.5 billion in nine years and a loss for the 2002–03 season alone of $224 million, a figure disputed by the NHLPA.

The union pointed to figures published by the influential *Forbes Magazine*. By its accounting, NHL management had incurred losses of only $96 million for the 2003–04 season and $123 million for 2002–03. The *Wall Street Journal* weighed in with yet another estimate when it reported that twenty of the league's teams had lost a total of $300 million over the same two seasons.

What are we to understand from these disparate figures? Certainly, we can say that the numbers game generally is confusing for manager, player, official, and fan alike. But I think we can also conclude, from whatever set of figures one chooses, that the situation was desperate and the league's survival was at stake.

The NHLPA wasn't convinced. Negotiations for a new collective agreement faltered and failed, and the 2004–05 season evaporated. It was the first cancelation of a full season in the history of major-league professional sports in North America.

In some respects, the NHLPA's actions were not remarkable. Players' associations in all professional sports have gained in strength in recent years, with those representing baseball and football players setting the pace. Both have taken their members out on strike, and in every case the owners capitulated. Football found itself with a salary-cap system that actually protected elevated salaries, and baseball's unique brand of free agency, fine-tuned over the years by such union stalwarts as Marvin Miller and Donald Fehr, made sure players like Alex Rodriguez could earn annual salaries of $25 million. Basketball, with its small rosters of twelve players and only three or four stars making big money, nonetheless moved in the same direction.

This trend put pressure on the NHL to pay its players more, but hockey franchises were not receiving, and still do not receive, the fabulous sums in TV revenue that basketball, baseball, and football teams enjoyed. It's arguable that the worst thing to happen to professional sports in North America was CBS's contract with major-league baseball in the early 1990s. The network agreed to broadcast even fewer games than had been shown in the days of NBC's *Game of the Week*, while paying more than $1 billion over four years for the privilege. That contract almost broke the network and threw salary scales in every sport out of whack.

Baseball and basketball have had mixed experiences with network TV over the years, but football has basked in ongoing lucrative broadcast deals worth hundred of millions. Today's NFL teams reap some $60 million each before they sell their first ticket. That league's total annual broadcast revenue is about $2.2 billion.

For hockey, the picture is very different, and "gate-driven" has become the synonym for "poor" in describing its position on the pro sports totem pole. It experimented with FOX-Sports, and vice versa, in the mid-1990s. The infamous glow puck had Canadian fans rolling on their floors for several seasons until the Australian in charge of sports for that network decided that Americans simply had trouble understanding the game. Then along came ESPN, its parent ABC-TV, and ESPN 2, and through the 1990s and into the new millennium the NHL earned some steady if gradually dwindling revenues from American television contracts.

More recently, the NHL was to receive some $200 million over three years from ESPN, with most games broadcast on the "deuce," ESPN 2. But that changed with the lockout, and in May 2005 ESPN announced it would not pick up its option for the 2005–06 season, assuming there was to be one. That decision left the NHL without an American national cable broadcasting partner for the first time since the 1970s—a cruel irony, given that the executive offices of the NHL left Montreal and Toronto for New York in order to be closer to the networks and the major sponsors.

The only network deal (in the loosest terms) the league could look forward to on its return to action was an NBC pact that appears to have the teams paying the network, instead of the opposite. Under the agreement, the network would have first dibs on advertising revenue to cover production costs, and both partners would split the remaining revenues.

The money game has winners and losers, and some of the latter were easy to predict. The Nordiques and the Jets are no longer with us, and the Oilers issued dire warnings during the 2004–05 lockout. It's my view that if the NHLPA does not back off in its demands, the storied Edmonton franchise will likewise be gone.

Early in the 1990s, the term "small-market team" made its appearance in the pro sports lexicon. It usually applied to those franchises located in medium-size cities where the numbers of fans were limited or the possibility of lucrative broadcast agreements remote. In major-league baseball, the Montreal Expos were labeled as such, an undeserved designation that eventually became a self-fulfilling prophecy. Today in hockey, the term is attached to Pittsburgh, Edmonton, Calgary, and Ottawa. Those market realities are one reason for their distress. Another is the absence of a team-owned or team-controlled facility that might provide much-needed additional revenues.

During the 1990s, more than seventy new stadia/arenas were built across North America. In the United States, they were financed primarily with public money and then either ownership or financial control was turned over to the prime tenant. Sports business analysts point out that there are some 115 professional teams in North America today and that almost thirty of them share facilities. This means some eighty-four or eighty-five teams enjoy substantial revenue streams.

In addition to such traditional cash cows as concessions and parking, image control (uniforms, pictures, posters, cards), and broadcast rights, a new source of money has lately contributed millions of dollars to team coffers, namely "stadium naming rights." The Buffalo Bills' stadium was renamed Rich Stadium in the early 1970s, making it the first beneficiary of such a deal. The football team received $1.5 million over twenty-five years. At the end of the century, an NFL expansion team, the Houston Texans, was guaranteed $300 million over thirty years for similar naming rights to its new facility, Reliant Stadium. Banks and investment brokers, telecom companies and energy suppliers, software and sports equipment manufacturers were among the many enterprises that sought to post their names and logos on the walls of modern sports facilities, while the teams that controlled those buildings happily pocketed the proceeds.

Today it is estimated that the value of naming-rights agreements in professional and amateur sport is nudging US$3 billion in North America and $4 billion worldwide. Some argue that this money is discounted by the conditions of the contract, that most of it is paid off in the first half of a long-term contract and inflation reduces the rest. My response is simpler: it is found money, something that didn't exist in pro sports a generation ago. Take it and invest it wisely.

THE WISDOM OF USING windfalls to enhance long-term assets was demonstrated to me close to home. When the Bronfmans sold the Canadiens to Molson in 1978, Edward and Peter Bronfman retained control of Canadian Arena Company (later Carena Bancorp), which in turn owned the Forum. The team occupied the Forum under the terms of a thirty-year "net-net" lease that permitted us to amortize improvements we made to the building.

However, one can do only so much with a building that belongs to someone else, and it had become obvious that the Forum was not suited to the needs of a modern hockey franchise. One of the league's older structures, it had been renovated in 1949 and again in 1968. But luxury boxes could not be added without removing large numbers of seats intended for more budget-conscious fans. Its narrow hallways were jammed at intermissions when people queued at the food concessions or smokers lined the walls for their between-period puffs. The very ice, once among the league's finest, had become one of its worst thanks to an ice plant that dated from the building's original construction in 1924 and a woefully inadequate air-conditioning system. Even the kids who skated there on Saturday afternoons complained. Furthermore, the Forum was hemmed in, located in a high-density area on the western edge of downtown. There were exactly ten indoor parking spaces, and parking revenues—a major income source elsewhere—were scooped by nearby private lots.

In 1982 Ronald Corey was appointed president of the Canadiens, and he was soon forced to confront the problem. He had to find the financial means to keep the Canadiens at the top of the league, while allowing us to maintain its standards as a class organization.

One morning he delivered a bombshell. "What would you think of putting up a new, state-of-the-art building on our own land?" he asked me.

I can't say that images of the existing Forum flashed before my eyes, like those appearing to the proverbial drowning man. I loved the building, but I also recognized its many shortcomings. I knew we needed a new building to ensure a solid revenue picture over the next decade and beyond. If we failed to do our duty now, another generation of managers in 2010 or so would rightly denounce us for having been asleep or irresponsible.

I also knew that hockey fans around the world regarded the Forum in the same way that Leaf supporters in Toronto viewed Maple Leaf Gardens, as a veritable shrine. Any replacement proposal would have to be meticulously planned, carefully marketed, and backed by reams of persuasive documentation.

"What do you propose to do, Ronald?"

"I'd like to have a feasibility study done," he said, "to see if we can upgrade the present building, and then we'll take it from there."

It seemed a prudent first step, and within days Ronald had commissioned SNC–Lavalin Group Incorporated, one of the world's top engineering design firms, to undertake the study. Six months later Lavalin's answer came back: it would take a $40-million investment to bring the Forum up to speed, after which it would still be a seventy-year-old building, albeit heavily renovated. Some of its liabilities—notably its size and location—could never be rectified, for any amount of money.

Lavalin concluded the Forum needed to double in size from its existing 300,000 square feet if it hoped to serve as a multifunctional, all-purpose entertainment venue for the 1990s. Plainly, another face-lift would not suffice. To remain profitable and competitive, the Canadiens needed a brand-new building.

The second phase of Ronald's plan sent engineers, designers, and Canadiens executives to visit facilities all over North America. Their ultimate mandate was to provide the team with a state-of-the-art building that would meet all of the needs identified by Lavalin's study, and to ensure that the team's new home would retain the warmth and ambience of the old Forum, the sport's most exciting venue.

The new arena, built just west of the historic Windsor railway station, opened as the Molson Centre in 1996 and was rechristened the Bell Centre in September 2002 in a twenty-year, $100 million naming-rights deal. It boasted the NHL's highest seating numbers—21,273, compared with 16,900 in the Forum—and more than 130 luxury boxes that should generate about $12 million in revenue a year. The building covers 168,700 square feet and features an on-site Metro subway station and a connection to the commuter trains at Lucien-L'Allier Station. It is a year-round venue, of course, booking acts across the entertainment spectrum.

Fans might be surprised to hear me say that the new arena could have been smaller, and a little more intimate to suit its patrons. The building would have been as successful with three thousand fewer seats, I believe, remembering that the last three thousand are the lowest-revenue seats in the building.

Success breeds success, and the long-term success that has been the Canadiens' good fortune for so many years has allowed the team to remain financially secure throughout the past decade. The new venue has already contributed to this process. Winners build up a store of goodwill and lasting strength that ebbs only a little when team fortunes dip. Although we have won only two Cups in the last eighteen seasons, the reputation of the Montreal Canadiens is hardly diminished, and the hockey show at the Bell Centre remains a spectacular one—especially when Toronto or Boston come to town. That said, I am the first to acknowledge that shrewd marketing can do only so much. This is professional sports, and while selling millions of dollars worth of team paraphernalia each year is highly desirable, performance is paramount in the end.

Certainly the money game is here to stay. You can begin to grasp how the sports world has changed in the last ten years simply by tracking the media coverage. In my day, business reporters had no interest in the Montreal Canadiens or the Toronto Maple Leafs. Today, they pay attention to sports franchises as they do to any other corporate or industrial sector.

Each spring, one of the most anticipated sports-cum-business stories was *Financial World*'s annual rating of North American sports franchises. In 1993, the Dallas Cowboys (repeat winners of the Super Bowl) were deemed number 1, with an estimated value of $190 million. The magazine factored in all the usual profit-and-loss yardsticks—revenues, players' salaries, operating costs, and so on—as well as something the publication called a franchise's "software value," the amount of revenue derived from broadcasts of the team's games and its value as a vehicle for the sale of consumer products.

The highest-ranked baseball team was the New York Yankees, in sixth place overall, at $166 million, followed by the Toronto Blue Jays at $150 million. The Montreal Expos were last in the baseball category, at a mere $75 million.

Nor was hockey doing all that well. The Detroit Red Wings were first among NHL teams at $104 million, followed by the Boston Bruins ($88 million), the Los Angeles Kings ($85 million), and the Montreal Canadiens ($82 million). The other Canadian NHL franchises checked in at $77 million (Toronto), $69 million (Vancouver), $50 million (Calgary and Ottawa), $46 million (Edmonton), $43 million (Quebec), and $35 million (Winnipeg). The Jets held the unenviable distinction of being the franchise with the lowest value in all four sports surveyed.

In April 2005, the annual list issued by *Forbes Magazine* held sway, and some of its numbers were staggering. First, the most lucrative sports franchise in North America had become the NFL's Washington Redskins, the only billion-dollar franchise ($1.104 billion) in sport. NFL teams averaged an astonishing US$733 million in 2004–05.

The second most valuable sports franchise overall was the New York Yankees at $950 million, almost $400 million more than the runner-up Boston Red Sox ($563 million) in its own sport, and edging out the NFL Dallas Cowboys and Houston Texans, at $923 million and $905 million respectively.

The Los Angeles Lakers led the NBA with a valuation of $510 million, almost double the NHL-leading New York Rangers at $282 million. While the NHL teams trailed the other sports, they nonetheless appreciated in value. As *Forbes* wrote: "Hockey franchises are worth an average of $163 million, up 3 percent from last year and 31 percent from when we first valuated them six years ago. The last four expansion teams—the Atlanta Thrashers, Columbus Blue Jackets, Minnesota Wild and Nashville Predators—went for $80 million each in 1997. These teams are now worth an average of $130 million each."

THOSE WHO KNOW ME know that I am a ferocious defender of the game and of what I believe to be right. Two editions of these memoirs have been written in the midst of the NHL's worst labor conflicts; it's a recipe for potential misunderstanding and strained relations between individuals who normally would be friends. Yet I've felt obliged to voice my opinion in defense of the game and let the chips fall where they may.

For the longest time, NHL management had the upper hand in controlling the league and its players, and they enjoyed wielding power. Many times I expressed my reservations about or outright opposition to some of the positions adopted by the league. It seemed to me that they embarrassed or humiliated the players at their peril, and I knew it would come back to haunt them. When the players started to wield power for their side, they would happily grind down the owners; they took a measure of revenge in 1992 and again in 1994 and 2004.

It was clear to me and to all neutral observers that the ten-year collective-bargaining agreement signed in late 1995 would put the sport in jeopardy. I publicly advised both sides to negotiate themselves out of a looming impasse earlier rather than later, while the league was still playing.

When the 2004–05 lockout got under way, I acknowledged that the act of shutting down the league came from NHL management. Nor were they blameless for the financial position in which they found themselves. The expansion well fed a false economy and eventually it dried up.

Nonetheless, I sympathized with league management because I believed their claims of losses in the hundreds of millions to be true. It was time for the players to make concessions, I felt, and significant ones. The pendulum had to swing back to the middle.

I wasn't alone in this assessment. Bob Pulford, formerly of the Toronto Maple Leafs, was a prime mover for the NHLPA during its renaissance in 1967–68. For almost a decade, no one worked harder than he to advance the cause of the players. In 2004–05, as a senior vice-president with the Chicago Blackhawks, he was vehemently against the union position and feared it would destroy the NHL. Other veterans, including the Bruins duo Bobby Orr and Phil Esposito, and Montreal's own Guy Lafleur, sounded the alarm during the winter of 2004–05.

When André Rousseau of *Le Journal de Montréal* called me for a statement two weeks after the lockout began, I felt compelled to raise my objections.

"The players and the players' association are making a terrible mistake," I told him.

"Why are you so sure of this?" Rousseau asked.

"Under the last ten-year agreement, I know that at least twenty teams lost millions of dollars in the final five years alone. How long can you operate with a deal like that?"

I've been involved with various organizations and companies in and out of hockey and could not name one in which 75 percent of revenues went to salaries. It's my contention that the only way to solve the situation in the NHL is to move toward a partnership between the parties.

Today's players have a ready answer when veterans like me advance such a notion: "Things are different today," they say. One thing is not different, though: When the owners don't have it, how can they pay it?

When that edition of *Le Journal* hit the stands, reaction came quickly. I could see that "handling the old guard" was a well-developed strategy for an NHLPA on a war footing, and they immediately went into action. Vincent Damphousse, one of the NHLPA vice-presidents, commented to the effect that those who had spent their entire playing careers with one team at the top of the heap couldn't understand the intricacies of the current labor dispute.

When I said I had always preferred to work inside a corporation or an organization that was wealthy and therefore stable and asked whether it wouldn't be better for the players to play inside a wealthy NHL, the players' association waffled.

Naturally, I responded with the observation that the union's answers were weak, that they didn't address all of the points I had raised. Damphousse in turn elaborated somewhat in a subsequent interview with David Stubbs of the *Gazette*, going so far as to say that he was sacrificing his own career for the well-being of the youngsters coming up in the league. I fear his legacy will be the bankruptcy of the game.

Martin Brodeur was also asked to comment, and although his statements were gentler, the gist was the same. That Damphousse and Brodeur made these comments was no accident; the NHLPA identified them as young, popular men in the francophone milieu of Quebec who would represent the association there much better than could Bob Goodenow or Ted Saskin.

Martin and I were together the next day at a charity event, and we talked a little bit. It wasn't the place for an in-depth discussion, but he didn't express anger or disappointment in what I had said. Remember, I had played with his father, and I had watched Martin grow up at the Forum when Denis became a sports photographer.

Then again, how could an individual player respond to the charge that all players were overpaid under the last collective agreement? There was no answer to that. He couldn't trot out his salary figures over the period and attempt to justify them, because the premise was that all salaries to players were bloated and dangerous to the league's future.

Martin is hugely popular in Quebec, and Vincent Damphousse is much admired as a good player and teammate. When Damphousse was with Montreal, he was the leading scorer for a couple years, and he and Kirk Muller, along with Patrick Roy, led the team to the Stanley Cup in 1993. A former captain, he never did anything that would slight the sport or the team. I regard him as an all-round fine citizen. But the fact remains that he and players like him who played under the previous agreement were overpaid. He may feel he is "sacrificing" his career, though surely it is less painful to do so with millions in the bank. And look where their last contract has left the game of professional hockey.

As for easing the way for future generations, we should take that pious wish with a grain of salt. The NHLPA has learned from the big boys how to keep their members in line. Its actions in this latest battle have reminded me of the Major League Baseball Players Association's handling of John Wetteland, the great Montreal reliever who went to the Yankees in the post-1994 sell-off of Expos talent.

After playing in the Bronx zoo at a much higher salary for a couple of seasons and helping the Yankees win a World Series, Wetteland was quoted as saying he would welcome a return to Montreal at a lower salary because he loved the city, the fans, and the team; it had been a great environment for his family. The MLBPA reacted to his comments with a stern reprimand: never again should he discuss "lower" salaries in a positive vein.

Pierre Dagenais, a fourth-line player with Montreal who had just come off his first season with the team in 2003–04, took stock of his immediate future when the lockout began. The Canadiens have many bright lights like Andrei Kostitsyn, Alexander Perezhogin, Jason Ward, Matt Higgins, and Tomas Plecanec in Hamilton and more players in the pipeline. Dagenais said publicly that the lockout was hurting him; he was on a minimum NHL salary and his spot might not be there for him when the league resumed play.

Dagenais was one of the fellows for whom Vincent et al. were apparently preparing the way. But the NHLPA brought Dagenais to Toronto and persuaded him to stop talking. That was it for him and other players on the bubble. Meanwhile, the new crop of young talent would graduate from the American Hockey League or from European or junior leagues directly to the big club. Would Dagenais be around when the next new season began? Who knew, but he was right to worry.

In Montreal, the situation was exacerbated by other concerns. Molson's merger with Colorado's Coors company in early 2005 was followed by the departure of Molson president Dan O'Neill in May. O'Neill was the executive who had helped broker the deal that sold 80.1 percent of Molson's interest in the team and the Molson Centre to George Gillett, a Coloradan, for US$183 million; one reason why Molson retained 19.9 percent was to guarantee the team would remain in Montreal. Not long after the merger and O'Neill's departure, it was announced that Coors was looking to get out of its guarantee to the Canadiens.

Ironically, the three major sports teams in Montreal—the Expos, the Alouettes and the Canadiens—all were owned by Americans. That list was reduced to two after the sad demise of the Expos, a situation that parallels the loss of the Nordiques. The truth is that no ownership situation can be regarded as safe or stable. Being the proprietor of a sports franchise these days is an entirely different proposition than it was in my era.

Interestingly, when the Bronfmans owned the team in the mid-1970s and were enjoying a string of Stanley Cups, one of their financial advisers told them it was time to get out of sports. The brothers asked why. His answer was two-fold: there were tax issues that mitigated against their continuing investment, and "we won't be able to control the players' salaries." They took his advice, persuaded that Carena Bancorp wouldn't continue to perform as well as it had if they stayed in the hockey business.

During the 2004–05 lockout, we heard much debate about salary caps, luxury taxes, and cost certainties. But a very basic question that was ignored or went unanswered may serve as a barometer of changed attitudes and realities: Can the average hockey fan afford to take his or her family to a hockey game? For the sake of discussion, let's make it a family of four. As I write, the answer is no. The price of tickets, parking, food, and souvenirs is simply prohibitive. If parents want to give their kids a great evening, it could cost them in the neighborhood of Can$500. I don't think the question even occurred to the players who were preoccupied with their rights and their bargaining positions and their wariness of the owners. They said nice things about the fans at press conferences, but those sentiments rang hollow to my ears.

We can quibble about what constitutes real dollars in 1953, 1971, 1994, or 2005, but even when those factors are allowed for, today's superstars come out miles ahead. Properly managed, the money they earn in their professional sports careers will last a lifetime. No superstar of my generation—Gordie Howe, Maurice Richard, Stan Mikita, Bobby Hull, or Frank Mahovlich—could say the same.

Many players of my era are baffled, even troubled, by what has happened to salaries in recent years. I have a somewhat different perspective, because I had a front-row seat as the money game took hold and, I think, developed a fuller understanding of how it came to pass. I'm not like the Rocket, who spent his retirement years raging against the salaries made by the modern players. Maurice had to retire to his basement to string fish wire and make lures and then work as a representative of a Montreal oil company to make ends meet. He was bitter, and he didn't hide it.

With all respect to Vincent Damphousse and Martin Brodeur, hockey players of my era were not naive, poorly educated, or the stooges of hockey management. We were, as they are today, the products of our generation; we reflected the attitudes and conduct of mainstream society at the time.

What confuses most of the players in today's National Hockey League Players' Association is the fact that there was so little money in anyone's hands in our day. The game was almost entirely gate-driven: teams sold tickets and may have received a small percentage of revenues from the concessions, or the sales of game programs, or marquee advertising around the building. That was it. Does that mean we must have been foolish to let management treat us so shabbily? No, it does not.

After missing an entire season, the league in 2005 faced a crisis and a challenge. It lost $60 million when ESPN pulled out of its commitment to broadcast the 2005–06 season, and its advertising partners were understandably nervous. With the possibility looming that hockey might return to the status of a gate-driven entertainment, perhaps this generation of NHL players will learn some of the hard-earned lessons we endured.

And if both sides wish to see the professional sport survive, perhaps they will remember the timeless recipe for success: form a strong team and learn to work together.

As these pages go to press amidst rumors of a pending agreement, it appears that the league will resume play in the fall of 2005 and that players' pay packets will be subject to a salary cap for the first time. Have the players lost the battle, then?

I feel this way: a balance between the league and the players had to be found if fiscal health was to be restored. All of hockey lost with the cancellation of the 2004–05 season; there was no single loser. Within two or three years, this labor dispute will be viewed as a "market correction" that needed to happen.

In the shorter term, does the episode warrant the dismissal of NHL commissioner Gary Bettman or NHLPA executive director Bob Goodenow? I couldn't say, but as it turned out, the players felt Goodenow had to go. Both men did their best to protect their constituents' interests, and that is the most that can be asked of them.

I read in the press that the Montreal Canadiens are expected to open the 2005–06 season in Boston on October 5, then visit Toronto the following Saturday. A pair of Original Six matchups, back-to-back, to get the juices flowing for players and fans alike.

Exactly what is needed. Game on.

VICTORIAVILLE

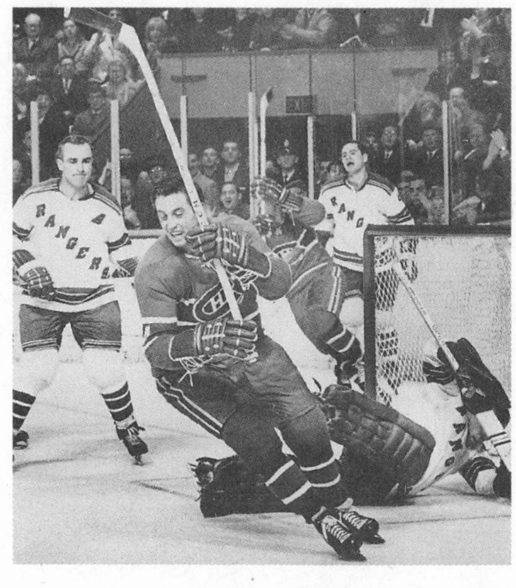

top left — Jean Béliveau, team captain in the late 1960s.

bottom left — Jean has just scored past New York's Eddie Giacomin, to the chagrin of Rangers defenders Harry Howell (center) and Arnie Brown (corner).

below — May Day 1965: Jean cradles the Stanley Cup, won earlier that evening in a 4–0 victory over Chicago at the Forum, and the brand-new Conn Smythe Trophy, offered for the first time to the play-offs' MVP.

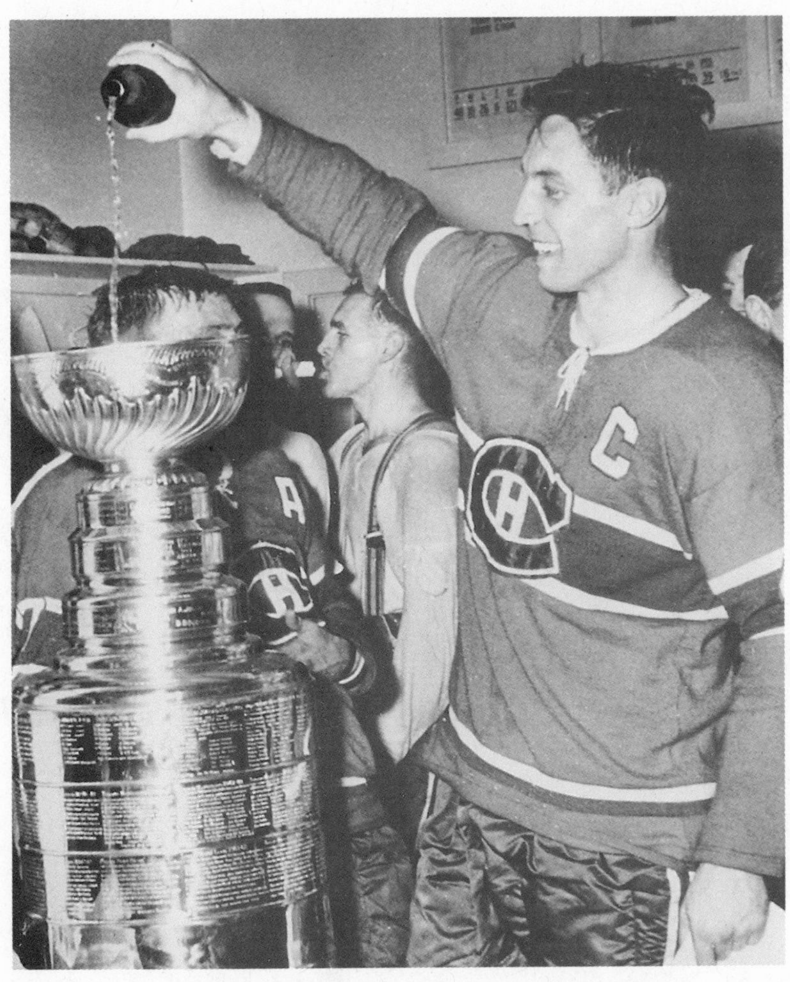

top left — Four on four: Jean is hot on the heels of the stellar Bobby Orr — the man, he says, who reshaped modern professional hockey.

middle left — Goalie Gerry Cheevers and defenseman Gary Doak, #26, protect the puck while a Boston teammate discourages Jean.

bottom left — Two Hall of Fame players, Jean and Chicago's Bobby Hull, in action.

above — On May 1, 1965, Jean celebrates Montreal's thirteenth Stanley Cup.

above — Bernard "Boom Boom" Geoffrion, Jean Béliveau, and Bert Olmstead (right).

right — Jean: A dressing room pose in the early 1950s.

top right — Rocket Richard and Jean.

bottom far right — Béliveau scores on the Hawks, as Pierre Pilote and Bill "Red" Hay look on.

above — The Canadiens' ambassadors, circa 1999: (left to right) Yvan Cournoyer, Maurice Richard, Jean Béliveau, Guy Lafleur, and Henri Richard.

right — Jean: A publicity still from the late 1950s.

top right — Jean Béliveau, team captain in the late 1960s.

bottom far right — Governor General Roland Michener oversees the induction of Officers of the Order of Canada Jean Béliveau and Gordie Howe in October 1971.

Jean Beliveau
#4

above — *On* March 11, 1996, fans gather on the last game night at the Forum. They saw a 4–1 win by Montreal over Dallas.

right — Jean Béliveau passes the torch to Henri Richard during closing ceremonies at the Montreal Forum on March 11, 1996.

left — A Béliveau family portrait: (clockwise) Jean, Mylène, Élise, Magalie, and Hélène.

above — During a pregame ceremony at the Montreal Forum, Jean Béliveau carries the torch for the 1988 Calgary Winter Olympic Games as it makes its way across Canada.

12

WE ARE ALL FANS

TO ECHO THE GREAT Lou Gehrig's farewell at Yankee Stadium in 1939, "I consider myself the luckiest guy in the world." I am a religious person, and I thank God daily for the natural abilities that enabled me to become a professional hockey player and for the countless opportunities that were presented to me during my career with the Montreal Canadiens.

The eighteen-year-old boy who left Victoriaville in December 1949 could not possibly have guessed that he was embarking on a voyage that would never cease to enrich him. Hockey enabled me to educate myself, to meet my wife, to pursue a career off-ice during and after my playing days. Hockey introduced me to wonderful friends: my teammates, the Côtés and the Byrnes, Roland Mercier, Zotique Lespérance, Jack Latter and Charlie Smith, the Molson and Bronfman families, the Selkes, Sam Pollock... the list goes on. I have been truly blessed, and I am grateful.

But hockey is also a business, and none of these things would have happened without the people who paid money to watch it. A player makes a decision early in a sports career as to how to balance his or her need for a private life with the public demands of the profession. A professional athlete should be involved in his community. He must treat the public with respect if he wishes to be granted respect in turn. It's not always easy. But anyone who thinks that he's there only for the paycheck and the good times will be bitterly disappointed.

As a hockey player and later as a member of various corporate boards, I was fortunate to travel to destinations around the world. First, however, I experienced the wonders of the country in which I live. I have crossed Canada many times over the past forty-five years and have come to know it well.

In my travels I am asked the inevitable questions about the country's political future, especially at times when events have created a climate of doubt. I think my actions over the years have made my own position clear; people know where I stand. I reply that I am first and foremost a Canadian—and a Canadien.

One of the proudest days in my life was December 19, 1969, when Gordie Howe and I were named Officers of the Order of Canada by Governor General Roland Michener. Strangely, my formal investiture in Ottawa didn't take place until almost two years later, on October 29, 1971, four months after I had retired from playing—possibly an indication of the demands of my schedule in those years. On May 6, 1998, Maurice Richard and I were elevated to the rank of Companions of the Order along with former prime minister Brian Mulroney; we were invested in special ceremonies on October 22 of the same year. If a man is known by the company he keeps, I could ask for no better than my partners on those occasions, two of the greatest players ever to don skates in the National Hockey League, Gordie and Maurice. The Order of Canada is a great honor, and I wear my pin every day.

We are so fortunate to call Canada home. However far I travel, however exotic the locale, I am always glad to return. Canada is the best place to live, bar none. And to my mind, the *Club de Hockey*

Canadien has always been a sort of metaphor for Canada, a fine example of different ethnic and linguistic groups working together to achieve great things.

Language and cultural differences never caused problems between the players. When I went to Quebec City, I couldn't speak a word of English. I picked it up from teammates there and, later, in the Canadiens' dressing room. I very quickly realized that there are good people everywhere, and I believe that part of the reason for the occasional friction between our "two solitudes" lies in the fact that the majority of Quebeckers have never had the chance to visit the rest of the country, to see its beauty or meet its people. Nor have many citizens from other provinces visited Quebec, to enjoy its culture and appreciate its history.

One thing is certain: the negative fallout, the climate of uncertainty, has lasted too long. For almost half a century, the people of Quebec haven't known where the future will take them. It makes a lot of people very uncomfortable to have to contemplate the possibility of unprecedented political upheaval every decade or so. Personally, I find it difficult to understand why, at a time when the world is made more accessible every day through communications, ease of travel, and a global marketplace, some people want to narrow their options and go the other way.

Politics is politics, and I am not so naive as to believe there are not occasional sorry happenings behind the scenes. In the spring of 2005, the daily revelations of the Gomery Commission examining federal sponsorship and advertising activities made Canadians cynical and angry. I would like readers to know that in my experience this situation is not reflective of political life generally. I've known hundreds of dedicated public servants at all levels of government in Quebec and all across the country, and I believe they are honest people with a genuine desire to serve. I hope this controversial episode will, in fact, make us stronger; above all, Canadians value truth and fairness, and it is worth reminding ourselves of the need to maintain those standards.

My most extensive—and exhaustive—tour of Canada came in the fall of 1994, when I took to the road to promote the first edition of these memoirs. Two topics were invariably raised in interviews and at autographing appearances: the first was the question of my candidacy for the position of governor general; the second was the 1994 NHL lockout. By 2005 and the release of this second edition, my aspirations to government service were long in the past; unfortunately, the suspension of play in the NHL was once again fresh in memory.

A couple of years before my 1994 "book tour," I had my first brush with politics. I had no political ambitions whatsoever, but through the years my name had appeared on various parties' "wish lists" of ideal candidates. I was approached in roundabout ways from time to time, but when I showed no interest these overtures ceased to come my way. It's true that I was twice offered a Senate seat by Prime Minister Mulroney, whom I knew quite well; the first call came in 1992 when there were several vacancies in the Upper House which he hoped to fill with Conservatives.

"First of all," I told him, "I've always stayed away from politics." I had—and have—no party affiliations whatsoever.

"Second," I said, "I wouldn't have anything to do with politics unless I was elected, not appointed. Third, I certainly wouldn't go to the Senate simply because the Conservatives need more votes." I didn't mean to disparage the Senate in any way; my old teammate and friend Frank Mahovlich entered that chamber in 1994 and has served with distinction ever since.

Former hockey players have also distinguished themselves in the House of Commons. Lionel "the Big Train" Conacher, who in 1950 was selected top Canadian athlete of the first half of the twentieth century, was twice elected a member of Parliament to represent the Toronto riding of Trinity. Sadly, this great sportsman and Canadian public servant died on May 26, 1954, during a softball game on Parliament Hill. Leonard "Red" Kelly was still playing for the Maple Leafs when he was elected MP in Toronto–York West.

Given that history, the prime minister wasn't stepping out of bounds by offering me a Senate seat. When I respectfully refused, he understood my feelings, and the matter rested. A year later, however, he tried again, just before he resigned as prime minister in June 1993 and at about the time that I was counting down to my corporate retirement. When word of the offer got out, I was in Toronto on business. I knew I couldn't hide from the press on this, so I asked my secretary, Louise Richer, to reroute all the calls. I sat in my room at the Royal York Hotel for two hours, answering reporters' questions.

Again, I had to refuse Mr. Mulroney, and I told him it was a question of consistency. "The Canadiens want me to stay, but I need more freedom. I want control of my agenda. If I accept your offer, I simply transfer my time at the Forum to Ottawa. And you know me; I wouldn't be a figurehead." I knew that nights and weekends would be absorbed by duties and travel. I was sixty-two years old, and I wanted to give more time to my family. And that was that.

The stories about my candidacy for the position of governor general surfaced in the early summer of 1994, and media friends told me that the original rumors, or "leaks," had started in Ottawa, which led some to believe that the Prime Minister's Office was floating a trial balloon. The story was that my name was on a list of candidates whom Prime Minister Jean Chrétien was considering in his search for a successor to Ray Hnatyshyn, whose term would end later that year.

"I don't know anything about it," I told my press friends. "I know how the sports media work, but I have no experience with the parliamentary press gallery. I really don't know what this is all about."

Trial balloon or not, the story found its way to the Canadian Press wire agency and from there to media across the country.

Élise and I discussed the possibility several times over the summer, and I would be lying if I said we were not attracted by the romance of the job and by the importance of it, too. I had spent many years in Quebec City, which is also Élise's hometown, and after Ottawa it is the city where the office of the governor general is most familiar. The incumbent customarily spends an average of two months a year in residence at the Citadel, and on several occasions we had been guests there of Governor General Jeanne Sauvé. I fully appreciated the significance of the office and its position, especially during times of national crisis.

In early September, I awoke very early one morning with the "will I or won't I?" quandary driving me from my bed. I went down to my office and, by the light of a lamp, began listing the pros and cons in two columns on a piece of paper. The two biggest arguments against it were the time it would take from my family and the state of my health.

I had just retired from the Montreal Canadiens after forty years with the organization. I was not tired of working at the Forum, but I felt I was less able to do the work in the way I thought it should be done. A seven-day-a-week schedule, year in and year out, exacts a price.

Élise has always teased me about being a perfectionist; never a hair out of place, never a phone call left unreturned. In recent years I had sometimes sat staring at a heap of telephone slips, wondering if one life held enough time to ever see the bottom of the pile.

We sat at the breakfast table and talked. It would be fair to say that both of us had Rideau Hall stars in our eyes and were extremely tempted by the possibility that we might occupy that viceregal offical residence in Ottawa. But we realized that it was an all-or-nothing commitment. If I accepted the job, I would plunge right in, coming up for air only at the end of the five-year appointment. That left little time for our daughter Hélène, or our granddaughters Mylène and Magalie in that period. Going to Ottawa would mean literally leaving them behind, and we couldn't do that. By the time the term was over, our grandchildren would be pretty much grown and independent, another opportunity missed—or so it seemed when I reflected on how quickly my daughter had gone from childhood to young womanhood.

On September 27, Élise and I were the guests of the prime minister and his wife, Aline, at 24 Sussex Drive in Ottawa. By this time, I had made my decision. At the end of the dinner, Mrs. Chrétien announced that we would have coffee in the salon; on the way, the prime minister asked me to follow him into the library.

"Jean, I have a very short list for the position of governor general, and I would like to meet each person on the list to discuss this possible opportunity," he said, perhaps testing the waters. I went more directly to the point.

"Just the honor of being considered is very special to me, Mr. Prime Minister, but I will not be able to have you further my candidacy."

I could see that he was a little disappointed, but Jean Chrétien is not an arm-twister. He quietly accepted my reply, and the rest of the evening was as cordial as it had been up to that point. I appreciated his understanding that circumstances and timing were against my considering any offer he might have made. Although he did not make me a concrete offer, I left 24 Sussex Drive that night feeling that if I had said I would be happy to remain on or move up a few spots on his shortlist, the job would have been mine.

A few weeks later, out on the book tour, the story of my candidacy was still regarded as newsworthy. It was truly heartwarming to be told by Canadians in all parts of the country, "We think you would have made a great governor general, and we wish you had accepted the position. You are a true Canadian."

One last word on the subject, because the question arose when it became known that I could not let my name stand: neither Canadian or Quebec politics, nor partisan sentiment of any kind, had a bearing on my decision. I would have been proud to serve had the situation been different. But I will say that a great many Canadians outside Quebec have taken the time to ask me to do what I can to persuade my fellow Quebeckers that we are all in this great national experiment together, as Canadians, and that other Canadians want that to never change. The quiet assurance and sincerity with which these sentiments have been delivered to me are inspiring.

That 1994 book-promotion tour was the longest trip of my life, fifty-six days from coast to coast. An especially treasured moment was the launch held in Quebec City. Unlike the situation in Montreal, where I was in frequent contact with former teammates and players who came before or after my on-ice days at gatherings of *les anciens Canadiens* and at casual get-togethers in the Forum's alumni lounge, keeping in touch with old Quebec City teammates from the Citadels and Aces had not been easy.

Thus it was a very special morning when a few Aces and Citadels veterans joined former Molson co-workers, media pals, and family friends at the Colisée to catch up and reminisce. Ludger Tremblay, Armand Gaudreault, Camille Henry, Bernard Guay, Claude Larochelle, and Butch Houle were among the 150 people who gathered to greet me in the city where it all started. Sad to say, many of these wonderful people have passed away since 1994, as has the alumni's room at the Forum. I miss them all.

The book tour brought me face-to-face with thousands of Canadians, and I've enjoyed countless similar encounters in the eleven years since. People are so friendly and genuinely delighted to meet someone from my NHL generation. The Montreal Canadiens have always had a huge following right across Canada, and wherever I go, I see the familiar *bleu-blanc-rouge* on caps, sweaters, pants, jackets, even running shoes. Many others are proud to tell me they are

Leafs fans, or that they support the more recently arrived Canadian teams such as the Flames, the Oilers, the Canucks, or the Senators. Their enthusiasm makes me realize once again just how large a part hockey plays in the lives of Canadians. Maybe Don Cherry is right; ice hockey takes us to another level and immediately gives strangers something to talk about, no matter where they meet in this country.

One comment that I heard and still hear from older fans, whether in Halifax or Victoria, is how difficult it is to follow the game today. Some favorite matchups they see only once a season (Montreal versus Detroit, for example), and they are unhappy with that. With an average of seven hundred players in the NHL, and maybe another hundred moving up and down between "the Show" and the minor-pro leagues during a season, the fans are also losing touch with the game's personalities. Add to that the tendency of helmets to hamper recognition, and the teams' much larger rosters, and you begin to feel the alienation of longtime fans, people who could once quote the statistics, both game and career, of the players who toiled in the six-team league and even in the post-1967 twelve-team league.

Back in the days of the Original Six, there were 120 players, with maybe another dozen or so subs who would come and go from other leagues, and fans didn't need the names written on our sweaters.

"If somebody was shooting the puck, we knew right away who it was," one fan told me. "We recognized players by their skating, shooting, and checking styles; there was an intimacy to the game that's been lost."

I PROMISED THAT I would reflect in these pages on the weaknesses of the modern game as I see them. Rather than express my reservations in abstract terms, I think it more important to consider the fans' viewpoint, so I'll do so here, distilling the opinions of thousands who have spoken to me.

On behalf of my fellow fans, I deliver to the league the following complaints. Fix them, please.

> Dumping the puck breaks the flow of the game and diminishes the skills of players. It is a useful tactic in the era of the neutral zone trap, but the fans hate it.
>
> The neutral zone trap, where teams line up all five players between the two blue lines to clog up the center of the ice, is a very effective defensive strategy. The result is a game that slows to a snail's pace.
>
> Stickwork, that is, using the stick to slash, spear, hook, or otherwise hinder puck carriers, brings out the dark side of the game. One simple question: why outlaw all such infractions and then ignore them when they occur? Again, it's a tactic that impedes the most skilled players, especially when opponents hold up their sticks as if to erect a fence in front of them.
>
> Refereeing according to circumstance. There is only one rule book, not one for every period in a game or every situation. Referees should whistle down all infractions when they occur, wherever on the ice they occur, no matter what the score or time left on the clock. The coaches of teams with larger, more physical players, or with larger, less-skilled players (witness Don Cherry's Bruins), long ago persuaded referees to "let them play," a euphemism for "let my bigger, less-skilled team use every device it can to slow or stop that much better team over there." The referees bought it, and the result was ugly hockey.

There have been many other excellent suggestions from Fan Row, and they deserve attention. These people have had a love affair with hockey all of their lives.

Meanwhile, the game's general managers have conducted tests of equipment size, goal measurements, and other rules in an effort to improve the state of play. Beginning with the 2005–06 season, goalie pads will shrink to 1990 levels; a decision to remove the center red line has been held in abeyance. My appeal to the league is this: don't worry about the size of the nets or the science behind composite sticks. Worry about the bigger problems that are equally within your power to solve.

CANADIAN UNIVERSITIES have been especially kind to me since I hung up my skates in 1971 and my pin-striped suit in 1993. *Honoris causa:* I haven't been confronted with so much Latin since my days with the Sacred Heart Brothers at L'Académie Saint-Louis de Gonzague.

My first honorary degree came from the obvious school inasmuch as my name is Béliveau, one of the original *Acadien* surnames. Conferred on May 7, 1972, it was an honorary degree in physical education from New Brunswick's University of Moncton, a primarily French-language institution. On May 30, 1995, I received the Loyola Medal from Concordia University in Montreal, and on June 6, 1999, an honorary doctorate from the University of Ottawa. What is especially gratifying is the fact that all three schools are bilingual institutions.

Three Nova Scotia universities chose to honor me next: Acadia in Wolfville, on May 11, 1998; St. Mary's in Halifax, in October 2001, and Ste-Anne's in Pointe-de-l'Église, in May 2001.

A life in and around hockey provides many opportunities to travel, and among my most memorable trips was the journey through western Canada with Élise in 1960. It was the year Molson's sent me to tour the western breweries they had acquired the year before. I could use any mode of transportation I wanted, but I suggested to Élise that we drive. "We'll have a second honeymoon all the way across the country."

Élise has always been an enthusiastic traveler, and she didn't hesitate. Her sister agreed to take care of Hélène, who had just turned three, and we were off to the west. We spent two or three days in each major city, and I visited hospitals, radio stations, and service clubs, representing both the brewery and the team. Near Regina,

I reconnected with those Béliveau uncles who had left Quebec for the wheat fields decades before.

A month later, we arrived in Vancouver. Molson's had offered us time to ourselves when we reached the coast, and we were ready for a few unscheduled days after four fully booked weeks on the road. We caught our breath, got back in the car, and drove all the way down the coasts of Washington, Oregon, and California, to San Diego. Then we took another month to return home.

After two months away from our daughter, we were content to stay put for a while. In retrospect, though, this was the adventure that gave us the travel bug for life. Later on, whenever I was offered the chance, I'd try to experience as much of our country as possible and especially its more remote areas. Of course, Canadians who live in these far-off corners don't consider themselves "remote" at all, but neither do they have the same opportunities to meet sports personalities. I was invited often to these communities and always tried to accept. For many years, the Canadiens were the only NHL team who had someone to perform this roving ambassador role.

One day, early in 1976, I received a call from the mayor of Dawson City, Yukon. "We're about to open a new sports complex and the major part of it is the arena. We'd be honored if you would come."

Montreal to Dawson was a marathon trek by anybody's standards, and I hesitated. The trip would involve three flights and an overnight stay in Vancouver.

"I don't say no very often, but this time I regret I must. Surely there's someone in Vancouver who could go?" I suggested.

I hung up the phone and immediately felt bad. The opening of the complex was a special event in the life of their community. If I could help, I should, even if it meant a long journey.

I called him back an hour later. "Have you found somebody else?"

"No, we still want you."

"Okay, I'll come."

The sights and sounds of so many destinations tend to blur with time, but I have a great memory aid when it comes to the Dawson trip. On the night of my Vancouver layover, I watched Darryl Sittler of Toronto set a league record with six goals and four assists for ten points in a single game.

I arrived in Whitehorse the next morning, February 8, changed planes, and flew on to Dawson. It was a crisp winter day. The mountains, lakes, and forests lay below a deep blanket of snow and ice. About eight hundred people wintered in Dawson City at that time, mostly Inuit and First Nations, but the population mushroomed to three or four thousand in the summer. The whole town and half the surrounding countryside came to the opening ceremonies.

The mayor began with an explanation. "Down east, you cut a ceremonial ribbon when you open a new building," he said. "Here, we do things differently." Two Inuit came toward us, one carrying a sawhorse and saw, the other a white birch log. The mayor and I each took an end of the saw and cut the birch in two. (Memories of Victoriaville and the cedar hydro poles!) When we were done, he presented me with a key to the front door of the sports complex and invited the crowd inside. We wasted no time in doing what every Canadian does in an inviting new arena—we went for a skate.

In those days, Dawson was the only place in Canada where gambling was legal. That evening, its casino was packed, decorated like an old saloon from gold rush days, complete with dance-hall girls and plenty of local color. An old prospector came by our table during dinner and showed me a gold nugget the size of my fist. It must have been worth thousands of dollars and he was carrying it around in his pocket. Later I was called up on stage and told to take off my jacket and roll up my sleeves. A bucket full of sandy water appeared and I panned for gold. I came up with about an ounce, all in tiny flakes.

I have them still, a souvenir of an unforgettable trip. It's not very often that you can make money during dessert.

I was up at seven the next morning, despite a late night. In the few hours before my plane back to Whitehorse, I walked through the town in weather 40 degrees below freezing, just me and the crunch of my boots in the half-light of a northern sunrise. Then I looked up and saw a family of huge ravens; they and a few dogs were my only companions until I spotted a lonely firefighter on duty at the firehall.

The North defines Canada for me. Several years later I was asked by the federal government to visit the community of Frobisher Bay, now called Iqaluit, for a weekend. I was to watch the *Hockey Night in Canada* game that Saturday with local residents and, after every period, answer their questions about the contest and about hockey in general.

Iqaluit—meaning "place where the fish are"—is on Baffin Island, a land mass that is 1,000 miles long and dotted with tiny settlements. It is home to the only hospital and high school in the region. During my visit, I was taken by plane to Pangnirtung on the Cumberland Peninsula, an important center for Inuit art, especially woven tapestries and soapstone carvings. It's said that the first Europeans landed there in 1585; by 1840, it was established as the northernmost port for whalers plying their trade in Arctic waters.

Pangnirtung sits at the base of a mountain. Flying in, the plane clears the peak, banks sharply, and then drops like a stone to land on a frozen clearing right in the middle of the village. When I disembarked, a group of kids were playing hockey in temperatures of thirty-five-below Fahrenheit. I joined them for a few minutes and then continued my tour, which included a visit to the local museum.

To fly out, we had to follow the course of a river canyon for several miles, with mountains flanking us on either side. All of a sudden we reached a pass, the pilot pointed the nose straight up, and we were out of there. A local guide had told me that Pangnirtung is Inuit for "place of the bull caribou," a name that is entirely appropriate; one of the sights below us was a massive caribou herd, hundreds if not thousands of animals moving across the landscape. Later, as we neared Iqaluit and darkness fell, I could see the lights of Inuit hunters, returning to their villages from all directions on snowmobiles.

At dinner in Iqaluit that night, the mayor introduced me to a dentist who had retired from his practice in Jonquière, Quebec, and had decided to experience the Far North for a year. Three years later, he was still there.

During the meal, I asked the mayor if I could see a dog sled.

"Sure, Jean, but I have to tell you that there's only one in town."

It belonged to the dentist from Jonquière. Everyone else relied on snowmobiles.

I EXPERIENCED WONDERFUL trips abroad, as well, the first in 1966 when I visited members of the Canadian Armed Forces who were part of a six-country United Nations peacekeeping contingent in the Sinai Desert. Every night, CBC Television provided footage of the latest Stanley Cup play-off game, and I provided the commentary. Our troupe numbered about twenty, including the entertainer Daniele Dorice and Miss Canada, Diane Landry, of St. Boniface, Manitoba. We were based in Rafah, on the coast, and visited the camps of other countries' contingents, as well as places that would become household names eighteen months later during the 1967 Arab-Israeli War.

There wasn't much ice available, so we played softball and golf. Our hosts set up a small course on the sand, and we'd tee off from carpets. To create greens, they emptied barrels of oil and rolled the surfaces smooth. Sand traps were self-maintaining.

A few years later, I arranged a European trip for purely personal reasons. In August 1971, two months after my last game as a player, I learned that my father had a touch of atherosclerosis and had apparently suffered a very minor stroke a couple of years earlier. Arthur Béliveau was nearing his seventieth year at that time, but, amazingly, he had never been on a plane. On the spur of the moment, we decided to take a five-week holiday in Europe—Élise, Hélène, myself, and my father and stepmother. The pleasure of seeing Dad's reaction to his first flying experience was worth the price of the tickets.

The plan was to motor through Germany, Switzerland, Italy, and France, taking five leisurely days in Nice on the Côte d'Azur, with a final stop in Paris. Before we left, seasoned travelers warned that we were foolhardy to visit Europe in high season with no reservations. Still, that was our intention. I wanted five weeks of freedom, gallivanting around with no itinerary.

We made reservations for our first morning in Frankfurt, but thereafter I dealt with the concierge of whatever hotel we happened to stop at. Before dinner on the eve of departure I'd tell him our next destination, and describe our requirements: a quality hotel, close to downtown, with two available suites. European concierges have a sophisticated network and they never failed us. Even in Nice in August we found accommodation at a four-star hotel a few blocks from the Promenade des Anglais.

In advance of our trip, I had contacted Louis Laurendeau, a Jesuit priest and former Montrealer then stationed in Rome, to ask if he could arrange a visit to the Vatican. Father Laurendeau was secretary to the director general of the Order of Jesus, headquartered right next to the Vatican. When we reached Rome, we met Father Laurendeau for dinner.

"Jean, I have good news for you." Not only would we see Pope Paul VI at the next day's regular public audience at Castel Gandolfo, his summer retreat outside the city, but we had been granted a private audience with His Holiness.

Needless to say, we were quite nervous when we left our hotel at eight thirty the following morning. Our driver informed us we had plenty of time. "It starts in the garden at ten," he said, "but the private audiences are at eleven." There was time for a tour of the catacombs before he drove us to the little town of Castel Gandolfo.

Twenty-three people, fifteen of them missionaries, were given private audiences that day. We sat in the marble reception chamber while the Pope attended to his audience in the garden. We could hear people cheering as he acknowledged the different delegations in their own languages. Then, shortly after eleven o'clock, there was movement at the end of the room, several cardinals walked by, and the Pope's assistants began calling us up by groups.

When our turn came, it was clear the Pope had been well briefed. He knew about my career and my work on behalf of various charities. He told me, "I was in Montreal when I was a young priest. I am very pleased that you have brought your parents with you." He then gave us prayer beads and medals.

The interview lasted no more than two or three minutes, but the memory of it is indelible. I will never forget the sight of the pontiff dressed all in white and the startling contrast of his robes with his blue eyes. While there is a no-camera policy at private audiences, the papal staff take discreet pictures to commemorate the occasion. Ours were delivered to us later that evening. When the hotel staff saw the envelope, their service became even better.

The next day, we visited Vatican City and, once again, everything had been laid on by Father Laurendeau. At the gate we were greeted by an imposing member of the Swiss Guard. He looked at me closely and said, "You have the shape of an athlete. Where are you from?"

"Montreal. What makes you say that I look like an athlete?"

"I'm sure you are one."

I admitted he was right and that I'd played for the Montreal Canadiens.

"The hockey club? You're Jean Béliveau of the Canadiens?"

He almost put down his halberd to shake my hand. As it turned out, he knew a great deal about hockey. We exchanged addresses and, later, books on our respective countries.

It was like that throughout our trip, an idyllic journey made even better for me by the pleasure of seeing my father's delight in visiting the Leaning Tower of Pisa, the Blue Grotto of Capri, the Pont d'Avignon, the Eiffel Tower, places he had only read about and never expected to see. I was so happy that I could share these things with him. He had been there in 1949 when his eighteen-year-old son set out from Victoriaville on the adventure that started it all, and in all the years since.

Our European trip together was, of course, scant repayment for all that he had done. But it was my way of saying, "Thank you, Papa. I hope that my best was enough."

IN 1997 I MADE another visit to the Middle East when Gary Ulrich, Eddie Wilzer, and Gordie Schwartz, all prominent members of Montreal's Jewish community, invited me to Israel to serve as honorary captain of the Canadian team competing in that year's Maccabeah Games, a sort of Jewish Olympics. Most events took place in Tel Aviv's Ramat Gan Stadium, with golf near Netanya and swimming in Jerusalem.

Because of the heat, the competitions were confined to early mornings, late afternoons, and evenings, leaving lots of time for Élise and me to visit other centers. Most days, we'd go to Jerusalem for the early competitions, then ask our driver to take us to the Dead Sea, the mountains, or to the ancient city of Jericho.

One afternoon in Jericho, I decided to look for a Bedouin teapot and asked our chauffeur to find a reputable antique shop.

"Antique shops are more numerous than people in Jericho," he smiled.

"Then take us to the best one," I said.

As it happened, we arrived at the shop just as units of the Israeli defense force appeared on the scene. Troop transports disgorged helmeted and flak-jacketed soldiers who fanned out in all directions. The canvas top of one two-ton truck was rolled back to reveal the most menacing piece of artillery I'd ever seen. The troops quickly secured the area immediately in front of us, roped it off, and took up their positions.

Of course, our destination was on the other side of the rope. Our chauffeur, who obviously had some kind of government, if not military, connection, hailed an officer. "What's happening?"

The officer pointed to a stone bridge not two hundred yards from where we stood.

"We just received a call that the bridge over there is mined with several hundred pounds of explosive."

There was nothing to do but wait while the sappers did their work. Meanwhile, our antique shop beckoned to us, a scant thirty yards away.

"Listen," our chauffeur said to the officer, "these people are from Montreal. Mr. Béliveau is honorary captain of the Canadian team at the Maccabeah Games. We want to go to that store. They'll be safer inside than standing here, should this whole thing explode, God forbid."

The officer thought for a moment, perhaps visualizing how much trouble would come down on his head if we were blown to bits because he had refused us shelter.

"Go ahead, but be careful," he said, waving us through.

We saw the modern Israel and also the country of biblical times: the Roman amphitheater at Caesarea, Masada, Galilee and the Jordan River, Bethlehem and Nazareth. I spent a few moments in contemplation and prayer at Manger Square and the Church of the

Nativity in Bethlehem. It was a shock at the ninth or tenth station of the cross to discover a Coca-Cola sign on the wall.

But the highlight of the trip to Israel was the event that had taken us there, the Maccabeah Games. Nothing in my professional career matched the march into Ramat Gan Stadium at the head of the Canadian team, with sixty thousand spectators cheering us on. Canada was given an especially warm salute, and everyone felt a surge of pride as we walked behind our flag.

In 1997, I was part of the Canadian contingent at the Maccabeah Games for a second time, and once again we had an adventure with a bridge. It happened as the national delegations entered the stadium in the opening ceremony processional. Because "Canada" is spelled with a *K* in Hebrew, our contingent was situated in the middle of the pack.

For some reason I don't know, the ceremony planners had constructed a temporary wooden bridge over a river and into the stadium, where a steel bridge had stood before. That night, Austria went first, with about 60 representatives, followed by the much larger Australian team with some 360. Midway across, the structure collapsed.

We were a good mile or so from the bridge and could only guess at the reason for the delay in the processional. We were able to see searchlights illuminating the river in an effort to find survivors, and finally word of the tragedy reached us: four or five people had drowned and many more were injured. The opening ceremonies were canceled and the games were carried out in an atmosphere of shock and mourning.

In December 1984, I was invited by the Canadian Association of Hong Kong to attend the then British colony's Canada Week and serve as honorary president of the festivities, which included a golf tournament, a press conference, and several receptions and parties. We were there just before Christmas, when the governor's wife threw a switch to illuminate the millions of holiday lights that decorated the city's buildings. Thousands of Chinese armed with tripod cameras added to the atmosphere, and a tremendous cheer went up when the lights blazed into life.

After Hong Kong we traveled to Beijing at the invitation of the recently installed Canadian ambassador to China. As our External Affairs contact put it, "Not too many Canadian sports figures ever get out his way. If you could come, it would give him an opportunity to meet the Chinese sports authorities, by hosting a reception or a dinner with you as guest."

Away we went, and we visited Tiananmen Square, the Great Wall of China, and the Forbidden City. The country seemed vast, and Beijing was spectacular, with wide avenues, huge squares, and swarms of bicycles everywhere we looked.

I told Élise I wanted to see all those bicycles in motion, so I got up at five thirty one morning, dressed quickly, and went downstairs to find the streets transformed into rivers of bicycles, their riders burdened with goods of every kind imaginable.

A humbling and wondrous thought came into my mind: the memory of a young boy, slapping pucks against the boards of the rink his father had built in their backyard, on a Sunday morning after Mass. That lad could never have imagined that a life in hockey would take him to this faraway place and to the extraordinary spectacle I witnessed that morning.

From Trois-Rivières to Beijing; it was more than a lifetime.

13

LEGACIES

IT OCCURS INEVITABLY in the life of every mature married couple that one day they sit down, perhaps at the kitchen table as we did, and confront a list of final matters about which they must make decisions. It is the last real service parents provide to their children; to us, it's the natural way of things: "We must determine how we are going to dispose of our worldly goods and, ultimately, of our worldly bodies."

The new millennium was well along when Élise and I had that "we're not getting any younger, honey" talk. Brochures and information kits at hand, we discussed burial arrangements, wills and testaments, life insurance policies, death taxes, and the distribution of our "goods and chattels" to our daughter and granddaughters. Several matters were decided, and others were put on the agenda of our next Sunday night dinner *en famille*.

We were most concerned about broaching the subject with the younger Béliveaus. Élise and I were in our early seventies, a time when people often become preoccupied with such issues, and Hélène was in her forties, a down-to-earth person who always tackled the hard stuff head on. But my two granddaughters were still pursuing their education, and I wondered if it might be a burden for them to deal with the mortality of close family members before they'd even launched their own lives.

Nonetheless, we agreed it had to be done and there was no delaying the process. The family met, and all the options were discussed, including the question of what should be done with the boxes and boxes of NHL paraphernalia I had accumulated over the years.

Hélène, as usual, went straight to the point. "What am I going to do with all that stuff?" she laughed. "Do you think you're going to empty your closets and fill up mine?" She requested only two things: the replica rink plaque Molson had given me in 1971 when I retired from playing and a bronze trophy commemorating my five hundredth goal, complete with the actual puck. She kept two Stanley Cup replicas for my granddaughters, along with several paintings I had received as gifts over the years. She had no room for the rest of it, and said so.

A few days after our family dinner, I contacted Classic Collectibles, an Internet-based hockey memorabilia auction house, to investigate the possibility of converting those boxes into something that would be of genuine value to my heirs.

AS MOST SPORTS FANS know, sports collectibles have become a serious business, one that dates from the 1950s. That was the golden age of player cards, packaged five to a pack with bubblegum and sold for a nickel. Millions of kids coveted, collected, traded, and played games with those cards.

From the earliest days of the twentieth century, various collectible items were distributed in small quantities alongside or inside particular products. Baseball cards came with Sweet Caporal cigarettes before the First World War and into the 1920s; Sportsman tobacco products and Beehive Corn Syrup offered hockey cards, and boxes of the renowned Wheaties Breakfast of Champions featured images of recent champions in all sports.

The passion for cards, especially baseball cards, took off in the fifties. For about twenty years, the cards themselves changed very little and were produced by relatively few manufacturers—Topps, O-Pee-Chee, and Fleer among them. While there were dedicated collectors out there, the usual practice was to amass cards by series, year, or sport and store them away in albums.

That changed in the 1980s and early 1990s when the major sports card manufacturers jumped into the competition by offering "specialty collectibles," cards that were sold in special foil packs without bubblegum and at much higher prices than a nickel a pack. What had been offered as premiums to enhance the appeal of cigarettes or food products were now products in their own right.

I never collected cards, but I've become almost an expert in the last decade or so, after viewing literally thousands placed before me for signing. Collectible cards opened up the sports memorabilia market, and today the exchange of autographed items and memorabilia of all kinds is a growing industry. Card shows and signing sessions attract thousands of eager fans and collectors who will pay to meet certain players. The athletes receive appearance fees from show organizers and happily turn up to sign cards, pictures, pucks, sticks, sweaters, and countless other items that are either brought to the shows by the fans or sold on-site.

It's a new business and one that could not be more timely for the sports world. It's a necessary business for hockey's veterans, because a lot of players who retired in the late 1950s or 1960s came out of the game with very little money. Back then, those who didn't prepare for retirement could have real difficulties. The salaries of that generation meant players could buy their houses outright, maybe a cottage as well, and put their kids through school. They might even be able to establish a small business for their post-hockey years, but many more failed than succeeded as entrepreneurs.

Almost twenty years ago, Gordie and Colleen Howe, Phil Esposito and other prominent hockey figures helped focus attention on retirement planning when it became obvious that many former players were in distress. One result was a much stronger and very active NHL Players Alumni Association, a group that provided all kinds of assistance to players who thought the "R Day" would never come.

The memorabilia industry is certainly a boon for all retirees, and when fellows from the Original Six appear at the shows they are always greeted enthusiastically. Likewise, they appreciate the attention. Many of them went home to small towns and smaller jobs, a far cry from the center-ice action they'd known for ten or twelve years in the NHL.

I have to admit, though, that this is a high-end, luxury business for the relatively affluent. Occasionally I attended the shows because I enjoyed meeting the fans. But I've watched athletes from other sports signing their names without even looking at people, let alone exchanging a few words. To me, that's not what it's all about.

One player who is often seen at these events is the ever popular Johnny Bower. I once told him that he and his Toronto colleagues were lucky: they didn't have far to travel, since a number of shows are held in that city every year. "I have to fly in and, most of the time, stay overnight. You take your car, and half an hour later you're back home for dinner."

He laughed. "Yeah, but I had to suffer with you and the Rocket in my face all those years. I've earned my break now."

Montreal stages perhaps two card shows annually, while Toronto hosts the most in Canada. Chicago, Detroit, and St. Louis each have several major shows a year. Needless to say, Bobby Hull, Stan Mikita, Gordie Howe, and other former Hawks and Red Wings are big draws at the U.S. events.

Most of the time, we're on our own or sharing the podium with someone like Bower. The last time I was in Detroit for a show, I had dinner with Gordie Howe. His marketing man, Dell Reddy, took pictures of the two of us in team jackets and sweaters. Some day these photographs, too, will become collectibles. In the meantime, I expect there will be fewer hockey figures at the memorabilia shows when the next generation begins to retire. Simply put, they won't need the money.

What started with playing cards and blossomed with memorabilia shows has become even more lucrative since the arrival of the Internet. Auction Web sites such as eBay are the drivers behind a growing hunger for sports collectibles.

One of the first to realize the monetary potential of his hockey assets was Maurice Richard. Late in his life, he engaged Classic Collectibles to set up an auction that sold 289 items and gave more than $1.6 million to the Richard family. This amount included the sale of various items to the Canadian Museum of Civilization in Gatineau, Quebec, just across the Ottawa River from Parliament Hill.

I admit to being shocked at first by Maurice's decision. It seemed a betrayal of his sport, his career, and his fans. A lot of the mementos he'd received over the years had been presented in good faith by associations, organizations, sponsors, companies, and leagues. Wouldn't selling them be some sort of repudiation of these gifts and institutions?

But when I thought about it for a while, Maurice's decision made all the sense in the world. He was maintaining the priorities that had guided his whole life: taking care of his family was number 1. Others who later followed his example with on-line auctions included Bernie Geoffrion, Guy Lafleur, and Jacques Demers. After a word with them and more discussion within the family, we decided to do the same.

I expected some controversy, but I was confident it was the right thing to do. The idea of my family sorting through hundreds of presentation items, mementos, and photographs after my death, uncertain of their value and uneasy with the responsibility for their disposal, was not attractive. Instead, I could ensure these items ended up in the hands of collectors who were prepared to invest and work hard so that their collections appreciated over the years.

In a way, it was recycling at its best. People who truly appreciate and enjoy owning trophies, awards, sticks, skates, and all the other material pieces of a hockey career would be happy, and my family would be taken care of. The "goods and chattels" would be converted into money for those I intended should have it, all taxes and fees paid. My granddaughters have something like four to six years of school remaining, but when they graduate they'll enjoy a greater range of options, to travel, to launch their careers, to establish their own homes.

Eventually the general public chimed in. Those who raised objections—thankfully, not the majority—were people who see life in terms of *la patrimoine,* the Quebec collectivity (not to be confused with collecting); in other words, those who favor shoving stuff into museums.

I had investigated the Hockey Hall of Fame in Toronto in the early 1970s and found that everything I had lent prior to that date was in storage. These included twenty or so items of interest, and my impression was that some had been displayed for a while and others had never left the cartons they were shipped in. When I made the loan, the HHOF was a part-time facility attached to the Canadian National Exhibition. It looked more like a forgotten archive than an active museum.

The physical plant improved when the Hall of Fame relocated to a heritage bank building in downtown Toronto and mounted a permanent exhibition of its own, but it still didn't have room to display everything in its collection. Some of the world's great museums—for example, the Louvre, the Smithsonian, or the Prado—are frequently compared to an iceberg in the open ocean: what you see on exhibit represents about 10 percent of its holdings; the rest is in the basement. The Hockey Hall of Fame was much the same.

Still, some commentators rallied to the museum solution, claiming that Québécois history—including sports history—belongs to the people. On one current affairs television show, a former Montreal Alouettes lineman railed on about *la patrimoine* and how the memorabilia of Quebec greats should be donated to institutions where everybody could enjoy them. The footballer wasn't upset that I was selling these items; he was angry because they would disappear into private, rather than public, collections. Because they are so attached to the collective-culture ideal, Quebeckers expect this stuff to be preserved in public institutions. They want a Quebec sports museum with a Jean Béliveau room, a Maurice Richard room, and a Rusty Staub room. They don't want to lose these iconic treasures to individuals who have no obligation to put them on display.

However, people who rarely visit museums or galleries don't realize that the major touring shows that come to their local museums are very often driven by important pieces from private collections, not public ones. A recent example was the Renoir exhibition that visited the Montreal Museum of Fine Arts. More than half of the significant pieces in that show were lent by their private owners.

What the ex-football player may not have known is that a gentleman named Edgar Théôret has been attempting to establish a permanent exhibition space for Quebec athletes, so far without success. He may have the best of intentions, but he has yet to open a facility. Why would we give our memorabilia to someone who can only keep it in storage?

It's been suggested that a company like Molson might support such a museum, buying and maintaining the building in question, but that seems less likely now with the merger with Coors.

Few other companies have shown any inclination to step forward, understanding perhaps that it's not just a matter of a building; there would be administrative, curatorial, and security staff to hire and train. And then there's the sticky question of how such a museum would make its acquisitions: would it purchase them like any other institution, and if so, with what source of funds?

Some have proposed that the Forum, now an entertainment and multiscreen theater complex, be converted to a museum site, although its success in drawing crowds is still in question. People shouldn't forget that a small museum was set up at the Maurice Richard Arena after Rocket died, but that it eventually closed because nobody went to see it.

I'm all in favor of a place that celebrates the accomplishments of Canadian athletes, but it will require a long-term commitment of financial support plus dedicated management, easy access for the public, and imaginative exhibits to make it successful.

The classifying and cataloguing of the 195 items in my "collection" took longer than I would have predicted, but the process was an education. Claude Juteau and his colleague Pierre Trudeau of Classic Collectibles taught me that certain pieces, or kinds of pieces, were worth more than expected; others, less so.

The auction was scheduled for a period beginning in late January 2005 and lasting until late February. Élise was in Barbados for our annual winter vacation at that time, and I was to join her after I got a few projects out of the way. The plan was that Hélène would monitor the auction activity closely, and I'd speak with Mr. Juteau or Mr. Trudeau every week or so for updates. With just under two hundred items on offer, we all agreed that a return of $300,000 was well within the realm of possibility.

The auction system itself was simple. A prospective buyer would go on-line to the Classic Collectibles Web page, then press the link to the Jean Béliveau Collection, just above the Rick Vaive Collection.

Up on the buyer's screen would appear the full listing of the items for sale, each one described and pictured with its accompanying bid number and suggested starting price.

For example, item number 33 was my 1956–57 Montreal Canadiens Stanley Cup championship pewter mug, bearing the Canadiens logo and my name. The bidding started at US$200, and after 3,011 page "hits" and thirty-four bids, it eventually sold for $4,367.12. Lot number 80 was my Quebec Aces number 9 green home-game jersey from the early 1950s. There were 8,485 page hits on this one and thirty-seven bids; it opened at US$1,000 and sold for $34,003.90, or Can$39,104.49.

"One thing you need to know about on-line auctions," Mr. Juteau advised us, "is that there is something called the 10-minute bid extension rule." He explained that many bidders lie low until the last few moments before the bid deadline and then plunge in, hoping to snatch away the item at a lower price. The 10-minute rule allowed for bidding to continue for ten minutes on all lots if a last-minute bid came in on an individual piece. The wisdom of this rule became evident on February 25, the final day of the auction.

On the evening of February 24, I went to bed in Barbados with some exciting news from my daughter. "It looks like the total may get up to $500,000," she said.

"A half million? U.S. or Canadian?" I can't remember hearing her answer, but I was surprised and delighted by the response of the fans and collectors.

Hélène was back on the telephone late the next afternoon. "The bidding is over, and we've got the final numbers," she said. "Are you sitting down?" I was.

"The final tally is $788,139.14 U.S., or $960,801.14 Canadian."

Almost a million dollars. I was stunned. This one auction of hockey memorabilia had brought in more money in real dollars, not accounting for inflation, than I had been paid in my entire NHL career.

In the midst of the auction, on February 11, I had been picked up by limousine and taken to familiar stomping grounds in Victoriaville. That evening, my old Quebec junior teams, Victoriaville and Quebec City, faced off in a regular-season game of the Quebec Major Junior Hockey League. The former team was coached by one time Canadien Stephan Lebeau, the latter was owned by one time Canadien netminder Patrick Roy.

My attendance that evening was in aid of a charity, and in appreciation they gave me a sculpture and a team sweater with my name and old Canadiens number 4 on the back. The presentation was broadcast on the late sports news and I was hardly in the front door when the telephone rang. It was Hélène.

"Don't tell me you're starting again!"

"I have a sweater for you," I replied.

We laughed like kids.

I WAS INVOLVED IN another good-news money story, though its origins date back more than thirty years.

On February 11, 1971, Frank Mahovlich was perched off the Minnesota net to the right of the goalie, and a puck I directed toward the goal was headed right for him. At the last second, he lifted his stick away from the puck, and it caught the corner just inside the right post. I had scored the five hundredth goal of my career, completing a hat trick against Gilles Gilbert in a 6–2 win over the North Stars. I was only the second member of the *bleu-blanc-rouge,* behind Maurice Richard, to reach this milestone. What made it even more precious was that it had come in my final year as a player. I had decided long before to hang up my skates at the end of the 1971 season.

About a week after the win over Minnesota, I was summoned upstairs to Sam Pollock's office. I assumed Sam wanted to discuss my presence at a dinner or similar public event; as the team captain, I was already traveling frequently as the Canadiens' representative.

When I arrived at Sam's door, he escorted me down the hall to David Molson's office.

"Jean, we want to give you a night to honor your five hundred goals and your career," David began. "This is your final season, and with everything you've done for the team, both on the ice and off, we feel that we owe you this."

I had a momentary flashback to some twenty years before in Quebec City, where I had received a brand-new car in a similar ceremony. I was touched by his offer, but I was uncomfortable with the vision of a sort of department store at center ice, where all sorts of appliances and gifts are presented, then topped off with a shiny new automobile, wheeled out by a slightly embarrassed friend as eighteen thousand onlookers oohed and aahed.

"All right," I said, "but with this proviso: I don't want a car full of gifts. I'll accept just four souvenirs: something from my teammates; the traditional silver tray from that night's opponent; something from *Hockey Night in Canada;* and something from the Canadiens organization. If there's any money involved, I don't want a penny for myself. Let me divide it among the four or five charities I've been associated with through the years."

David and Sam agreed and mentioned something about a date in late March. I didn't think much about it after that. We were in the thick of a play-off race against Boston and New York, after missing the play-offs (for the first time in my career) the previous spring. I wanted no distractions in my quest for a tenth Stanley Cup title.

Back then, a hockey team's public relations department generally confined itself to rather basic tasks such as issuing the occasional press release. No one was equipped to handle a major promotion like a celebratory night for a retiring player. The team's management usually went to the player's friends for advice. In this case, the Canadiens cornered two of the very best friends and organizers a man could wish for—Zotique Lespérance, the former broadcaster, columnist, and Molson's executive, and Raymond Lemay, a prominent Quebec businessman and president of Montreal's Blue Bonnets Raceway. They agreed to help, and my celebration was scheduled for the night of March 24, 1971.

Shortly before that date, the three of us got together to discuss their progress. Zotique and Raymond had been given less than a month to publicize the event, and during that time Montreal had been brought to a virtual standstill for a week by a severe blizzard. Nonetheless, Raymond began with an optimistic forecast.

"I don't know what you have in mind, Jean, but the money that comes in for your charities might be a lot more than you are expecting."

I was doubtful and told him so. "You've lost a week because of the snow, so how much could it possibly be? If you pick up $25,000 or $30,000, at least each charity will get $6,000 or $7,000 apiece. I can't see it being any more."

"Maybe we should have a backup plan, just in case," Zotique cautioned, and he suggested the creation of a foundation. That same afternoon, he called in Jim Grant of the law firm Stikeman Elliot to create the Jean Béliveau Fund, as it was first known.

On March 24, when I was presented with a poster-sized check for $155,855 at center ice, I could hardly believe my eyes. Thankfully, all that money had worthy purposes to fulfill. I later discovered that Zotique had enlisted the help of Molson's sales representatives in every region of Quebec, while Raymond had used his connections to the upper echelons of Quebec corporate management, securing the first donation from financier Jean-Louis Lévesque in the amount of $10,000. Together, Zotique and Raymond did a fantastic job, and the fund was off and running from the start.

The Jean Béliveau Foundation operated for more than twenty years, until we closed the books in 1993 when I retired from the Canadiens' executive offices. Zotique, Raymond, and Ron Perowne, the original trustees, were onboard throughout, along with Marcel

Lacroix, who replaced my friend Jacques Côté when he perished in a plane crash; Jean Bruneau, who took over from Sam Maislin when he passed away; and my daughter Hélène, who joined us for the final five years. In two decades, we'd managed to pass along almost $600,000 for charitable good works and still had almost $900,000 remaining.

The extraordinary thing was that, after the initial $155,000 was presented to me at the Forum in 1971, we never again had to solicit money. I managed to raise a fair amount by presiding over golf tournaments and the like. I donated any honoraria that I received for personal appearances, and ten or twelve friends would send $1,000 or so every year. The largest donation we ever received was $25,000 from the estate of a couple I had never met.

One morning, I received a call from a gentleman with an accounting firm in Mont-Joli. "Mr. Béliveau, I'm the executor of the will of an elderly couple from Priceville, a little town up past Matane. The wife died a year ago and the husband just passed away. They left their estate of $200,000 to eight charitable organizations, and your foundation is one of them."

"You're sure there are no encumbrances? No long-lost cousins or nephews somewhere?" I didn't want any of our resources spent on legal fees in an expensive probate battle.

"No family, no children, nobody. Everything is clear."

With $25,000 from these wonderfully generous strangers, our bank account began to grow. At the end, we decided to transfer the foundation's entire assets—the remaining $900,000—to the Quebec Society for Disabled Children, earmarking the money for its summer camp northeast of Joliette. The only condition for the society was that it follow the foundation's long-standing practice of purchasing equipment and materials, tangible items that directly benefited the recipients. No foundation money ever went to salaries or administrative costs. My assistant at the Forum, Louise Richer, handled the day-to-day operations, making sure that I saw every request for funds.

If the trustees approved the expenditure, I would authorize the charity involved to make the purchase from a local supplier and have the bill sent to me. That's the way it operated for twenty-two years, and I like to think it worked out reasonably well.

As I close this edition of my memoirs, I am proud to report that the Quebec Society for Disabled Children has been able to carry on our original program of donations, distributing some $60,000 a year without touching the principal, which continues to grow. I am reminded of that old advertising slogan, "the gift that goes on giving," and I am proud.

It is one thing to benefit personally from a career in a public milieu like professional hockey, and certainly my family will benefit from the sale of that career's memorabilia. But the ongoing distribution of the foundation money to people who really need it, today and long after I'm gone, is a gratifying legacy for me. I am humbled, honored, and immensely grateful to everyone who has been involved with the Jean Béliveau Foundation over the years and to the wonderful people at the Society for Disabled Children.

Like the Montreal Canadiens, they have been members of a very special team, and I am proud to acknowledge them as teammates for life.

Appendix 1

TOP SALES ITEMS OF JEAN BÉLIVEAU MEMORABILIA

JANUARY–FEBRUARY 2005

ITEM	TITLE	PRICE	BIDS
1	1958–59 Stanley Cup ring	$69,045.40	27
79	1967 game-used jersey	$42,900.00	19
7	1957–58 Stanley Cup replica trophy	$37,135.80	26
80	Quebec Aces home jersey, number 9	$34,003.90	37
5	1985–86 Stanley Cup ring	$28,531.10	25
21	1965 Conn Smythe trophy	$27,964.30	23
6	1992–93 Stanley Cup ring	$27,086.50	27
3	1977–78 Stanley Cup ring	$25,701.80	26
10	1970–71 Stanley Cup replica trophy	$22,547.10	10
48	Hockey Hall of Fame ring	$20,182.60	32

Appendix 2

JEAN BÉLIVEAU'S SEMI-PRO AND PROFESSIONAL STATISTICAL RECORD

QUEBEC ACES (QSHL)

SEASON	GP	G	A	TP	PIM
1951–52	59	45	38	83	88
1952–53	57	50	39	89	59
QSHL Totals	116	95	77	172	147

MONTREAL CANADIENS (NHL)

SEASON	GP	G	A	TP	PIM
1950–51	2	1	1	2	0
1952–53	3	5	0	5	0
1953–54	44	13	21	34	22
1954–55	70	37	36	73	58
1955–56[ab]	70	47*	41	88*	143
1956–57	69	33	51	84	105
1957–58	55	27	32	59	93
1958–59	67	45*	46	91	67
1959–60	60	34	40	74	57
1960–61	69	32	58*	90	57
1961–62	43	18	23	41	36
1962–63	69	18	49	67	68
1963–64[b]	68	28	50	78	42
1964–65	58	20	23	43	76
1965–66	67	29	48*	77	50
1966–67	53	12	26	38	22
1967–68	59	31	37	68	28
1968–69	69	33	49	82	55
1969–70	63	19	30	49	10
1970–71	70	25	51	76	40
NHL totals	1125	507	712	1219	1029

PLAY-OFFS

SEASON	GP	G	A	TP	PIM
1953–54	10	2	8*	10	4
1954–55	12	6	7	13	18
1955–56	10	12*	7	19*	22
1956–57	10	6	6	12	15
1957–58	10	4	8	12	10
1958–59	3	1	4	5	4
1959–60	8	5	2	7	6
1960–61	6	0	5	5	0
1961–62	6	2	1	3	4
1962–63	5	2	1	3	2
1963–64	5	2	0	2	18
1964–65[c]	13	8	8	16	34
1965–66	10	5	5	10	6
1966–67	10	6	5	11	26*
1967–68	10	7	4	11	6
1968–69	14	5	10*	15	8
1969–70	–	–	–	–	–
1970–71[d]	20	6	16*	22	28
NHL totals	163	79	97	176	211

[a] Won Art Ross Trophy.

[b] Won Hart Trophy.

[c] Won Conn Smythe Trophy.

[d] NHL record for assists in Stanley Cup play-offs.

* Highest individual total in NHL for season.

ACKNOWLEDGMENTS

THE GREATEST FEAR of a team captain is to overlook the contribution of a teammate or, for that matter, of a worthy opponent. Therefore, I would like to acknowledge all of my teammates, stars and otherwise, who helped me throughout my career. My success is their success. In addition, I would be remiss if I didn't thank the media, led by the late Jacques Beauchamp and Danny Gallivan, as well as René Lecavalier, Red Fisher, Marcel Desjardins, and Dick Irvin, who are still with us. I also cannot forget the fans who were very good to me throughout more than forty years of hockey.

On a more personal level, I would like to acknowledge the friendship and contributions of the following persons in my careers, both within and without hockey: Roland Mercier, Raymond Lemay, the Byrne family, Roland Hébert, Jack Latter, Rita and Jean Proulx, Punch Imlach, Jacques Côté and the entire Côté family, Father Leonard Murphy, René Corbeil, Camil DesRoches, Pierre Roux, the Sacred Heart Brothers of L'Académie Saint-Louis de Gonzague and Collège de Victoriaville, Raynald Deslandes, Thérèse and Yves Robitaille, Irène and Paul Brouillard, Paul Aquin, George Lengvari, Doug Kinnear, MD, David Mulder, MD, Maurice Godin, MD, Senator Hartland de Montarville Molson and the Molson families, Peter and Edward Bronfman, Zotique Lespérance, Frank Selke Sr., Dick Irvin Sr., Toe Blake, and Ronald Corey.

And, in a very special category of one, there is Louise Richer. This book, and many of the memories it contains, are as much hers as mine.

INDEX